EARLY
WARNING

EARLY
WARNING

Using Competitive Intelligence to Anticipate Market Shifts, Control Risk, and Create Powerful Strategies

Ben Gilad

AMACOM
American Management Association
New York • Atlanta • Brussels • Chicago • Mexico City • San Francisco
Shanghai • Tokyo • Toronto • Washington, D.C.

Special discounts on bulk quantities of AMACOM books are
available to corporations, professional associations, and other
organizations. For details, contact Special Sales Department,
AMACOM, a division of American Management Association,
1601 Broadway, New York, NY 10019.
Tel.: 212-903-8316.   Fax: 212-903-8083.
Web site: www.amacombooks.org

This publication is designed to provide accurate and authoritative
information in regard to the subject matter covered. It is sold with
the understanding that the publisher is not engaged in rendering
legal, accounting, or other professional service. If legal advice or other
expert assistance is required, the services of a competent professional
person should be sought.

Library of Congress Cataloging-in-Publication Data

Gilad, Benjamin.
        Early warning : using competitive intelligence to anticipate market shifts,
    control risk, and create powerful strategies / Ben Gilad.
            p.   cm.
        Includes index.
        ISBN 0-8144-0786-2 (hardcover)
        1. Risk management.   2. Risk.   3. Strategic planning.   I. Title.

    HD61.G533 2003
    658.15′5—dc21   2003006506

Printing number

10   9   8   7   6   5   4   3   2   1

To my family—
Shirly, Corinne, and little Jonathan (Milo)—
with all my love.

Contents

List of Tables and Figures

Preface

"There are risks and costs to a program of action. But they are far less than the long-range risks and costs of comfortable inaction."

—John F. Kennedy

Do you know the Sarbanes-Oxley Act of 2002? If you don't, you are not alone. But many very powerful, rich, and influential people know this act intimately. It is the law that required CEOs to certify that their companies' financial statements were true. Violating this law would send those people to jail.

Now imagine if there were another law that required CEOs to certify that their forecasts and strategic plans relied on a careful examination of the external environment. Furthermore, they would have to back up their oaths with proof of a serious competitive intelligence capability that monitors emerging structural changes in their industries. The lines to the county jail would be backed up to the local K-Mart.

There is a process that brings management closer to external focus. It is called competitive early warning. It helps companies decipher early signs of trouble before they mushroom into a full-scale crisis and identify early signs of opportunities before everyone else sees them. It makes planning more realistic and raises the prospects of success for strategies. It just might save your company and your career.

This book may not move any cheese, but it is a must for reasonable companies and smart managers who deal with uncertainty and competition. The competitive early warning process is a minimum insurance against strategic surprises. It allows managers to control risks—those risks that are controllable. If I were an institutional investor, I'd make sure the companies I invest in instituted one of the early warning models detailed in this book. If I were a manager, I'd put my company to the test in Chapter 10. If it fails, I'd run for my life. As an old saying goes, "Who is so deaf or so blind as he that willfully will neither hear nor see?"

Acknowledgments

There are thousands of graduates of the Academy of Competitive Intelligence who toil in large and small corporations in the United States, Europe, Asia, and Australia, and without their insightful observations my model of early warning would never have come to life. I can't name them all, but I sure can thank them all.

Then there are a few individuals whom I have the good fortune to call friends and whose brilliant execution of my concepts and ideas made them real. I would like to take the opportunity to thank them in public: Wayne Rosenkrants and Deni Deasy of AstraZeneca Pharmaceuticals, Karl Rose and Ceri Powell of Shell, and David Sheehan and Lars von Kantzow of Pergo. Your friendship means a lot to me. Wayne and Karl deserve special thanks, as they contributed sections to Chapter 9, at a cost of time and effort they could hardly afford. All I can do is promise to do the same when you write your own books!

EARLY
WARNING

PART ONE

COMPANIES AT RISK

CHAPTER 1

Surprise!

"Man's basic vice, the source of all his evils, is the act of unfocusing his mind, the suspension of his consciousness, which is not blindness, but the refusal to see, not ignorance, but the refusal to know."

—Ayn Rand

Take a minute to carefully read the responses to the two survey questions in Table 1-1 on the next page. Then consider their amazing findings. Ninety-eight percent of respondents predicted their companies' exposure to business risk would increase over the next three years. Ninety-two percent reported that their company was surprised by *at least* one significant event in the past five years.[1]

The first part is not surprising. There is a consensus in the business world that the environment has become much riskier over the past three decades. Executives lament about globalization, technology change, regulatory shifts, and consolidations making competitive pressures substantially higher. Yet, despite the fact that everyone knows the world has become riskier and expects even more business risk in the future, fully 92 percent of the managers surveyed reported that their company was recently (last five years) *surprised* by at least one event that was

Q. To what extent does your company anticipate an increased level of business risk in its markets and industries in the next two to three years?

44.1%	Very likely
36.3%	Likely
17.6%	Somewhat likely
2.0%	Not likely
0.0%	I don't know

Q. How many times would you say that your company was, in the past five years, surprised by events that had the potential for a significant impact on your long-term market position?

8.0%	a. Never
68.0%	b. 1–3 times
24.0%	c. More than 3 times

Early Warning Survey results, Feb. 2002, Academy of Competitive Intelligence.

Table 1-1: Early Warning Survey results: risk and surprise.

significant enough to affect their organization's long-term market position!

The survey was taken at the beginning of 2002. The respondents were middle managers working mostly in Fortune 500 corporations. How come their large, sophisticated organizations were surprised by events that posed a strategic threat?

The answer is not for lack of signs. Signs for emerging risk are almost always out there.

Surprise Attacks

Surprise plays a significant role in decision processes. In military history, for example, surprise attacks have almost always proved successful beyond expectations. From Pearl Harbor to the Allies' landing in Normandy on D-Day, from the Barbarossa offensive (Hitler's invasion of the Soviet Union in 1941) to the Yom Kippur War (the Arab attack on Israel in 1973) to the September 11 Islamic terrorist attacks on New York and Washington, surprise has enabled the attackers to achieve far more damaging results than what one would have expected from judging initial "objective" odds, taking into consideration relative strengths of the opposing parties, defensive measures, etc.

In business, surprise is as damaging. The failure of Jack Welch to foresee the determined resistance of European regulatory authorities to his plans to take over Honeywell resulted in significant loss of money and prestige by General Electric and Welch himself, who until then had been considered infallible. The swiftness with which doctors and hospitals moved away from using Johnson & Johnson's stents (medical devices that prop open clogged heart vessels) to using those made by Guidant took J&J by complete surprise, resulting in market share decline from 91 percent in 1996 to 8 percent in 1998, and prompting an analyst to describe it as "the most dramatic transfer of wealth between two companies in medical device history."[2] The disastrous merger of Daimler-Benz with Chrysler and the surprise departure of most of Chrysler's management over the next two years cost Daimler billions of dollars and has shaken markets' valuation of the merged company.

However, surprise has a surprising side. Academic research into surprise military attacks spanning the last seventy years shows that their success was not due to cunning deceptions and lack of early signs. Instead, those studies found that surprise attacks were successful because the other side was the captive of obsolete assumptions and beliefs that led, in the absence of countermechanisms, to *ignoring signs of risk.*[3]

In other words, surprise is often not really such a surprise. This may sound like a trivial statement, but it may not be so trivial. It means that those whose responsibility it is to act early on—but not necessarily *everyone else*—ignore early signs of an impending "surprise." The failure is in lack of action, and in most surprise attacks there were indeed some who foresaw the risk and warned about it, but often they were simply ignored or dismissed as doomsday prophets. The existence of early signs is good news for those whose role is defending their enterprises from nasty surprises. It means that defending against surprise is not an impossible task. Instead, it may be a matter of having an effective mechanism to identify early signs of risk and forcing the decision makers to heed the warning. Not an easy task, but not as forbidding as trying to know the unknowable.

Naturally, decision makers must cooperate in order to have such an effective system. If you were a decision maker, wouldn't you like to have an early warning capability at your fingertips? The answer may not be as simple as it seems. Terry Smith, a famed British analyst with a large following who predicted the demise of the stock market bubble of the 1990s, says CEOs "often don't know what is going on in the business."[4] To that we may add that CEOs often don't *want* to know.

The Supremacy of Internal Convictions

The finding that surprise is often a result of ignoring available signs of risk leads to the realm of executive judgment. In this realm, many books and articles document the supremacy of internal convictions over facts and findings.[5] In the broadest sense, I call this a blindspot. "Blinders" worn by decision makers represent a critical source of failures in their judgment and decisions and are a major reason that organizations are "surprised." Performance failure is a direct consequence of bad surprises. The logical chain is straightforward: Obsolete internal convictions—blindspots—lead to the adherence to wrong strategies, ignoring market evidence that they should be modified or replaced, and then the company's sales or profits or market share "surprisingly" declines.

Ignoring signs of risk is a substantial problem facing all those planning for the future, be it in government or in business. Invariably, the people at the head of the pyramid, those who must accept or reject evidence for emerging risks, are the ones most susceptible to such a failure. For reasons that will be described shortly, leaders—especially business leaders—are those whose internal schemas are more prone to internal blinders than those of their subordinates.

If those whose duty it is to act on signs of risk look at the wrong things—*or fail to look at the right things*—disasters follow. When convictions of powerful leaders clash with evidence, the problem multiplies. This is because powerful leaders evoke powerful mechanisms to explain away the facts, sustain the denial, and dismiss the signals from the outside world that reality is changing. In the name of "team spirit" they encourage groupthink that further supports their views. They intentionally or unintentionally block internal debates from becoming too loud by limiting the forums available for subordinates to interact directly with the top (for example, by prohibiting them from going over a supervisor's head). They surround themselves with acquiescent consultants. This is how it happens, again and again, that smart and experienced leaders and commanders who turn a blind eye to what is happening *under their noses* "succeed" in leading their organizations toward decline and losses. When it happens in business, investors and employees pay the price.

Blind Executives?

A surprising number of powerful executives at the top of leading corporations are captive to a special class of internal convictions that relate to the future direction of the industry in which they compete. When these convictions and "visions" are out of tune with the evolving market, they obscure the ability of otherwise smart and knowledgeable executives to adjust their strategies accordingly. When a company's strategy no longer fits market reality, I call the situation "industry dissonance."* The risk of industry dissonance is the risk that executive assumptions can lag behind industry reality and that companies' strategies therefore do not reflect the new conditions.

Inevitably, when industry dissonance arises out of changing industry conditions, new competitors, or more agile ones, take advantage of these changing circumstances to offer customers a better deal or a new route to serve their needs. Industry dissonance offers opportunities to some and grave risks to others. Such was the case when PC networks took the market away from large and expensive mainframes, and IBM, refusing to admit the new reality, suffered large losses. At the same time, it practically handed the market to Sun Microsystems. Such was

* I am indebted to Leonard Fuld for coining this term.

the case when small, efficient Japanese cars took over the American market and left General Motors in the dust. GM simply gave the market away with its strategy of gas-guzzlers and old-style unreliable cars, despite technological changes, consumer changes, and supply-chain changes ("just-in-time inventory management," for example) that were already available to it.

A "new" industry of bottled water replaced cola drinks for many younger people, while Coke fixed its attention for many years on its hated rival, Pepsi. Canon took global leadership away from Xerox with, first, smaller and cheaper machines, and then with better features and reliability while Xerox stuck to its failed strategy of expensive-to-service leased copiers, and later an empty theme of "the document company." Such was also the case for Kodak, which was busy with a disastrous diversification strategy, including a misguided venture into the pharmaceutical industry, all the while assuming its lead in film technology would be sustained indefinitely. Fuji came from behind and took over the global lead, damaging Kodak's monopoly in the U.S. market as well. Polaroid rested on its laurels, selling high-margin instant cameras and film and refusing to see the new digital age as the end for its instant film market, until Sony and HP and Canon and Fuji and Kodak's advanced digital products bankrupted it. Industries do not stay static, and companies that fail to see the dynamics of change and adapt to it are overrun by others who do.

The failure to identify the risk of industry dissonance and act on it is not related to a specific industry, company size, or even how slow or fast a market changes. It does relate to the culture inside a company, its market position, and the organizational mechanisms it uses to identify and control strategic risks. Dominant players and arrogant cultures are always more susceptible. In Table 1-2, I present a very partial list of companies that suffered severe performance crises when their leaders failed to bring their expectations up-to-date with reality.

Executives who are trapped in their obsolete assumptions often refuse to believe the intelligence flowing from their own people, who deal with the markets, the customers, the suppliers, and the competitors on a daily basis. In the absence of a formal system capable of overcoming their convictions and alerting them to dissonance risk *early enough to make a difference*, they

Leader	Company	Leader	Company
John Akers	IBM	Eckhard Pfeiffer	Compaq
Bob Allen	AT&T	Wolfgang Schmidt	Rubbermaid
Jill Barad	Mattel	Jürgen Schrempp	Daimler-Chrysler
Gary DiCamillo	Polaroid	Fred Smith	GM
Bob Haas	Levi Strauss	William Smithburg	Quaker Oats
Douglas Ivester	Coca-Cola	Bob Stempel	GM
Durk Jaeger	P&G	Barry Sternlicht	Starwood
Paul Lego	Westinghouse	Richard Thomas	Xerox
Richard McGinn	Lucent	Kay Whitmore	Kodak

Table 1-2: Dissonance failure hall of fame (some famous examples of executives whose internal convictions and market realities did not agree).

wake up only when the crisis hits and performance is down. By that time it is often way too late for them, their companies, their employees, and their shareholders, who often pay the price of blindspots.

Can Companies Do Better?

Senior executives could overcome some of the obstacles to "staring reality straight in its face" if they assumed responsibility for the active management of industry dissonance. The mere admittance that this risk is a strategic issue—*their issue*—and requires specific attention, resources, system, and culture to handle can bring many companies to do a better job of identifying and reacting to early signs of change. The system approach outlined below provides an effective relief for most companies. It replaces an empty slogan of "external focus" with specific activities aimed at bringing the outside world inside.

Middle managers can do even better. Because the convictions that trap most large organizations and their powerful leaders do not usually apply to the individual manager in a mid-level position, the tool offered in this book can serve to substantially improve his or her performance on the job. Free of many of the limitations confronting senior executives, such as large egos, insularity from negative intelligence, and a public commitment to a "vision," and equipped with a tool to assess and track risk to their products, areas, or projects, individual managers can largely avoid nasty surprises and the resulting performance disasters. *Since the signs of risk are out there, and since the problem is a mindset*, a systematic approach that attacks "fixated" mindsets head-on can save jobs, wealth, and the mental health of many managers.

Mind you, I do not offer a panacea. Many powerful decision makers are prisoners of their own convictions and proud history, and no method will change their view of the future or their unshakable belief in the validity of their strategy. No book and no system would have made Mike Armstrong of AT&T admit he was wrong as his vision for an integrated phone-cable company crashed about him, bringing AT&T's stock tumbling down and sending its debt skyrocketing. But for most readers and most companies, following the straightforward process suggested in this book, which has been tested in high-risk environments for many years, will mean a better preparedness to face the future. As the French scientist Louis Pasteur once said: "Luck favors the prepared mind."

The toolbox presented in this book is based on a sophisticated and tested military doctrine of early warning. Just as the U.S. Air Force can detect missile launches thousands of miles away and warn of an impending attack on the United States, businesses can detect signs of strategic risks (and opportunities) years ahead of time and prepare to act on them. A few leading corporations, such as Citigroup, Shell, Daimler's DASA, AstraZeneca (United States), and Visa, facing changing environments and markets, have in recent years applied this approach to create a line of first defense against nasty market surprises. Their systems quickly interpret intelligence from the market about emerging trends that pose substantial future risk to the company and in a feedback loop bring this intelligence to bear on their company's planning. The essence of these systems is the seamless marriage of planning, intelligence, and action, integrating them across products and markets, coordinating and systematizing them all the way to the top. In many cases, the output of the early warning system *forces* action upon senior management.

These experiments offer companies and individuals a method for fighting future uncertainty and the risk associated with industry changes better than existing methods of planning. Short of having a crystal ball, cultivating a culture of early warning can be companies' best defense against performance decline.

At times, managers may be able to compensate somewhat for the failure of risk management in their company's executive suites. Using their own early warning process, managers can prevent surprises in their corner of the world despite an inferior organizational early warning system, blinded leadership, and a growing industry dissonance. They may not be able to forestall an eventual decline if their company does not address the risk they expose, but at least they will be regarded as smart enough to have identified it early on. If they do it five minutes before everyone else does, this book will pay for itself many times over.

Manager's Checklist

❏ Early signs always precede surprises. The problem is that they are ignored as often as they are recognized.

❏ Many research studies show that when reality and convictions are at odds with each other, convictions often win. This is the risk called a *blindspot*, and it is the gravest risk for planners.

❏ Industry dissonance is the risk that as the industry changes, the company does not.

❏ Many businesses lose out to more agile competitors not for lack of early signs of risk, but because of their executives' mindsets. Executives and managers can avoid lagging behind simply by addressing the mindset issue head-on with the help of the straightforward process offered in this book.

❏ The essence of the new business-based early warning system is the integration of strategy planning, intelligence, and action in an unprecedented, seamless way. In many cases, an early warning system "forces" action upon management.

There are few surprises in life, but there are many blind executives who confuse their own grand visions with reality and then make others pay for their confusion. Can you count examples? Send the stories to bsgilad@netvision.net.il. I'll compile a list of those who receive the most "votes" and post it on my Web site, www.bengilad.com. Maybe it will wake them up. At the least it will allow investors to demand explanations.

Notes

1. Tables 1-1, 2-1, 3-1, 4-1, and 5-1 show results from an on-line survey conducted in 2002 among CI managers by the Fuld-Gilad-Herring Academy of Competitive Intelligence, of which the author is one of the founders and serves as its president. The Academy is located in Cambridge, MA, and one can access its site at *www.academyci.com*.
2. Ron Winslow, "How a breakthrough in Cardiac Treatment Broke Down for J&J," *Wall Street Journal*, 23 Sept. 1998, p. 1.
3. For example, Roberta Wohlstetter, *Pearl Harbor: Warning and Decision* (Stanford, Calif.: Stanford University Press, 1962), and Richard K. Betts, *Surprise Attack: Lessons for Defense Planning* (Washington, D.C.: The Brookings Institution, 1982).
4. Stanley Reed, "When Terry Smith Growls, the Markets Listen," *BusinessWeek Online*, 26 Aug. 2002.
5. For a sample of readings on politicians' blinders, see: *The March of Folly: From Troy to Vietnam* by Barbara Tuchman (New York: Random House, 1984). For business examples, see "Why CEOs Fail" by Ram Charan and Geoffrey Colvin, *Fortune*, 21 June 1999, and *Business Blindspots* by Benjamin Gilad (Tetbury, U.K.: Infonortics, 1998). For psychological theories and studies about the phenomenon, see Amos Tversky and Daniel Kahneman, "Judgment under Uncertainty: Heuristics and Biases," *Science* 185 (1974): 1124–1131.

CHAPTER 2

What Do You Know About Strategic Risks?

"Prediction is very difficult, especially about the future."
—*Neils Bohr*

Table 2-1 on the following page sums up management handling of major risk categories. Blindspots affect individuals' ability to perceive risks. But organizations don't live or die by individual behavior. They create organizational mechanisms and processes that replace individual perception with a more reliable collective perception. Why can't organizations do the same for strategic risks?

The Various Types of Risk

The reason companies and their executives so often fail to systematically manage strategic risks is rooted in the way companies define the risks they face.

A dictionary defines risk as "a prospect of loss." A more precise definition found in financial theory is "the potential for a *worse* outcome than one is expecting." Better outcomes than ex-

Q. Which of the following risks would you say your company least manages? Risk of . . . (Please check all choices that apply)

10.3%	a.	Currency fluctuations
5.6%	b.	Health hazard to employees and customers
6.0%	c.	Negligent work by employees
6.4%	d.	Stock market fluctuations hurting your marketable securities
6.9%	e.	Public relations flop by an executive
10.7%	f.	Customers' needs not being met by future products/services
17.2%	g.	Competitors introducing a proprietary or alternative breakthrough product/service
16.3%	h.	New competitor entering your segment with new skills
8.6%	i.	Suppliers integrating into your markets
12.0%	j.	Alternative technology replacing the need for your offering

Early Warning Survey results, Feb. 2002, Academy of Competitive Intelligence.

Table 2-1: Early Warning Survey results: risk types.

pected do not constitute risk (though economists may refer to them as "upside risk").

If risk is clearly defined in the literature, strategic risk is not. Surprisingly little research has been done into strategic risks. The more notable works in recent years have been by two professors, Robert Simons and Elizabeth Teisberg. Teisberg's work will be discussed in Chapter 5.

Simons defines strategic risk as "an unexpected event or set of conditions that significantly reduces the ability of managers to implement their intended business strategy."[1] He recognizes three main types of strategic risk: operational, asset-impairment, and competitive. The first two have to do with the company's assets and processes. The last relates specifically to external events—changes in the competitive environment.[2] For reasons outlined below, I will focus on the latter, as this has been the weakest link for many companies. Moreover, while it is clear that operational and asset-impairment risks—a defective manufacturing process or a reduction in the value of a firm's financial assets—can hamper managers' ability to *implement* their strategy, my concern is not limited to implementation. *The risk I call strategic is the risk that the strategy itself is misaligned with market conditions.*

Companies find it easier to deal with Simons's first two categories of risk. This is because risk management in large companies has always been defined in functional terms and then compartmentalized. Companies recognize financial, operational, and public relations risks, and these are handled separately by various departments in the organization.[3]

Financial risk, for example, is the most familiar type of risk to most corporations. It deals with the risk that financial markets and default by debtors pose to the firm's cash flow and balance sheet. A famous example of financial markets' risk is Procter & Gamble's loss of $157 million on two interest swaps with Bankers Trust back in 1994. Other examples include UBS, the Swiss-based global bank, which bought $1.2 billion of Japanese banks' shares in 1997 and lost $600 million when the Japanese banks collapsed during November 1997. LTCM (Long Term Capital Management), an investment company, lost a cool $2 billion betting on the wrong spread between rates on various financial instruments. It also faced another financial hazard— liquidity risk—when it could not sell its assets fast enough to cover $3.6 billion of margin calls. A credit risk example is Chase Manhattan, which almost collapsed in the 1980s when Brazil defaulted on its debt. The financial community, being the leader in researching (financial) risk, has devised sophisticated tools (not all successful, however, as the examples above demonstrate) to manage it. Nonfinancial companies followed, with the chief financial officer (CFO) taking the role of chief risk manager in the typical large company, protecting the firm against the variability of currency, stock, and bond markets as well as changes in the prices of essential raw materials.

Businesses recognize another class of risk: operational. This is the risk that originates from operations. Exxon's *Valdez* oil spill in Alaska and Union Carbide's toxic explosion in its Bhopal plant in India are examples of health and environmental risk from operations. Most companies (at least in the Western world) have devised elaborate procedures and processes to deal with operational risk, including crisis management contingency routines.

Then there are public relations risks. Johnson & Johnson's famous handling of the Tylenol poisoning demonstrated how companies that are prepared to handle a PR crisis can do well despite the initial customer reaction.

Strategic risk stemming from the competitive environment, especially the strategy risk I term "industry dissonance," is much more difficult to manage. Its identification is no one's job and everyone's job. Its management is the responsibility of executives (especially business unit's executives), but they are often too busy to worry about matters as ambiguous as future strategic risks. Existing financial policies and operational safeguards are helpless against the risk of industry dissonance because assumptions about the industry's future direction, which underlie industry dissonance, are cross-functional. These assumptions underlie companies' overall strategies, not just their financial or operational strategies. When a company's strategy no longer fits the emerging reality of the industry and the market in which it competes, risk becomes a strategic rather than a functional issue in that the company's overall strategy must be adjusted. Since strategy is a pattern of functional policies and activities, not just one overriding vision, many different adjustments may be needed. For example, marketing, human resources, production, and sales activities and policies may have to change in response to a change in buyers' preferences. Purchasing, manufacturing, logistics, and selling policies may have to be adjusted in reaction to or in anticipation of a significant change in the structure of the supply chain.

Functional "silos" in corporations dictate that no one in particular is actually in charge of managing this risk of industry dissonance. Companies need a system that cuts across functions. In the case of corporate strategy, when a corporation is made of related businesses so strategy is not a mere portfolio shifting, tensions between business units and the parent company create substantial barriers to the systematic management of strategic risks that cut across several units or sectors. Presidents of divisions or general managers of business units are as "siloed"—i.e., insulated inside their areas—as functional managers are when it comes to looking at the overall external picture in the industry. Balanced Scorecards and other recent management tools have had almost no effect on this endemic problem.

The Most Neglected Risk

All the financial maneuvering in the world will not save a company whose strategy does not fit reality. Implementation is not the problem, adaptation is. Protecting revenues from currency fluctuations is an irrelevant remedy when the disease is the disappearance of revenues themselves. While P&G lost $157 million in a financial debacle in 1994 (derivative trading), P&G's stock lost more than half of its value in the stock market during the first three month of 2000, leaving the shareholders $35 *billion* poorer. The decline of P&G's market value was the result of years of slipping in its various consumer product markets. Kimberly-Clark was giving P&G a run for its money in diapers with the Huggies brand. Crest was being beaten badly by Colgate-Palmolive's Total. Private labels and local brands in household cleaning products and processed foods have risen in market share over the years as global brands weakened. Unilever and L'Oréal were gaining over P&G in cosmetics and hair care. Its pharmaceutical division was a nonplayer in the industry of giants. Its early technological lead, which was evident in the 1960s and 1970s, evaporated in all but a few categories.

In short, P&G's strategy, which had hardly changed since the 1960s, did not fit P&G's market leadership aspirations given the much tougher competitive environment, and investors—seeing that the management of P&G was not responding—devalued the company accordingly. In comparison, the financial debacle mentioned above can be justly seen as immaterial. Ironically, during the 1990s P&G spent *much more* time and corporate thought on managing its financial exposure than on managing its growing industry dissonance.

Adjusting strategy to changing conditions, especially those that require sacrificing current profits for long-term profits is the most difficult of tasks, especially in very large companies. It requires executives to balance the protection of their existing assets with the need to stay ahead in the game. This is especially clear in late stages of market change, when incumbents fight tooth and nail to preserve their customers. However, if one can feel sympathy toward the dilemmas of management in reacting to change late in the game, what should not be acceptable to both management and shareholders is companies that do not have an effective system in place to identify dissonance risk signs *early enough to try and make a difference.*

Shifts in industries and markets that give rise to industry dissonance are not always clear, especially early on. Often the signals are ambiguous, hard to distinguish from mere "white noise." White noises are the daily changes and developments in every business's markets. Industries are dynamic. Markets are dynamic. Who knows when an innocent datum showing a rise in data transmission is a trend that will explode to exceed voice transmission and annihilate Lucent, or when the appearance of bell-bottom jeans signals the end to "normal" jeans among teenagers and the resulting near-demise of Levi Strauss?

It is much easier to manage other risks. Take a look at the responses in Table 2-1 to the question about which risk is *least* managed in our respondents' companies. While for operational, public relations, or even financial risks, the percentage is mostly a single digit, it jumps to double digits when the issues involve customers' needs, competitors' moves, alternative technologies, and new players. These changes create truly strategic risks in the sense that they do not interfere with the implementation of the existing strategy—they may negate the company's strategic concept itself.

Industry dissonance risk is not programmable. One cannot use mathematical modeling, computer programs, or known probabilities to calculate divergence of assumptions from reality. In assessing the risk of a stock, analysts use past distributions of returns. In assessing the future direction of the industry, past outcomes are often irrelevant. Therefore, assessment of the risk of external events is by its nature subjective.

Industry dissonance poses a complex picture that is hard to decipher. It emanates from the external world, where multitudes of external forces including competitive, technological, macroeconomic, global-political, and demand and supply determinants operate for or against the company's strategy. Information-wise, however, it requires *less* collection of data—less of the mass of structured data (the so called "data mining")—but more in-sight into what is relevant and what is not in the world around the company. Companies have systems in place to collect mass data. Software companies sell solutions they call "business intel-ligence" that are actually not about business and not about intel-ligence but about structuring mass quantitative data into databases. Busy executives may find solace in reading the reports generated by this data mining software, but the hard tasks of identifying and acting on strategic change are still very much labor intensive. Inundated with internal issues—memos and meetings, fire fighting in a zillion operational problems per day—executives find it hard to spare the time needed to reflect *systematically* on the big picture and arrive at an insight about where their assumptions might be straying. Sometimes, they are not even aware of what assumptions they work on. Without a conscious attempt to reveal hidden assumptions developed over years of experience working in an industry, management may have no chance of exposing obsolete models.

Because of its amorphous nature, the subjectivity in assess-ing it, and the complexity of looking at the big picture across products or business units, the risk of industry dissonance tends to fall between the cracks. This is the most neglected risk in busi-ness. Billions of wasted dollars reflect how deep this oversight can run. Sears, Montgomery Ward, Levi Strauss, Swissair, American Express, General Motors, Chrysler, Digital, Polaroid, Lucent, Nortel, AT&T, Ericsson, People Express, TWA—shall I continue? Sometimes the failure is what Robert Simons called "franchise risk," where the entire enterprise disappears. Some-times a failure involving industry dissonance results "merely" in losses of hundreds of millions and the layoff of thousands. For example, before its current chairman and CEO, Carlos Gutierrez, was appointed to his position, the Kellogg's Company lost mar-ket share and sales in the hundred of millions when it failed under Arnold Langbo, its previous CEO, to address the crucial trend of a steadily declining ready-to-eat breakfast market with alternative options to cereals. By acquiring Keebler, Gutierrez was the first to dare to acknowledge that Kellogg's future can no longer be in cereals alone—*and* to do something about it. For Kellogg, this was nothing short of a revolution.

Top Teams and Top Problems

It is the role of the entire top team, especially the heads of businesses and the heads of corporations, to manage industry dissonance. Since they are responsible for charting their business's strategies (at least in theory, unless they yield even this role to McKinsey or Booz Allen Hamilton or Bain, as some have been doing), they should be responsible for *refining* those strategies when they notice that changing circumstances in their industry render them less effective. They should be the ones to take advantage proactively of opportunities arising from changing conditions. This is the notion of strategy "Kaizen," the continuous improvement process, which became a familiar term in another sphere, that of quality improvement techniques, but never took hold in strategy, where it is often most needed.

Even if time were not a problem for busy executives, they are often the last to recognize changing circumstances. They are especially vulnerable because of several unique factors:

- They are the least objective about the risk of divergence between assumptions and reality because they are personally involved in formulating the company's assumptions (so-called ego involvement).

- They are the most insulated from field intelligence about developments in their markets and industries by virtue of their roles, the company they keep, and the hierarchical reporting in their organizations (which is rife with window dressing, massaging of reports, and filtering of important information).

- Surprisingly enough, despite their power, no one really helps them (Who wants to be a "bad news bearer" or an "alarmist"?) and the intelligence they seek comes from people as insulated as they are.

Recall that when executives *refuse* to change strategy even though market conditions have changed significantly, I call it a blindspot. Such were the cases of Richard McGinn at Lucent and Gary DiCamillo at Polaroid, which are described in Chapter 3. Denial and arrogance often go hand in hand, but these are the extreme cases. Often, neglect of strategic risks is due to a mundane problem of having no effective system to ensure that industry dissonance is identified early on and acted upon before it is too late, while the executive attention is on operational problems of much less long-term significance. It is hard to blame executives who are misinformed, ill-informed, or uninformed and are therefore the last to recognize signs of risk to their strategies. On the other hand, if they consciously refuse to create an early warning mechanism to help them stay on top, and blame everyone else (including the "bad economy," a common excuse for failing executives) after the fact, they should bear the consequences directly. Executives make frequent mention of the concept of "external focus," which is supposed to be a magic term signifying that they are aware of the importance of monitoring the outside world. For many the concept means little. Perhaps it is time to define it more precisely. This is what Tim Koogle of Yahoo! did.

The Case of Yahoo!

Yahoo!, the leading portal company, survived and prospered in one of the fastest-changing, most turbulent industries in business history. While its rivals Excite, Infoseek, and others were either going out of business or being swallowed up by giants such as Microsoft, NBC, Disney, etc., Yahoo! stayed independent. And while even Disney and NBC failed to make their portals profitable, Yahoo! was the *only* portal to show consistent profits until the recession of 2001. In 1999, Tim Koogle, then CEO of Yahoo!, defined external focus as follows: "As a company, we're heavily externally focused. We maintain a level of paranoia about the environment that is pretty healthy, and we seldom actually get surprised. If anything tectonic is going on, [we] get word of it before it occurs. When it happens, we come back to fairly basic fundamentals. Are we still doing the right thing?" (quoted in "Yahoo! Business on the Net," by Jay Girotto and Jan Rivkin, Harvard Business School Publishing, 1999.)

The three legs of Koogle's definition of external focus were as follows: paranoia, no surprises, and revisiting strategy often. These three principles are simple enough. Why doesn't everyone abide by them? Perhaps because the whole of Yahoo! had 3,300 employees at its peak in 2000. The management of small, focused companies has fewer problems staying on top of things. It is a different matter for a division head of a company with 30,000 employees to know what's going on before it occurs, and even worse for a CEO of a parent company with fifty divisions spread across the globe. For them external focus must be backed up by a clear, systematic, and fully supported early warning process, a few models of which are presented in this book.

Manager's Checklist

☐ Companies manage risk as a functional issue: financial, operational, public relations. Yet the worst risk—industry dissonance—cuts across all functions, and no one actually *manages* it.

☐ Top executives are especially vulnerable to industry dissonance since they are often the last to know and the first to deny it. Industry dissonance is therefore the most neglected risk with the consequences that are most damaging to careers and wealth.

☐ Industry dissonance cannot be managed through data mining software and other technology toys. It requires human insight.

☐ Strategic response to change should come early, in the form of the "Kaizen" strategy to avoid painful trade-offs.

☐ It is *not* always possible to react to change with a brilliant move that will turn around a bad situation. But management owes it to its shareholders and employees to *always* be on top of the strategic risks and to let them know if and when it has no solution.

There are several software firms that deliberately confuse their clients with offerings of "business intelligence" software, while in essence these are nothing more than data mining tools or storage and classification mechanisms. Business intelligence comes from a network of human sources—people. Can you name a particular software piece whose value as "business intelligence" is especially disappointing? Send it to bsgilad@netvision.net.il. I'll post the names on my Web site, www.bengilad.com, in order of number of "votes" received. The companies will keep selling them to the higher-ups who approve those huge expenditures, but at the least we'll spread the word.

Notes

1. Robert L. Simons, "A Note on Identifying Strategic Risk," Harvard Business School, note # 9-199-031, 1998.
2. Ibid., p. 4.
3. For evidence of this compartmentalization, see chapters 16 and 17 of *Risk Management* by Michael Crouhy, Dan Galai, and Robert Mark (New York: McGraw-Hill, 2001).

CHAPTER 3

The Internal Dynamics of Early Warning Failures

"When a blind man bears the standard, pity those who follow."

—French proverb

This chapter tells the story of some spectacular early warning failures. The purpose is not to degrade the companies mentioned or their executives, but to shed light on the internal dynamic of such failures. Table 3-1 shows that the destructive behaviors described in this chapter are presented elsewhere as well. The detailed stories provide a perspective that was not always available to the public. They should help the reader answer the following questions: Is it top management's fault alone? Could the company have done something differently? Was the dissonance within a changing industry inevitable? Finally, and perhaps most important, could an early warning mechanism have saved the companies from the competitive disaster?

Technology "Golden Boys"

Arzoo.com

Bazillion.com

Q. What is your management's typical attitude toward "bad news"? (Please check all choices that apply).

2.2% a. Does not want to know and will potentially punish the messenger.

13.2% b. Denies it as poorly thought-out or presented.

27.2% c. Says it knows it already and does nothing.

33.8 d. Encourages debate about the news.

23.5% e. Encourages fast delivery and distribution of the news.

Q. If you have identified the potential for a structural change in your industry, which of the following describes how your management typically responds? (Please check all choices that apply.)

8.1% My management will discuss it with its outside consultants only.

19.6% We are the embodiment of "paralysis by analysis"—everyone takes part in the debate.

16.2% The issues will disappear into a "black hole"—no discussion, no action until crisis.

38.5% Management will react but slowly and almost always late.

12.8% We have a method of "forcing quick action" in our company.

4.7% Our company is very proactive.

Early Warning Survey results, Feb. 2002, Academy of Competitive Intelligence.

Table 3-1: Early Warning Survey results: management response.

Buildnet

Carclub.com

Collabria

Cybergold

CyberRebate.com

Dantis

eToys.com

eVoice

eYada

FoodUSA.com

Handtech

Headlight.com

Homebytes.com

iDervie.com

iMotors

Kozmo.com

marchFirst

Mercata

Musicmaker.com

MyBiz.com

NorthPoint Communications

OnlineChoice

PlanetRx.com

Radnet.com

Rival Networks

Rx.com

Savvio.com

Spaceworks

Struxicon

Suck.com

theglobe.com

Themestream

TotalE.com

Voter.com

Webvan

Wwwrrr

Zing.com

The preceding is but a *very* small portion of dot-com companies that failed in 2001 alone. It was published on the now defunct site of *www.upside.com* under the heading: "the dot com
graveyard." Some of these dot-com ventures like Webvan and
eToys burned hundred of millions of dollars while they were
making headlines with visions of cosmic change in the way people shop. Some disappeared without so much as a trace, leaving
behind optimistic statements of a technology breakthrough.

One failure's legacy is worth quoting here. The oldest online
publication, Suck.com, posted the following message of departure on its defunct Web site: "Every day for six years we've been
shucking and jiving for the amusement of a bunch of retards
and you say we're not suffering enough?"

Were the entrepreneurs the ones who suffered? I doubt it.
No one can blame the dot-com founders and executives for failing to observe elementary economic rules of profit and cash flow
while investors were pouring funds down their throats as if it
were Monopoly money. It was the investors who were the actual
"retards." Those who got out in time made millions. The vast
majority of investors, including some very "sophisticated" investment bankers and venture capitalists, lost their shirts.

For about a year, I was a member of the board of directors
of a public venture capital (VC) fund. During my short tenure,
the board approved several investments in new startups. I voted
against those whose business plans were especially ludicrous
and argued strongly for the need to strengthen the analysis of
others, and I was considered a nuisance by the fund management. If I had not been representing a minority shareholder in
this fund, I would have been ousted quickly. It was enough that
the fund management brought an investment for approval for
the majority of board members to trust it to be a worthwhile
investment. Most members of the board were respected members of the community—retired generals, former government
officials, a businessman or two—but almost all were ignorant as
to the fundamental structure of the industries where the investments were made and the competitive strategy needed to prosper
under these structures. Most business plans prepared by the ventures looking for investments had a half-page description of the
industry and its main drivers, and even less on competition,
which was almost universally discounted as insignificant. The

bulk of those proposals were devoted to the *technology*, as if technology brings in the buyers and overcomes competitors *on its own*.

The fund managers were respected for their knowledge and experience in the VC business. The fact that they were mostly technology experts and had little to zero understanding of business strategy was immaterial. Instead of looking at the industries in which they invested and judging each company's prospects based on its strategy *relative to* the forces in its industry, they operated on the vaunted principle that a VC only needs one success in ten to make it big—a principle that cost investors billions of dollars.

Dot-coms failed because the structure of their industries was never attractive, and their strategies did nothing to change this fact. According to Michael Porter's universally familiar model, all industries confront the same five forces, which together constitute an industry structure.[1] These forces are buyers and their bargaining power, suppliers and their bargaining power, new entrants and their ability to overcome entry barriers, substitute industries competing for the same customers with alternative services/products, and rivalry, which is the interaction of incumbents setting the "rules of the game." In the dot-com industries, the bargaining power of buyers was so high that often buyers just did not want to pay for services they could get free from competitors or with better value from substitutes (e.g., advertising in traditional media versus Internet advertising). Entry barriers hardly existed, what with VCs pouring billions into silly ideas as long as someone said the technology was "interesting." Substitutes were readily available. For every dot-com retailer or Asymmetrical Digital Subscriber Line (ADSL) provider or Internet e-commerce there were bricks-and-mortar retailers, slower but sufficient Internet Service Providers' (ISP) services, and old-fashioned, much less expensive Business-to-Business (B2B) transaction routes. Rivalry was ruinous as differentiation was impossible and ease of imitation was so obvious. The inevitable result was the simple fact that cost was higher than revenues for so many dot-coms. One needn't even do industry analysis on a rigorous level to wonder how those dot-coms were going to cover their huge expenses on research and development (R&D) and their lack of any experience in marketing. My experience showed, again and again, that brilliant technologists couldn't replace a sound business strategy. Therefore, one generalization I drew from the "new economy" was that companies that are run by technologists without a great deal of influence by business professionals on finance and strategy are prone to fail the industry dissonance test. Their leaders are too often in love with their technology and are inclined to ignore signs that the market is moving away from it or that substitutes offer the buyers better value. This is true of large companies as well.

The dot-com hallucinations came crashing down very fast. Sometimes, however, the failure of technology-based companies comes decades after the original technologist made a commercial breakthrough, left the company, and moved on. His successors, alas, are left holding the candle in a "one-product" company. The story of Polaroid is one classic example.

Polaroid

Polaroid was founded by Edwin Land, a brilliant inventor and technologist and a researcher of polarized light. In 1948 he invented the instant camera, and instant photography became the core business for Polaroid. For many years, Polaroid was the sole player in the field of instant photography, enjoying strong protection through patents. In 1976, Kodak made an attempt to enter the market but was forced out three years later by a court ruling. The only substitute for instant photography was conventional photography that required long processing time. As a result, Polaroid enjoyed monopoly profits on its product and was Wall Street's darling throughout the 1960s.

The first sign of trouble came in the 1970s. Processing technology of traditional film advanced to the point where "one-hour" development time was possible. That was close enough to offer many customers a reasonable tradeoff. Then in the late 1980s came cheap disposable cameras that appealed to the same consumer desire for alternatives to traditional expensive 35-mm cameras. But the final blow came with digital technology. Starting in the 1990s, instant photography became available, but this time it required no film and none of Polaroid's products. With digital defining the new instant industry, competitors became both camera manufacturers and consumer electronics manufacturers. Polaroid was now competing for the consumer's pocketbook with Sony, Canon, Kodak, Fuji, HP, Epson, and many others. As a result, the buyer had more alternatives and a much higher bargaining power.

Polaroid's industry—instant photography—showcases an evolution led by changes in the force of substitutes. Industries such as steel, horse buggies, and eight-track music players suffered similarly from the emergence of a dominant substitute (aluminum for steel, the automobile for buggies, and tape cassettes for eight-track tapes). In terms of Porter's five forces, if we define the industry as *instant w/film* the evolution looks as shown in Figure 3-1; darker shades signify increasing pressure on the firms in the industry.

If we define the industry more broadly as *all* instant photography, the former substitute (digital photography) becomes part of rivalry, and the diagrams change (see Figure 3-2 on page 32).

The difference in shading of the five forces between the two figures represents the fact that with the broader definition of instant photography to include digital, entry has become much easier for anyone with digital expertise, from consumer electronics to traditional photographic companies, increasing the pressure on incumbents such as Polaroid. Both methods, however, show a clear rise in the power of at least two structural forces. If a company does not take brilliant, bold, proactive, preemptive moves to forestall the effect of such structural hits, it will, *inevitably*, pay dearly. On October 12, 2001, Polaroid filed for bankruptcy. Its stock was trading for a few cents, down from a high of $60 in 1997. Its famous art-deco headquarters on the Charles River was empty and up for sale.

The bankruptcy was the culmination of a process that had started fifteen years earlier. Edwin Land left the company in 1985 after the disastrous failure of his instant motion picture system, Polavision, into which the company poured millions. Polavision lost out to the video camera, an alternative to Polaroid's technology. An executive at Polaroid told the press "everybody but Land knew video was on the way."[2] This is quite typical of strong, charismatic, and autocratic technologists who become leaders in the industry.

As is true of several other companies built around a once-

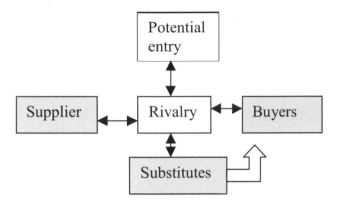

Polaroid's industry structure in the 1970s

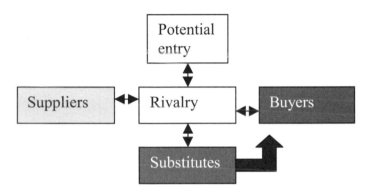

Polaroid's industry structure in the 1990s

Adapted with the permission of The Free Press, a Division of Simon & Schuster Adult Publishing Group, from *Competitive Strategy: Techniques for Analyzing Industries and Competitors* by Michael E. Porter, Copyright © 1980, 1998 by The Free Press.

Figure 3-1: Changes in the instant w/film industry, 1970–1990.

brilliant technology, Land's blindspot persisted for fifteen years after his departure from the company. The signs of a changing industry were mounting everywhere. Polaroid's post-Land leadership just did not want to see them clearly enough.

Consider this:

❐ In 1988, Roy Disney and his Shamrock Holdings Company launched a bid for Polaroid. Shamrock offered $40, which

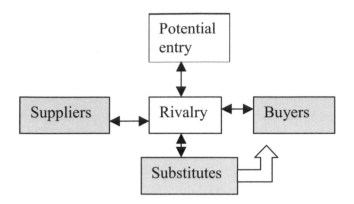

Instant photography industry in the 1970s

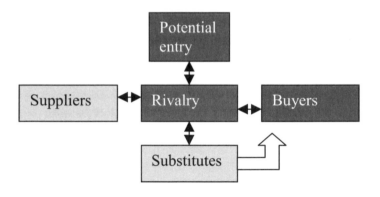

Instant photography in the 1990s

Figure 3-2: Changes in the instant photography industry, 1970–1990.

was $6 above market value at the time. That acquisition would have allowed Polaroid to invest in several promising technologies that would have gotten it out of its core business, which faced increasing challenges from conventional and (at that time) an emerging digital substitution. Instead, Polaroid's management, led by McAllister Booth (a loyal Land follower), borrowed $300 million through its ESOP program (an employee ownership program) and beat back the bid. That was hailed at the time as an innovative use of employees' stock ownership. Alas, it also started what would later be called Polaroid's mountain of debt. In 1986 Polaroid's debt was $171.3 million, by 1989 it was $830 million, and by 2001 it grew to $948.4 million and crushed Polaroid. Fighting such a costly battle to hold off an acquirer as one's industry was slowly but clearly fading away was not a strategic decision that was in the best interests of shareholders. It was a personal blindness. Industry dissonance with the company's strategy was not even acknowledged as possible.

❏ In 1995, as the situation worsened, Polaroid brought in a new CEO, an expert turnaround executive from Black and Decker named Gary DiCamillo. He tried various strategies of revival but mostly cut cost and employment across the line. The market was changing rapidly now, and not in Polaroid's favor, but DiCamillo refused to see it. One of his lieutenants, Carole Uhrich, who headed the commercial division, advised DiCamillo in 1998, with shares still at $40, to sell the company. Her recommendations came on the heels of a long internal debate over the speed of advances in digital technology. The advance of digital technology meant the company's strategy of relying on high-margin instant cameras and film was quickly becoming incongruent with the changing market. Her conclusion, based on an internal report, was that digital's progress would leave Polaroid's in the dust (which it did, very quickly for commercial customers). DiCamillo's response, which became famous as blinders go: "The board did not hire me to sell the company."[3] It surely did not bring him in to bankrupt it, either . . . Again, personal blinders prevailed over clear signs that Polaroid's strategy was failing to address the fundamental changes in the instant industry.

So what *was* Polaroid's strategy in those last few years? On the surface it might have looked like a reasonably successful strategy. Under DiCamillo, Polaroid introduced a big hit product, the I-Zone camera, which produced stamp-size "sticker photos" that were very popular with teenagers, even though the camera was of low quality and some employees called it "junk." Polaroid was also producing digital cameras and selling many of them—1.3 million in 2000 alone. And then Polaroid had two winning technological aces up its sleeve—new digital image printing technology known as Opal and a handheld device called Onyx that printed high-quality instant monochrome prints.

However, upon closer examination—*relative to the industry's changes*—the strategy was obsolete. The industry dissonance just grew larger.

❐ The I-Zone was still just an attempt to revive the dying instant camera with film industry, not to address the fundamental reality of a fading technology. Alas, the teenage market does not use much film (it's a fad, not a functional use), and the I-Zone produced lower margins than previous instant products (much of the profit in instant comes from the film). The I-Zone also required significant outlays on marketing. Overall, it did not change the picture of a sliding instant camera with film market. Instead, it gave the illusion of "success" to the old guard at Polaroid who wanted to stick by the old technology. The strategy of high-margin cameras and film was replaced with a strategy of low-margin cameras and film. By the second quarter of 2001, Polaroid was losing $109 million on revenues that fell 33 percent.

❐ Polaroid's digital camera was a halfhearted attempt to enter the digital age. It was on the low end, bringing in very little (if any) profit. Manufacturing was outsourced, and Polaroid just added its software. Polaroid did not have the technological savvy, manufacturing economies, or marketing deep pockets to compete with Sony, Kodak, Canon, Fuji, HP, and Epson on the high end. As will be seen later though, the main problem was that Polaroid's leadership did not have the serious commitment to moving into a new industry. The changing nature of rivalry with the entry of digital instant required much more than a hesitant, halfhearted effort on the part of management if Polaroid was to survive.

❐ The two new printing technologies needed a lot of cash to move forward fast. Even if the cash was available (not spent on marketing low-margin consumer products), rivalry was much stronger than in the instant camera with film industry. Kodak and Fuji locked most channels of distribution for the Opal technology, which aimed at printing high-quality images for consumers who brought in their digital cameras. It required space in kiosks and shopping centers that was already occupied. The Onyx technology required very strong partners, and at that late stage in the game, Polaroid had little to offer them.

It is unfair to lay the blame on Gary DiCamillo's shoulders for all of Polaroid's troubles. The decline started under Land himself, and Polaroid's refusal to look reality straight in the face dates back many years. Instant cameras with film were a stagnant industry back in the 1980s. It just took twenty years to die off. But unlike Land, neither Booth nor DiCamillo had any reason to stick blindly to their old instant technology, the "core business." When your core business is disappearing under your feet, it should be your core business to *change* cores. . . . The popular management trend of "going back to one's core" or "core competency" as an instant remedy to a company's problems is based on a fundamental fallacy that ignored the environment. Core competencies must fit a changing world to be worth developing or sticking with. But most of DiCamillo's efforts between 1995 and 2000 were focused on preserving or reviving the old "core business" that had no future. Anything that did not fit this obsolete "core" was jettisoned or got shuffled in endless reorganizations.

For example, Polaroid was an earlier developer of holographic technology, held the number-one position in the market, and had products that were superior to those of other competitors. Holography is heavily figured in security tags as well as backing for displays on cell phones, two examples of markets with a large upside potential. In 1998 it was estimated to be in the range of $2.8 billion, up from $1 billion in 1997. Yet inside Polaroid, the holographic division was limping along. It never received serious investment. Its people were put on notice that the division was not performing. At a security conference, a U.S. government expert testified that in his eight years on the job, he had never seen a forgery of a Polaroid hologram, yet Polaroid shut down its hologram division and spun off its holographic storage portion because it drained resources from the "core business." If anyone had made a serious analysis of the industry structure for holography, it would have been immediately clear that it was a much better industry to be in than the dying instant camera with film. If anyone did make such an analysis, no one at the top at Polaroid listened.

Could anything have changed Polaroid's fate? I believe that an effective, culturally supported, early warning system used by DiCamillo and his top aides would have helped significantly, especially in his earlier days at Polaroid. It is clear, though, that Polaroid did not have *any* such systematic process, and as a result, DiCamillo and his top aides had no chance at all: They were operating on the basis of wrong assumptions, insulated in their intuitions and beliefs and "vision" of a better future until the company collapsed. Evidence of that can be found in the way Polaroid's competitive intelligence worked (or did not work).

Competitive intelligence analysis of the industry was carried out at Polaroid in the business unit level, not at DiCamillo's level. As one former manager described it to me, it was obvious to everyone that digital would one day replace Polaroid's instant technology, and the only question was *How fast?*

This is a critical question for a company whose livelihood depends on the answer. One would expect that following basic rules of risk management—and Polaroid was facing significant risk—DiCamillo and his top aides would build a serious early warning capability that would track this issue constantly and alert management to significant developments, so that management could follow Yahoo!'s philosophy described in Chapter 2 and ask frequently and honestly: "Are we (still) doing the right thing?" One would also expect emergency meetings at the top to debate and act decisively when the alarms went off. None of it happened at Polaroid. Instead, a siege mentality of "we stick to our core" took effect and pushed all others efforts aside.

By 1998, digital was taking away a significant chunk of Polaroid's commercial business, from real estate to medical to drivers' licenses. Instead of concluding that consumer business was going to follow suit, Polaroid's management of the consumer side made rosy forecasts. It urged corporate management to shift its focus from commercial to consumer, where the pace of adoption of digital would be much slower. A 1997 report on Generation Y's fast adoption of digital technology was completely ignored. DiCamillo did not even see it. Strategy sessions at the division paid lip service to competition in digital. DiCamillo and his staff ignored recommendations of an internal task force on digital strategy. Competitive intelligence (CI) reports that said over and over "the world is changing, we must act now" did not lead to action. Instead, in one of the cost-cutting rounds, CI was basically *eliminated*.

In one illuminating incident, a presentation made in 1998 to the consumer division on future trends that would affect strategy encountered a chilly reception. The president of the division sitting at this meeting dismissed the suggestions as "fun" futuristic stuff without many *actionable* implications. Four years later the future was there with plenty of action. . . .

The absence of a rational approach to risk management using an early warning system cost Polaroid's investors their investment and Polaroid's employees their pension funds. Executives who listen only to the voices inside their heads make very poor risk managers.

If Polaroid's saga is mainly the failure to properly manage the rise in the power of substitutes, Lucent's story is a classic sad example of the failure to understand changing buyers' needs.

Lucent

In 1996, when AT&T spun off Lucent Technologies, the company became an instant market leader with considerable power in the telecom equipment industry. AT&T was the leading producer of voice communication infrastructure for the telecommunications industry. The customers—Regional Bell Operating Companies (also known as RBOCs)—were all dependent on AT&T infrastructure in which they invested billion of dollars.

Lucent walked right into this legacy. The buyers had little choice but to buy from Lucent. Lucent therefore formulated a strategy that made a lot of sense. It aimed to become a one-stop shop for their "captive" buyers, offering a wide range of products. It also insisted on producing all those products in-house, a vertically integrated strategy, because it wanted to ensure the quality of its voice communication products. It was an admirable goal, and a successful strategy.

For about a year or two.

The first sign of risk to Lucent's strategy was completely lost on Lucent, but not on Nortel, which was at the time Lucent's relatively smaller Canadian competitor. That sign was a faster growth rate in the data communication market in 1995–1996. It was still light-years behind voice communication, but it should have raised a red flag for Lucent, which was totally dependent on AT&T's voice communication technology. Data communication required much faster equipment with greater capacity than voice. In 1995, looking into the future, Nortel developed a revolutionary product just for this market, a fiber-optic network system called OC-192. OC-192 carried 10 gigabits a second. Lucent's optical equipment carried 2.5. OC-192 also had 400 percent more capacity.

The second sign of risk showed in signals sent by the government about deregulating competition in the markets served by the Bell companies. In 1996 these were mere noises, nothing to worry about—unless, of course, you had an early warning system that forced you to worry about the future. Lucent had none.

Fast-forward to 2001. In the short six years that had passed, the change triggers (technology and regulations) had had a huge effect on Porter's five forces. Data communication had become the market to be in. Voice had been flat for quite a while. Local competition to the RBOCs had emerged in the form of Competitive Local Exchange Carriers (CLECs). Eventually the CLECs proved a flop, and most disappeared or merged. But between 1996 and 2001 they created panic among the RBOCs.

Anyone working with the giant Bell companies knows these are bureaucracies that operate at the speed of a snail on Valium. Yet the appearance of the CLECs changed them in one important dimension. The CLECs had no infrastructure from old AT&T, and therefore had no loyalty to Lucent. In their bid to serve business customers (the cream of the market), they bought fast fiber-optic networks from anyone who could provide them with the hottest products, e.g., Nortel, Ciena, and other new players in the market for data communication equipment. The RBOCs had to respond or lose their choice customers, those who could afford to pay for faster traffic. The RBOCs responded by breaking the age-old tie with Lucent and buying optical equipment from the "best of breed" instead of a one-stop shop. Lucent's strategy was in tatters. It did not have the products to compete or the technology to develop them. New competitors were entering fast as barriers to entry were falling with the new technology.

Worse, the new fiber-optic technology brought about a host of new specialized suppliers. The new players in the (data) communication equipment industry preferred a strategy of outsourcing as a method of keeping up with fast-changing technologies. As a result, component manufacturers gained power. Their cost was lower than Lucent's by as much as 32 percent. This changing constellation of forces is depicted in Figure 3-3, again using Porter's model for simplicity. It is amazing how changed an industry can look in just six years (see Figure 3-3; darker shades signify rising pressure).

The results of the changes in the industry were disastrous for Lucent. In 2001, it reported about $16 billion in losses including special charges. In one quarter alone it lost $8.8 billion. It started 2001 with 123,000 employees and ended it with 57,000. Forty thousand people lost their jobs (the rest retired or left). Richard McGinn, chairman and CEO, was ousted amid allegations of misleading accounting practices and misleading statements to security analysts. Lucent's debt was rated "junk." Its stock, which had traded at $84 in January, plummeted to below $10 by September 2001. Remember—this was Lucent, the giant, global market leader in the important industry of telecommunications equipment, and its market cap was less than some Internet ventures!

The failure of Lucent's leadership to manage industry dissonance was total. First there was the complete disregard for the changing circumstances of their main buyers. Then it was total lack of attention to competitors, both old and new. In entering the data communication race, Lucent chose an inferior product (OC-48) and stuck to its in-house production strategy in an industry where the race demanded outsourcing. The in-house strategy resulted in quality problems, a lag in incorporating new technologies into the product line, and prices that were outright uncompetitive. When eventually, in 1999, it decided to outsource, Lucent faced a surprise: component shortage. The market was hot, and suppliers had the upper hand. They placed

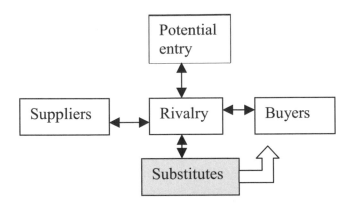

Telecommunications equipment industry in 1996 (voice mainly)

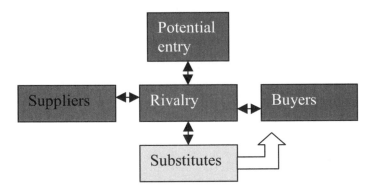

Telecommunications equipment industry in 2001 (data & voice)

Figure 3-3: Changes in the telecommunications equipment industry, 1996–2001.

Lucent low on their list. Its competitors, who had been buying for years now, had priority.

Was Lucent a case of wrong bet on technology? You bet. Was it an issue of fear of cannibalizing one's own profitable products? Sure. In his best-selling book, *The Innovator's Dilemma* (Harvard School of Business, 1999), which pre-dated the Lucent fiasco, Clayton Christensen details several famous similar cases. Christensen's model explains convincingly how internal pressures to satisfy existing customers can prevent companies from innovating in time to save themselves. What is clear in all his examples but especially in our example of Lucent is a simple but powerful realization: Without an early warning approach to industry dissonance, innovators' dilemmas are inevitable and immensely destructive. With a strategic early warning process embedded in its culture and supported and used by top management, Lucent's profits and stock might have been spared the total crash of 2001. To see that, consider the following.

As early as 1996, Lucent's competitive intelligence professionals warned management that the data communication market was heating up and posing a serious threat to Lucent's reliance on exploiting voice communication sales to loyal RBOC customers. Intelligence reports on Nortel's OC-192 product were accurate and timely. Lucent's intelligence knew early on about Nortel's first transaction of OC-192 with Qwest, shipped in 1997, totaling $150 million, and the frenzied acceptance of new optical equipment by the market. Yet Richard McGinn and the top optical division executives, who met only once a month (!) during those years, chose to ignore these reports. Competitive intelligence managers were tucked down below in Lucent's enormous organizational structure, had no direct reporting line to any senior executive and no effect on senior decision making, and never once came even close to making a presentation to the board. The result was that in August 1997, in a meeting in Red Bank, New Jersey, McGinn and his lieutenants decided to postpone the development of OC-192 by Lucent's R&D lab. Instead, Lucent offered the RBOCs its inferior OC-48 product, which was produced in-house. Following this meeting, and up to 1999, Lucent's plant managers and the CI managers warned about outsourcing as a competitive advantage of Lucent's competitors and pointed at Lucent's lack of competitive pricing on OC-48 due to the in-house production cost and quality problems. Top management ignored these warnings.

It is hard to know how much of his company's competitive intelligence actually reached McGinn himself, how much he personally ignored, or how much was massaged and blocked by the optical division executives and never made it to his attention. It is easier to state unequivocally that Lucent did not have a systematic, effective, early warning process that forced top management, especially corporate, to pay attention to tectonic changes in the structural forces. At the least, such a process would have forced McGinn and his lieutenants to schedule strategic discussions more often than once a month in an industry that was changing at the speed of light

The "Old Economy" and the "Light Brigade"

Failure to manage industry dissonance does not occur only in technology companies. True, the pace of change in technology sectors is so fast, and the decision makers are so enamored with their technology, that industry dissonance is always a risk. But consider this: Change in the environment does not have to be in the form of a "big bang" to destroy a strategy's fit. It can accumulate bit by tactical bit until over time it simply overwhelms a company. Take for example the case of Procter & Gamble (P&G).

The Old Economy—Procter & Gamble

In January 2000, P&G's stock price hovered around $120. By March 6, 2000, it had fallen by 28 percent to $87. Then, as if that wasn't bad enough, in one day, from March 6 to March 7, it collapsed to $60. I was in P&G's headquarters in Cincinnati on that date. It was not a pleasant day. Many of P&G's middle managers had significant amounts of stock and options as part of their savings and retirement plans. These savings were massacred.

P&G has always been a solid company. Its portfolio of brands includes such famous products as Tide, Pampers, Crest toothpaste, Cover Girl cosmetics, and Charmin and Bounty paper products. What made the market judge it so harshly?

The announcement immediately preceding the worst-day-in-its-stock-history event was that P&G's earning growth would be 7 percent. The market expected 13 percent based upon CEO Durk Jaeger's earlier forecast.

That was Jaeger's third time of missing an earning forecast.

Following the market reception, Jaeger resigned after only eighteen months on the job. The former CEO and chairman, John Pepper, was called back from retirement to save P&G. The stock hovered between $60 and $70 for most of 2001. Under a new leader, A. G. Lafley, it rose back in 2002 to the $80 range. (more on Lafley in Chapter 10).

There is an element of absurdity in this story. Durk Jaeger was actually the CEO who was trying to fix the problems created by his predecessors. He was decisive and innovative. He just missed his forecasts, and the market judged him to be out of touch—more even than the general market crash would explain.

Markets can be fickle, hysterical, and downright silly, as the Internet bubble proved. But over time, the market's valuation of companies is rather rational. The reason P&G's stock was dumped was not the 7 versus 13 percent growth, and it was not a result of a general collapse of the market. The reason for the crash was that P&G's market leadership position had been eroding continually in the 1990s. Actually, some will claim that P&G's last big invention was in 1961, when it introduced Pampers!

Let's look at changes in P&G's industry over those years. The biggest force of change in the consumer products industry was the changing character of the buyers. From mom-and-pop grocery stores and small department stores with little bargaining power, the buyers changed into huge discount chains such as Wal-Mart, and huge grocery chains such as Albertson's. The change in buyers' characteristics shifted the balance of power from the manufacturers of consumer brands to the retailers, and most important, caused a brutal fight for shelf space. The manufacturer could no longer dictate the terms of trade to the retailer. If the merchandise did not move fast enough, the retailer pulled the product off the shelf and gave the space to others. The result was not apparent overnight. It took years. It moved slowly, trend after trend, but it was consistent, persistent, and inevitable.

The rising buyers' power made the rivalry for the crowded shelf space ferocious. To stay a dominant leader, manufacturers had to be innovative, unique, fast, and bold. P&G was *none* of those. Looking at P&G's portfolio in 2000, the market saw nineteen out of thirty core brands bleeding. A former market-leading brand, such as Crest, was losing badly to aggressive competitors such as Total, a Colgate product. Pampers was facing tough and successful competition for market leadership from Kimberly-Clark's Huggies. In both cases, P&G was late to catch on to market trends and late to innovate. In toothpaste, the aging baby boomers had fewer cavities but more gum disease. Total came out with an anti-gingivitis ingredient, got approved by the American Dental Association as the only toothpaste containing it, and buried Crest. In diapers, Huggies came out with pull-ups, catching Pampers, well, with its pants down. In cosmetics, L'Oréal was leading with a unique hair salon distribution system that posed enormous barrier to entry to its markets, and P&G's Cover Girl and Oil of Olay were losing share to Maybelline and Revlon in what remained of the segment in the mass merchandisers. In food, Nestlé and Unilever were growing, acquiring everything that seemed to move, while P&G's share was shrinking. As an overall portfolio of brands, *BusinessWeek* calculated that P&G's value declined by 6 percent in August 2001 as compared to August 2000, while Nestlé, Unilever, and Colgate grew by 2 to 5 percent.[4] The bottom line was that, unlike the situation in1960, by 2000 P&G did not have *any* significant technological *or* competitive lead over its main competitors.

Competition from other brands was not the only rising pressure. Substitutes for global brands in the form of private labels had been giving P&G a headache for over two decades. From insignificant phenomenon, private labels grew through the 1980s and 1990s reaching 35 percent in some markets. In several large non-U.S. markets, especially in Asia, strong *local* brands lowered P&G's share. Since P&G brands were global and standardized to a large degree, they could never fully account for local preferences. Taken together, the loss of technological lead and the fierce competition from substitutes of local and private brands meant price competition was much worse in 2000 than in 1961.

So where could growth come from? Maybe pharmaceuticals? The pharmaceutical industry grew at a healthy rate throughout the late 1990s. P&G was a small player because its pharmaceutical division had always been a stepchild to P&G management, who grew up in consumer goods. It was rumored that P&G would make a play for a large pharmaceutical company (names mentioned were AHP and Warner-Lambert) to get into this growth sector seriously. By February 2000, however, it was clear that no such deal was going to happen. The assessment was that P&G just did not have the resources or expertise to execute such a huge move. That doomed the last venue for fast growth. The market came to terms with P&G's less appealing position in a much less attractive industry (see Figure 3-4).

Could P&G have done anything *differently* to prevent the slow but persistent loss of market leadership, especially when it accelerated in the late 1990s? Could it have prevented the industry dissonance with its strategy? Can any market leader defend its dominance and attractive margins forever in a contestable market? This is a hypothetical, and therefore largely irrelevant, question for P&G. Strategy gurus such as Gary Hamel of the London Business School and Michael Porter of Harvard claim it can be done with forward-looking, innovative strategies. What is clear to me is that P&G's management never actually internalized the severity of the change in its industry. P&G management has traditionally been composed mostly of "lifers." It hardly ever recruited from the outside to its senior positions. As leadership expert Warren Bennis claims, lifers tend to believe that their *unique* vision is the only route to success. "When they feel threatened," Bennis told *Fortune* magazine, "[lifers] focus even more on what brought them their success. They get that narrowing of the eyes. They dismiss anything that clashes with their beliefs."[5]

"Narrowing of the eyes" is, of course, just another term for our "blindspots." At P&G, fierce politics and a very strict hierarchy played a significant role in shaping strategy and internal debates. As discussed in Chapter 10, these two are red flags for the lack of an early warning culture. Autonomous business units' rivalries also contributed to lack of a systematic effort at strategic risk analysis. Management was not known for taking criticism nicely. Action was slow, external focus was low, and loyalty was cherished above all. I can only suggest to lifers, as well as other executives, that a systematic early warning system may be the only sensible and practical way to prevent their eyes from being wide shut in such strong, proud, and internally focused cultures.

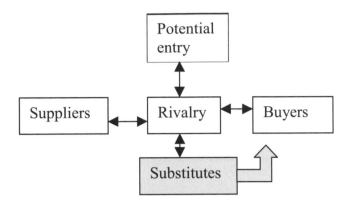

Branded consumer products industry in 1960

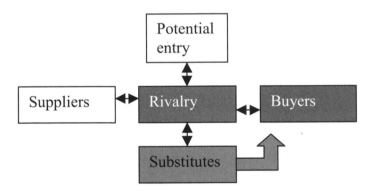

Branded consumer products industry in 2001

Figure 3-4: Changes in the consumer products industry, 1960–2001.

The Light Brigade—Levi Strauss

The Light Brigade was an elite cavalry unit in the British army, which was fighting a war against Russia in the Crimea on the Black Sea in the 1850s. During one night, the Russians overwhelmed the British front line and captured some territory, including many British cannons. The Light Brigade was ordered to take it back. Proud and disciplined, driven by blind loyalty and inner convictions, the cavalry charged the enemy line, ignoring intelligence and physical evidence that the Russians had turned the cannons around. Sitting straight in their saddles, never once flinching in the face of the enemy, the lightly armored cavalry was slaughtered. The battle has become a symbol of bravery but more so of silly pride and blindness—both on the part of the high command who sent the cavalry in without knowing (or caring) what it was up against, and on the part of the brigade's leadership, who ignored all signs of risk in the name of tradition, pride, and a vision.

Some business cases can only be described as examples of the Light Brigade's total foolhardy blindness. This is the case of Levi Strauss.

Say you entered a company's chain store looking for a product you wanted. You look around and the merchandise seems to be familiar—you've seen it there while growing up. You may conclude, correctly, that the company who owns the chain has not changed much with the times. If everything else in this industry has been changing, you don't need an industry analysis to tell you management is focused more internally than externally. This was the case of Levi Strauss under Bob Haas.

Levi Strauss is a 150-year-old company that was for many years the clear dominant player in the jeans and business-casual clothing markets. Three out of four red-blooded American males own at least one pair of Levi's Dockers khakis. In jeans the company owned the market until the 1990s. It has been one of the strongest brand names among teens and their parents for decades.

Bob Haas, a descendant of the founding family and the son of a former Levi's CEO, took over the CEO position in 1984. In 1996, he completed a move that turned Levi's private through a management-led leveraged buyout that started in 1985. From then on, what Haas did to this proud company in his capacity as CEO can only be described as a massacre.[6]

First the statistics: In 1990, Levi's had 48.2 percent of the jeans market. By 1998 it had 25 percent, by 2000, about 17 percent, while the jeans market expanded by 4 percent. Its brand awareness among teens dipped to 7 percent. From sales in the $7 billion range in 1996, it dropped to under $6 billion in 1998, and as Haas resigned (but stayed as chairman—after all, his family owns the company), it dropped to $5 billion in 2000. In 1999, it laid off 15,000 employees and shut down thirty out of fifty-one plants, and its mounting debt had been downgraded by debt rating agencies.

Levi's was a classic case of a leader with a vision, but the vision did not match reality, and the leader did not let that obstruct his actions. Surrounded by like-minded executives such as Gordon Shank, head of Levi's North America and later Levi's chief marketer, the leadership of Levi's was completely blind to changes in the industry. Throughout the 1990s it continued to produce Levi's traditional straight-legged, five standard-size pocket, shrink-to-fit blue jeans, ignoring almost every style trend imaginable from baggy pants to big-pockets denim to carpenter pants to stretch fiber. Haas and company looked down on or outright ignored competitors, which numbered in the single digits prior to 1990 but came in the dozens by 1999. They ignored a major shift in the power of Levi's traditional buyers, the department stores, whose fortunes were declining, and who eventually turned out to be worse competitors of Levi's with their own private brands of jeans (such as Arizona from JCPenney). By 2000, young people were buying their jeans in specialty stores, from the VF Corporation (Lee and Wrangler), Gap, Calvin Klein, Tommy Hilfiger, Diesel, JNCO, Kikwear, Bongo, Stussy, Fubu, Mudd, and many, many more. But to Haas and Shank, the five forces never existed.

How could top management miss *all* the signs? How can anyone ignore a decade of slipping numbers, a complete annihilation in an important segment (youth), and a collapse of its other leading brand, Dockers, which was late (no kidding . . .) in adopting wrinkle-free technology?

The answer is insularity. There are some companies where top management is just *sure* it knows it all. It is sure it knows it better than anyone else. It has the solutions, and it is just a matter of time until they prove right. It steadfastly refuses to listen to objective outside observers. In the case of Levi's, it was the company's own distributors who tried to convince management of changing trends, to no avail. They showed Levi's executives their numbers, shared their focus groups, and begged the arrogant and insular managers to look around, but Levi's executives refused to believe!

But even the most insular management could not miss the rise of more than a dozen new competitors, could it? Well, that depends on whether one is a member of what I call the "Cocoon Club." One of chaos theory's famous claims is that a butterfly moving its wings in Singapore will have an effect on the climate in North America because even the smallest event has repercussions. The Cocoon Club is composed of executives such as Haas and Shank who believe the exact *opposite* (that's why I call them "cocoonuts"): It does not matter what competitors are doing, it only matters what you are doing. There is a healthy dose of "cocoonism" in all the great leaders who plow forward refusing to imitate competitors, but keeping their companies in the lead with bold, unique moves that transform the five forces. Members of the Cocoon Club, however, bring their companies to the brink instead.

What makes a cocoonut? A vision so vivid, so urgent, that reality just does not matter anymore. Haas was not interested in running a competitive company. His vision was to re-create capitalism in his humanistic image of utopia. Since the day he took over, he was obsessive about making the company and its employees more "inspirational." More than eighty task forces diligently worked on the great social experiment of remaking the workplace into a more spiritual environment, saturated with values of love, community, and political correctness. Maybe for some, Haas's humanistic management was an admirable goal, but it replaced an external focus with an internal obsessive-compulsive culture that made no decisions and was busy exploring its navel.

The pinnacle of Haas's vision was a mammoth project, initiated by Haas, to reengineer the company's customer supply chain. The goal? To reduce development time for new products from fifteen to three months and to reduce restocking of their stores from three weeks to seventy-two hours! To accomplish this "Miracle on Thirty-Fourth Street" (no other description can fit it), Haas, a former McKinsey consultant, brought in the big boys—Andersen Consulting. For two years, from 1993 to 1995, 100 of Andersen's and 200 of Levi's best people set out to revolutionize Levi's. The army of outside and inside consultants took over the third floor in Levi's headquarters in San Francisco and was labeled by disbelieving insiders "the Third Floor Brigade" (very fitting for our Light Brigade file).

The project cost $850 million, befitting a project managed by one of the big consulting firms. It kept the best Levi's managers occupied for three years. It turned employees into an anxious crowd who did not know what jobs they would have the next day and whether or not they would have to reapply for them. It produced the incredible result of increasing Levi's restocking time from twenty-one to twenty-seven days. That's not a joke.[7]

On Early Warning Failure and the Big Consultants

The folly of reengineering, restructuring, and other "re" diseases is not so much in their often nonsensical but very hyped goals and outcomes. I am always amazed how much companies pay the outside "experts" for the simple advice to merge a few business units just so that several years later they can again pay them exorbitant prices to break the units apart. Instead of spending money on a first-class early warning system, many large U.S. firms focus their attention on the next restructuring mayhem. The irony is that those big management initiatives destroy any shred of attention to the outside world, in the name of being more *adaptable* to the outside world. . . . At Levi's, the consultants and the internal team of vice presidents and other powerful people pasted on poster board huge photos of magazine covers dealing with companies that were in trouble for ignoring changing markets. The absurdity did not end there: The team published a 145-page handbook titled *Individual Readiness for a Changing Environment*.

The theater of the absurd in the ritual of bringing in the big hired guns to restructure companies is not unique to Levi Strauss. Lucent and P&G have been avid users of the big consulting firms over the years, as have many of the Fortune 500 companies. The prestigious consulting firms employ an army of extremely talented people, and no one can fault them for carrying out their work in their own business interests. Their effect on companies, however, is another matter. A prudent use of outside consulting is beneficial. It brings an external perspective, which, if combined with an internal dialogue and careful listening to customers, suppliers, and competitors, can help management stay ahead of the game.

However, "serial" use of consulting, especially the big strategy consulting empires, as I have found again and again, can be quite destructive. The blame is squarely on management, not on the consultants. First, by handing over strategy to the big guns, management abdicates its *main* responsibility for independent thinking and creative strategy making—and don't be fooled by the common window dressing claim that "we bring them in but *we* make the decisions." Second, and more pertinent to our subject matter, management ability to manage strategic risks is critically diminished with "serial" use of the big consulting firms.

The essence of an effective early warning system, as will be described in detail in Chapters 5 through 8, is that it relies on the company's own people, a whole organization working together diligently to identify early trends and predict significant future developments that can threaten the company's viability. It requires a perspective from within, looking outside, and it requires continuity—a patient build-up of internal knowledge. Most of all, it requires management that *trusts and listens* to its people. This is naturally an antidote to the role of the big consulting firm, which comes in and gets out, leaving the company with little but its perspective, which it then takes to the next client. In the process, however, it severs the direct link between junior-middle management and top executives. However, many of the executives in Fortune 500 firms feel compelled to use the consultants to cover their collective rear ends, as if employing the most expensive and useless advice around makes them more credible as managers.

In my years of training top competitive intelligence managers, I observed that frequent use of the big consultants usually signals the *opposite*—management that is directing its attention away from its fundamental role of managing the company's strategic risks. The process takes different shapes in different companies, but its common properties are familiar to almost every middle manager working for a large organization. First, management stops listening to the "small guys" in its environment—distributors, customers, etc. Then it ignores competitors' signals, and as the big consulting firms are called in, management stops listening to its own middle managers as well. Everything must go through the consultants who control the channels to top management thinking. Internal dissent against the consultants' recommendations is squashed. The consultants, especially the senior project leaders (usually partners in the consulting firms), mold management perception of the outside world, modifying "harsh" conclusions that may meet resistance with more politically acceptable ones. Finally, as the consultants depart, they leave a company behind with little or no intelligence capability. The dependency is so complete that executives must bring them back to survive. Therefore, one clear signal of a company at risk of developing industry dissonance is one with "flavor of the month" initiatives and an obsessive, serial use of big consulting firms. No executive can pay attention to the changes in the environment when his mind is on a big corporate "re" project and the consultants are running around freely in his company. Just imagine the U.S. government contracting with a foreign intelligence service to provide it with an assessment of its national security . . . how much trust would you have in it?

Getting over the big consulting firms may be difficult. The way top management in large U.S. companies thinks and operates has become a force of habit to a whole generation of executives who may need to be replaced before behavior changes significantly. Even the tremendous success of the Japanese multinationals against Western companies several times their size, and their obvious *dis*inclination to use the large consulting firms (a disinclination they abandoned in the 1990s) did not persuade U.S. executives to kick the habit and rely on their own human resources. However, as the business environment becomes riskier, business will need to build a more effective *internal* competency in managing strategic risks. The competitive early warning process described schematically in Chapter 4 is one excellent alternative to the old reliance on the Big Five or Big Three or Big Two (the final number depends on the latest scandal . . .).

Manager's Checklist

❑ The dot-coms' collapse suggests one broad generalization: Companies run by strong "technologists" without significant influence by business professionals (finance, marketing, strategy) are prone to fail the industry dissonance test. Their leaders are too much in love with the technology to pay attention to market forces.

❑ Polaroid: "Everybody but Land knew video was on the way." Gates, Allison, McNeal, Chambers—are you listening?

❑ Polaroid: Executives who listen only to the voices inside their heads make very poor risk managers. Executives who listen only to the voices of the large consulting firms and the large investment banks make equally poor risk managers, but cost their shareholders a lot more.

❑ Lucent: Executives who meet once a month or less to discuss the industry and how their strategy fits it within a high-tech environment going through gut-wrenching technological change are poor risk managers.

❑ P&G: Lifers tend to put a lot of faith in what they see as their unique experience in the company and its industry. Any evidence to the contrary is dismissed.

❑ A competitive early warning system may be a sensible and practical process to avoid having executives' eyes wide shut. Lifers, technology visionaries, and passionate entrepreneurs should consider it a first aid kit—maybe the *only* aid kit—for visions going astray.

❑ Levi Strauss: Do you know the type of companies where management already knows it all? And they are already busy solving the "temporary" problems with initiatives and new initiatives and more initiatives, and they don't need anyone telling them what's wrong with them and "Yes, we took our eyes off the ball for a while, but *now* we are coming out with this initiative and it will solve the problems"? They are typically as blind as a bat.

❑ There are those executives who sincerely believe that it does not matter what competitors are doing, but only what the company, i.e., they themselves, are doing. I call this theory the cocoon theory, and these executives, cocoonuts.

❑ Companies and executives who are known for using the big consulting firms frequently are prone to industry dissonance. Management that is a serial user of the big consulting firms or their personnel tends to ignore first its own people, then its own markets.

> I would like to start a collection of stories about companies where the large consulting firms left a trail of destruction, took a lot of money, and provided no proof of value. I will post one such story periodically on my Web site, www.ben gilad.com. Send the story to bsgilad@netvision.net.il. If you are convincing enough, the market may open the executives' eyes.

Notes

1. See Michael E. Porter, *Competitive Strategy: Techniques for Analyzing Industries and Competitors* (New York: Free Press, 1980), Chapter 1.
2. Nolan Young, "How Polaroid Lost Sight of the Bigger Picture," *Scotland on Sunday*, 28 Oct. 2001.
3. James Bandler, "Polaroid Banks on New Inventions," *Wall Street Journal*, 22 Aug. 2001.
4. *Business Week* cover story, "The Best Global Brands," by Gerry Khermouch in New York, with Stanley Holmes in Seattle and Moon Ihlwan in Seoul, 6 Aug. 2001. While no one should take the measures of global brand power too seriously, this story reinforces the problem facing P&G.
5. Ram Charan and Geoffrey Colvin, "Why CEOs Fail," *Fortune*, 21 June 1999, p. 39.
6. *Fortune* labeled it "How Levi's Trashed a Great American Brand," by Nina Munk, 12 April 1999, pp. 33–38.
7. See *Fortune*, 12 April 1999, p. 37.

CHAPTER 4

The Analytical, the Tactical, the Couch Potato, and the Blind

"Planning is an unnatural process; it is much more fun to do something. The nicest thing about not planning is that failure comes as a complete surprise, rather than being preceded by a period of worry and depression."
—*Sir John Harvey-Jones*

Chapter 3 presented a few extreme cases of failure to heed clear signs of impending disaster. The internal dynamic of these failures showed management that was dangerously out of touch with trends and developments in its industry. Table 4-1 shows that many more companies are potential candidates for failure. Recall that industry dissonance is the risk that a company will become misaligned with its changing environment, i.e., the company's strategy and its underlying assumptions and convictions are or will be out of sync with the evolving reality of its market(s). Identifying signs of industry dissonance as early as possible should therefore be one of executives' main priorities and one

---

Q. Does your company have a systematic approach (an early warning process) to mitigate or reduce structural risk (risk to your strategy)?

2.9%	Yes, fully formal and systematic
62.7%	Some components of a systematic process but not all
33.3%	No systematic process at all
1.0%	I don't know

Early Warning Survey results, Feb. 2002, Academy of Competitive Intelligence.

Table 4-1: Early Warning Survey results: process and system.

of the reasons why executives are so highly compensated with stock options.

But how does one identify the risks of industry dissonance? There are additional related questions:

‣ Where do the highest risks lie?

‣ What can one do to track these risks in "real time"?

‣ How does one force management to act on early signs?

These are the issues that any early warning mechanism must address directly and effectively. The approach taken in this book is to treat each of these questions as a step in an integrated early warning cycle. To understand the importance of integration as a basic requirement of early warning, let us examine the current methods used by organizations to get a handle on strategic risks (and, yes, opportunities as well).

Prioritizing risk must be the first step in ensuring rational managerial action to address threats, given a company's limited resources and management attention. In most large Western companies, identifying strategic risks and then prioritizing them is the role of strategic planning. Strategic planning is a discipline that has ebbed and flowed over the past thirty years. It knew better days in the 1960s, declined significantly in the 1990s, and is now making a comeback *of sorts*. Many management researchers have documented the process of strategic planning and strategy-making in large companies.[1] Their conclusion was that strategy is often the result of a sequence of decisions that move incrementally, rather than a formal planning process. Thus, while many companies devote time and resources to formal planning that yields a document (the "strategic plan," the "five-year plan," etc.), strategy is often emerging out of many moves, initiatives, and experiments in the market.

Moreover, a company's strategic vision emerges more out of the endless informal discussions that take place between top management, middle management, and outside consultants than from the formal executive "retreat." These dialogues (or debates, or lectures—depending on the company's culture) are carried out in meetings, on the plane, in project and special study teams, and so on. Still, most companies hold one or more formal "planning retreats" per year—usually in a nice warm place in mid-winter or a cool place in mid-summer—to discuss strategic issues and to deal directly or indirectly with strategic risks and strategic opportunities facing the company. These formal retreats more often than not are divided into two parts: a day or two devoted to briefings on issues and market trends (sometime done by outside consultants) that touch upon the state of the industry, buyers' needs, competitors' moves, alternative technologies, etc., with the rest of the retreat basically a political negotiation process in which the various business heads vie for resources.

Over the past thirty years, there has been very little change in the way companies and executives approach the task of identifying strategic risks. Though business trends have come and gone, technologies have changed and changed again, and global issues have risen and fallen, strategic planning methodology has remained incredibly fixed. When it comes to addressing the much more risky environment of the twenty-first century, however, the current methodology of endless informal discussions and its associated retreat for formal planning suffer from several inherent weaknesses:

> ▶ They are based more on intuition than on a rigorous framework.

▶ They are not backed by competent intelligence work—most companies have a serious disconnect between their intelligence activities and their strategy making—and therefore easily fall prey to armchair reasoning, "academic" reports, and, most significantly, internal blinders.

▶ They are pulled in various directions according to the "pet concerns" of various influential parties (business unit heads, vice presidents, etc.) and therefore lack a systematic perspective.

▶ They are often susceptible to "groupthink," internal politics, and external consultants' agendas.

▶ Inevitably, they reflect present conditions more than future estimates. Present concerns are more prominent, easier to analyze, and often more pressing than vague trends of future impact.

▶ They are haphazard, and they lack continuity. They are picked up because of looming threats and then dropped as more pressing operational issues take front stage.

▶ Finally, they are mechanisms that were appropriate decades ago. Can it be that a thirty-year-old methodology serves the most pressing needs of management? Common sense dictates that new global competitive pressures, regulatory changes, and speed of technology evolution pressure management to move to a more sophisticated form of strategy formulation and execution. And I do not consider better PowerPoint presentations or faster desktop access to sales figures a new planning methodology. . . .

There are two broad methods of managing strategic risks: before they happen and after they happen. The second method is known as crisis management. My method aims to prevent crises. This means that risks must be managed proactively, at the first sign of a problem, or at least reacted to quickly when the loss is not yet substantial. Few companies are truly proactive. Our survey shows that only 5 percent of the respondents rated their companies as proactive, and 13 percent rated them as action-oriented (see Table 3-1). The approach I detail in this and the next four chapters calls for strengthening exactly these two qualities:

proaction, before the events unfold completely or, at the least, quick response to occurring events. To accomplish this lofty goal, I prescribe a powerful integration of competitive intelligence activities, strategic planning, and management action in a systematic, seamless, organizationwide effort to identify and address risk and opportunity early enough to make a difference in the future of the company. I term this approach broadly as competitive early warning (CEW) to separate it from military, health, or environmental hazard warning mechanisms. Several leading global companies that operate in high-pressure competitive environments have adopted it. It requires coordination between business and corporate units and among various functions inside each business unit. It also:

▶ Calls for management attention in a specific form and substance and a change in top management culture.

▶ Advances new thinking on the way strategy should be formulated in companies, advocating a reduction in reliance on the big consulting firms *and* increasing reliance on particular networks of employees and managers.

▶ Calls for speeding up action through "action triggers" in high-risk/high-opportunity situations. In return, it offers executives and companies an unprecedented protection from competitive surprises and performance decline that is unavailable from existing organizational planning mechanisms.

CEW relies on three interlocking steps that move continuously toward a better and better refinement of strategy as signs of early risk, as well as opportunities, appear. These steps are depicted schematically in Figure 4-1.

The three steps in the CEW framework begin with identification of broad areas of strategic risks (and opportunities), proceed through monitoring for early signs, and end up with inducing management action. Each of these three steps is crucial: I know of companies that excel in one or two of the steps but not all three, and the result is that performance still falls short. At times a business unit may come close to having a good CEW approach, but corporate has none, and the result is failure at the business portfolio level.

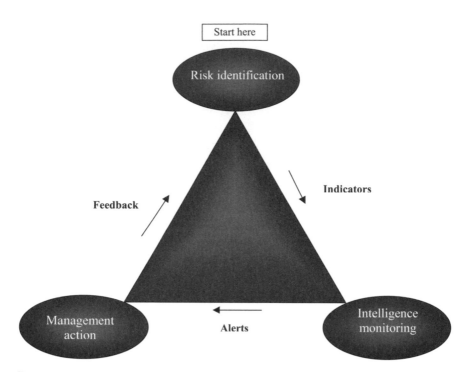

Figure 4-1: The competitive early warning triangle.

Broadly speaking, in analyzing cases of surprise and early warning failures over the past twenty years, I have found that companies tend to fall into one of four categories based on their strength and weakness on the three CEW components of Figure 4-1. While this is not a statistically significant research result, many readers may find similarities to their companies. The four main categories of CEW *under*performance are shown in Table 4-2.

1. *The Analytical:* Companies that do a good job on the identification side, which is typically carried out in the planning departments, but fail to monitor the environment with effective intelligence activities and fail to act in time. These companies are noted for excellent team projects producing ample position papers and blue ribbon committees, but nothing actually happens as most of the positions are theoretical. Our survey shows that 20 percent of the respondents characterized their

Category of companies	Risk identification and prioritization	Intelligence monitoring	Management action	Most common risk failure
"The Analytical"	Excellent	Weak	Weak	Surprise; late response
"The Tactical"	Weak	Excellent	Weak	Surprise; missed opportunities
"The Couch Potato"	OK to good	OK to good	Weak	Late or slow response
"The Blind"	Weak to nonexistent	Nonexistent	Weak to nonexistent	No response to market changes

Table 4-2: Typology of most common early warning underperformance.

companies as too analytical (Table 3-1). Infamous example: Polaroid.

2. *The Tactical:* Companies that build good intelligence capability but divorce it from strategy and limit its effect on top management action. These companies' intelligence activities are put to use in supporting sales and marketing's tactical goals but have little impact on long-term performance. These companies react fast to tactical moves, but slowly and late to strategic changes. Our survey shows 40 percent of respondents characterizing their companies along these lines. Infamous example: old IBM (Prior to Gerstner. Post-Gerstner IBM is yet to be tested but is much improved over the old one).

3. *The Couch Potato*: Companies with reasonable risk analytics and good intelligence monitoring but management that just will not act. Such companies are noted for dragging their feet for years, eventually paying dearly. The lack of action at the top emanates typically from a "disconnect" between top and middle management. Top management pays a fortune to a parade of consultants but fails to heed anything from below a VP level. It is arrogant and insular. It acts, eventually, when a crisis hits, and its favorite mode of action is reorganization. About 23 percent of our respondents characterized their companies as couch potatoes. Infamous example: Lucent.

4. *The Blind:* Companies that pay little attention to identifying
   or prioritizing strategic risk, ignore competitive intelligence
   or hardly use it all, and have a management living in total
   denial, surrounded by consultants and yes-sayers. The result
   is a disastrous collapse of the value of the stock because Wall
   Street always catches up. At times, the result is franchise disappearance altogether. Infamous example: Levi's.

One may note the absence of Enron from our list of infamous examples. This is because, at least while this book was
being written, Enron's management activities bordered on the
criminal. Enron was not a case where management was surprised. On the contrary, preliminary evidence suggests Enron's
top executives, from the former McKinsey consultant turned
CEO Jeff Skilling, to his fellow Harvard graduate CFO Andrew
Fastow, knew exactly how bad their strategy was, but chose to
profit from it while bankrupting the company.

Few companies do a good job on all three steps. In our survey, no respondents graded their company's intelligence capabilities as excellent. However, 3 percent said they have a formal
early warning system (Table 4-1), and 8 percent reported zero
surprises in the past three years (Table 1-1). The truth must lie
somewhere in between, so my estimate based on the survey is
that around 5 percent of companies carry out CEW effectively.
Chapter 9 of this book describes several cases of an effective application of the CEW model, including two special contributions
by practicing heads of such systems. Given the state of risk facing companies in the twenty-first century, companies should
take a close look at these cases, and adopt the model, or combination of models, that best fit their circumstances. Though
many details had to be left out for confidentiality reasons, and
companies that employ this approach guard its disclosure
closely as a source of competitive advantage, I have provided
sufficient technical details for managers who want to establish a
CEW in their companies to take the necessary steps to accomplish this task.

Manager's Checklist

❐ Strategy retreats and informal discussions of risks are organizational mechanisms for managing industry dissonance

that have been used for over thirty years. They are deficient on several important fronts. To manage strategy risk in this day and age of global competition and rapid technological change, companies must do better.

❐ The three steps of a competitive early warning system taken together create a capability. Companies without this capability fall into four broad categories of early warning underperformance. If one step is weak, a company will most likely suffer some early warning failure. If all three are weak, shareholders can kiss their investment goodbye.

> I love the strategy retreats by senior management. Three to seven days full of camaraderie, good food, networking, the symbolic outsider corporate-clown's presentation (I made a lot of money being that clown), and always the best location for the season. Where does your management go and in what season? Send the details to bsgilad@netvision.net.il. I'd like to correlate locations and seasons to company's performance. Should be fun to see if warm locations on cold winter days cause better performance or if these are just added perks. . . .

Note

1. For a collection of classical articles on strategy and strategic planning in large organizations, see *The Strategy Process: Concepts, Contexts, and Cases,* edited by James Quinn, Henry Mintzberg, and Robert James (Englewood Cliffs, N.J.: Prentice-Hall, 1988).

PART TWO

THE
COMPETITIVE
EARLY
WARNING
SYSTEM

CHAPTER 5

Step 1: Identifying Risk (and Opportunities)

> "May you live in interesting times."
>
> *—Chinese curse*

Chapters 5 through 8 present, step by step, the essentials of the competitive early warning (CEW) process. The process is described in details that should be sufficient to enable readers to apply it in their companies. While each company may do it a bit differently based on variations in internal culture, politics, organizational structure, and scope of operations, the universal principles presented below apply to every company in any industry—service, manufacturing, high-tech, low-tech, global, or domestic. Chapter 9 provides real-life case studies of how several companies adopted and applied each step to their own specific circumstances.

CEW relies on three steps—the triangle in Figure 4-1—consisting of risk identification, intelligence monitoring, and management action. Table 5-1 suggests that many companies manage these steps rather poorly. This chapter and the following chapter deal with Step 1: the identification of the relevant risks (see Figure 5-1). The identification of potential risks produces a

Q. How would you rate your company's ability to monitor and track changes in the business environment and bring them to management's attention before they occur?

0.0%	Excellent
22.5%	Good
60.8%	Needs improvement
13.7%	Minimal
2.9%	Nonexistent

Q. Which of the following describes your company's approach to analysis of competitors' future moves? (Please check all choices that apply.)

15.7%   a. My company has a systematic analytical process for predicting competitive shifts.

29.4%   b. We informally discuss competitors' plans mostly within sales and marketing meetings.

22.5%   c. We try to anticipate competitors' strategic moves in our annual planning meeting(s) but have no specific, consistent methodology for it.

12.7%   d. Competitors are not considered a strategic threat, and we have no regular discussions of their intentions or capabilities.

19.6%   e. We know very little about our competitors' long-term plans.

Q. If you have identified the potential for a structural change in your industry, which of the following describes how your management typically responds? (Please check all choices that apply.)

8.1%   My management will discuss it with its outside consultants only.

19.6%   We are the embodiment of "paralysis by analysis"—everyone takes part in the debate.

16.2%   The issues will disappear into a "black hole"—no discussion, no action until crisis.

38.5%	Management will react but slowly and almost always late.
12.8%	We have a method of "forcing quick action" in our company.
4.7%	Our company is very proactive.

Early Warning Survey results, Feb. 2002, Academy of Competitive Intelligence.

Table 5-1: Early Warning Survey results: components of the CEW.

list of potential opportunities as well, as *these two are always two sides of the same coin*.

Identifying risks and opportunities is not enough, however. One has to prioritize the list according to some predetermined criteria. This is obvious to anyone working under time and budget constraints in an organization. Perhaps a less obvious benefit of prioritization is the focusing of management attention on the worst risks, which may be events with large potential damage but smaller probabilities and may be discounted by overworked management focusing on more immediate issues.

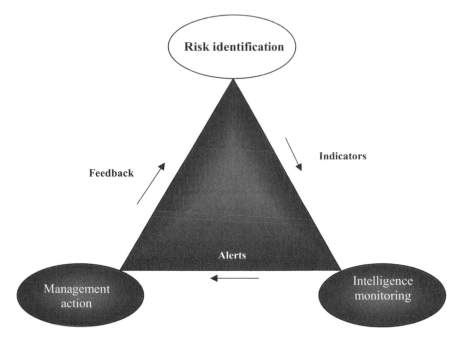

Figure 5-1: CEW's Step 1—Identifying strategic risks (and opportunities).

Identifying potential risks and opportunities is the most "analytical" step in the CEW framework. Here, companies employ a myriad of methods, as seen from Figure 5-2.

The intriguing finding of this survey is that, despite the critical role of identifying risks and the availability of systematic methods for doing just that, many companies still rely on an ad hoc, nonsystematic approach. In response to the question about which tools their companies used to anticipate industry and market shifts—the precursors of strategic risks and opportunities—respondents rated informal discussions as the most popular method. Market research came second. Scenario development and war gaming, which are probably the most effective methods of identifying future risks, have not yet taken root in most companies. Only 15 percent do scenarios, and even fewer, 5 percent, do war gaming! Apparently, companies' constant complaints

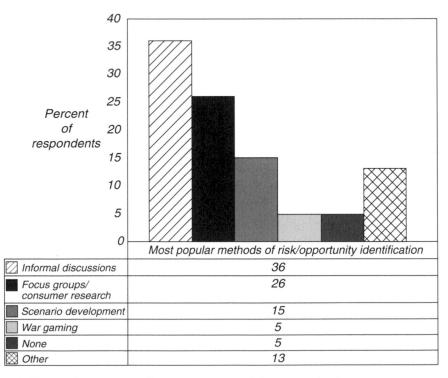

Most popular methods of risk/opportunity identification	
Informal discussions	36
Focus groups/ consumer research	26
Scenario development	15
War gaming	5
None	5
Other	13

Early Warning Survey results, Feb. 2002, Academy of Competitive Intelligence.

Figure 5-2: Risk identification methods.

about rising competition, frequently found in their glossy annual reports, have yet to translate into a significant adaptation in internal planning mechanisms. More troubling for Western businesses is the fact that the influx of MBAs into managerial positions at inflated wages has not raised companies' analytical profile. If the use of analysis remains at the level that can be carried out by non-MBAs in informal discussions, why do companies pay higher rates for MBAs?

Thinking Systematically About Risk

So how should a company identify its strategic risks in a systematic way? By following the logic behind the creation of risk.

What creates risk? Uncertainty. According to Elizabeth Teisberg uncertainty creates "the potential for change in the firm's relative position" in its market.[1] Uncertainty implies that future events can move in different directions, and no one knows for sure which one. Uncertainty creates the possibility that plans and strategies will not work as expected, which is risk

What creates uncertainty? Change. Identification of change is therefore at the core of the assessment of the potential for risk. In order to assess the specific risk of industry dissonance, for example, change identification must start with industry *change drivers*.

Industry change drivers are events or variables that drive the evolution of industries. For example, in the pharmaceutical industry, the science of genomics is an industry change driver. If genomics, which is the study of human genetic makeup, progresses as hoped, it will make the application of drugs much more accurate. Patients will not be given the same drug just because they show the same symptoms. Instead, the genetic makeup of a patient will determine which drug works best, with the fewest side effects, for him or her. The implications for drug companies are significant. Both drug development and drug manufacturing will be affected as markets fragment. The uncertainty is how well genomics' commercial technology delivers on its promise. No one knows for sure whether this new technology will fulfill its promise or when it will be available.

If genomics evolves rapidly, and if its commercial application is successful, it will present both risk and opportunities. The risk is for fragmentation of the patient market. This is a particularly large risk for megabrands, which in 2001 accounted for 20 percent of world sales and rely on mass manufacturing and marketing of one formula to all patients. This is a particular risk for companies such as Pfizer that depend heavily on blockbusters. The opportunities, on the other hand, are for the development of market segments and of niche players who can service them, and for better outcomes for patients. This will lower buyers' bargaining power (those who can afford the customized drug), and alleviate government pressure for price-cutting. If a company continues to rely on a strategy of developing and marketing megabrands while genomics shows rapid progress, this company may eventually face a misalignment with industry conditions, i.e., industry dissonance. Consumers will demand specific tailoring of their prescription drugs, and companies will have to comply if they want customers to shoulder growing out-of-pocket payments.

This example shows that the causal chain behind the creation of risk is simple enough (see Figure 5-3).

Industry Change Drivers

Change drivers differ from industry to industry. In most industries, however, four classes of drivers drive most of the change. These are new technology or science, new regulations or other governmental/political action, new social/demographic trends, and new competitive behavior. The importance of these drivers is in their effect on the underlying industry structure (see Chapter 3).[2]

A *new technology/science* can affect buyers' power or barriers to entry. Incumbents' responses to the new technology—quick adoption of the technology, for example—will determine

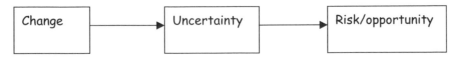

Figure 5-3: Flow chart of risk/opportunity causal chain.

how much the structure of their industry actually changes and *how fast it changes*. Take the Internet for instance. This new technology was hyped beyond all reason partially because analysts wanted to sell shares in the IPOs organized by their investment houses. On closer examination, it became clear that the effect of the Internet would be much more modest and much slower, but it still had a significant effect on the power of buyers to bargain for lower prices with sellers. Buying through the Internet presented consumers with easier and quicker price/product comparisons (comparative shopping). That said, it is clear that buyers' power vis-à-vis sellers increased mostly in those industries where the product or service could be sold directly on the Web, and less in industries where shipping was required because shipping made bulk purchase (by bricks-and-mortar chains) cheaper to the buyer overall. Thus, travel services, brokerage services, music, and software were the first to feel the impact of the new technology. But retailers offering garden tools and laundry detergents still enjoyed an advantage over pure online sellers, since the buyer could elect to pick the items up in the store and enjoy the savings of store bulk-purchases. Naturally, products that require feel and touch were even less affected.

The second change driver for most industries, *regulatory change*, or a broader driver of *government action*, (regulatory action is but one way government can impact markets) can impact entry barriers—as was the case in the airline and utility industries in the United States when deregulation allowed new players to enter and in Eastern Europe when artificial barriers were dropped with the privatization of many industries. Regulations can make substitutes attractive—for example, Ethanol or solar energy as a substitute for gasoline in Europe. Regulations can also make substitutes less attractive—for example, train versus air travel in Europe, where the skies are still pretty much regulated. Regulations can affect buyers' power, as happened when broker services were deregulated, allowing brokers to compete for buyers' demand, with the result that discount brokerage houses emerged. And naturally, government action and regulatory moves can affect rivalry, as was the case with favorable rulings and mechanisms put in place by the Bush administration that helped a specific player by the name of Enron.

Social and demographic changes, a third major change driver in many industries, work their way through changing customer profiles and therefore customer preferences. The rise of the supermarkets became a major trend that transformed the grocery industry when women in the United States moved into the labor force in large numbers. Their rising opportunity cost made the convenience of one-stop shopping a major benefit over shopping separately for meat, vegetables, pastry, and cleaning items. The bargaining power of the shoppers actually declined as their opportunity cost rose, and supermarket chains took advantage of this shift in industry structure. Early on, the chains charged premium prices for convenience, and people were willing to pay them. Later, as they grew in scale and their costs decreased, supermarkets brought prices down to accommodate increasing rivalry.

Finally, *competitive action*, the fourth industry change driver, comes as a response to other changes, or as an independent discovery process of buyers' hidden preferences. In the first instance, competitors' response to new technology, new regulations, or new social/demographic trends will determine the actual course of these changes and the shift in the underlying industry structure. Rate of technology adoption, lobbying for or against regulations, and the introduction of new products or services in response to changing customer needs would influence the uncertain outcomes of drivers in the environment and thus the risk facing the company. At the same time, competitive action can bring about a change that people did not even know was needed, as consumers are not always aware of their needs until someone comes out with a product to address them. Apple's innovation of an affordable personal computer created a significant change in the computing industry, while consumers did not even know computers could be useful at home (some readers may still disagree about their usefulness . . .).

Change drivers are so fundamental to understanding risks that an early warning system lives or dies depending on its success in compiling an *agreed-upon* list of the most significant change drivers. As long as this list is prioritized according to specific criteria and then used to form a target list for the monitoring operations, this will be a marked improvement over existing unsystematic and ad hoc efforts of many corporations.

Scenarios

A more sophisticated risk identification method moves beyond a "watch list" of industry change drivers by adding the tool of scenarios. Following a list of change drivers, analysts and managers can hypothesize about the possible direction they will take. There is no point in trying to map out all possible future directions, however. Two or three different drivers' end states may suffice. In some instances, a driver can be assumed to take on only two extreme positions, i.e., be bipolar (high-low, fast-slow, etc). Drivers' hypothesized future values can be quantitative or qualitative. If one is in the commercial aircraft business, airport capacity is an important driver of demand, and one that will assume specific numerical capacity. Similarly, the growth rate of the youth segment in the population, an important change driver in the fashion industry for example, can be assigned numbers based on official demographic statistics. Most of the time, however, drivers are qualitative. Generation Y's preference for shopping channels, for example—Buy where parents buy? Buy anywhere *but* where parents buy?—is a qualitative driver (with more than these two possible future options, naturally). A combination of the main drivers' outcomes will chart a scenario for an industry's future.

Scenarios are by definition hypotheses about how the future will turn out. Unlike statistical forecasting methods, which project a trend from past events, scenarios are not limited to trajectories of history. As a tool for dealing with massive uncertainty, scenarios are superb. A scenario *set* is a small group of scenarios that offers contrasting views of the future and can serve as a management tool for decision making. The scenarios in a scenario set are selected to maximize contrast, which enables a company to decide which strategies will best fit the evolving future. A company can bet on one particular scenario, or it can spread the risk by opting for a robust strategy that will work in all scenarios and, most important, protect the company against especially bad scenarios. A company can also elect to invest in several options covering a range of possible scenarios.[3]

In deriving a set of scenarios, two independent drivers—also known as orthogonal drivers—each with two possible outcomes can produce four different scenarios. Say driver A has fast and slow outcomes and driver B has fast and slow outcomes. The four theoretically possible scenarios are shown below in Figure 5-4.

A set of three independent drivers can produce eight scenarios. The numbers can get very large very fast (2^n, where n is the number of bipolar drivers). It is therefore useful to select major independent drivers (other drivers that depend on them can be subsumed under them) and either limit their number, or have a mechanism for selecting a handful of scenarios for the final risk discussion with management (see "Prioritizing Risk" below).

Scenario development can be a huge, intellectually challenging, costly undertaking, or it can be an internal exercise of a team of bright minds. The former method is what turned most of the business world against scenarios. In the early 1980s, it was not atypical to run into companies that spent a million dollars or more on a computer-driven simulation producing scenarios no one ever used. The result was that most companies abandoned scenario construction early on.

My experience with scenarios is different. They don't have to be big. They don't have to involve system dynamics and computer modeling and all the latest fads. They *do* involve creative reasoning and imagination. Imagination, not computing power, is the true limiting factor in scenarios. For early warning purposes, sophisticated statistical techniques such as econometric

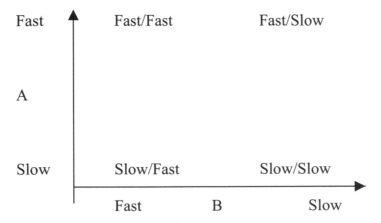

Figure 5-4: Scenario set, two bipolar drivers.

modeling and Monte Carlo simulations are mostly a waste of time and money.

Scenarios are best constructed by a cross-functional team of experts. They can be done solely with internal resources, with or without external input. A form of external input I have found useful is an assembly of an in-house conference of internal and significant external experts aimed at charting future industry paths.

A specific scenario, known as worst-case scenario, has a special role in CEW. The worst-case scenario combines the change drivers' most damaging future outcomes into an internally consistent pessimistic picture of the world. According to one expert who worked in a bank, most companies' worst-case scenarios are still too optimistic.[4] Yet a worst-case scenario offers one advantage: It serves to prod management to pay closer attention to strategic risks. If management can ignore one or two strategic risk areas, it finds it hard to ignore a worst-case scenario composed of an entire set of things that can go wrong. WorldCom CEO Bernard Ebbers could have benefited from such an early warning tool.

The benefits of scenario construction lie in the facilitation of a discussion on strategic risks. Scenarios allow for the exploration of alternative future environments that are not restricted to the "most likely" future. By conversing about possible futures, executives are made aware of a range of potential risks and opportunities. Most respond very favorably to the opening of possibilities. Notwithstanding the value of exploring a host of divergent scenarios, the question of which scenario is actually emerging in the market is, of course, one of the most important questions answered by an early warning process.

Industry Changes and the Elusive "Strategy"

Following the identification of change drivers or the construction of scenarios, one still needs to identify risks. In identifying the risks of industry dissonance, one must keep in mind that the dissonance is between market conditions and the firm's strategy (and its underlying assumptions). Strategy, however, can be an elusive term. What is a firm's strategy? Often, employees them-

selves can't answer this question. The situation is further con-
founded by the distinction one should make between corporate
and business unit's strategy. Corporate strategy addresses portfolio issues: In which industries should we compete? What
businesses should we or shouldn't we own? As long as the corporation competes in one industry or in a set of closely related
industries, one may meaningfully speak of the existence (or non-
existence) of industry dissonance. For unrelated conglomerates,
industry dissonance will apply only in relation to the various
divisions or business units composing the parent corporation, as
corporate strategy has no underlying industry to relate to.

On the business unit/division level, the concept of industry
dissonance is easier to grasp if one treats the firm's holistic
"strategy" as a collection of its functional strategies, such as its
marketing strategy, R&D strategy, human resource policies, etc.
Ideally, policies and functional strategies come together to support a particular direction or the firm's overall "strategy." Internal consistency of the various policies and actions is a known
test of the coherence of a firm's strategy. Even if not all functional policies and actions are consistent, however, often a strategy is reflected in a pattern of the more important policies and
initiatives.

In identifying the risk of industry dissonance, therefore, one
needs to identify a company's major functional policies and initiatives before comparing them to market conditions. This is
demonstrated below in an example from the dot-com industry.
A change in customers' willingness to pay—an industry driver
for most industries—had an impact on the effectiveness of important marketing and financial actions and policies for this particular set of companies.

Many young dot-com companies adopted a marketing
strategy of quick branding. Some spent the largest percentage of
their venture capital funds—larger than the percentage they
spent on creating their product or service—on creating "brand
awareness." The assumption behind this important marketing
strategy was that market share was critical to the economics of
the business. The particular policy adopted to achieve this critical
mass was to use TV advertising because it conferred the fastest
mass recognition. There was only one problem. While *early mov-
ers* like Amazon and Yahoo! benefited from brand awareness,

later waves of dot-coms showed no return on their expensive marketing activities, specifically their TV advertising policy. Many young dot-coms kept spending heavily on TV advertising (including spot ads during Super Bowl broadcasts) while their buyers were not willing to pay anything for a "brand." This is an example of an industry dissonance: a misalignment between a functional strategy (in this case, branding through TV advertising) and the market condition (in this case, customers' preference—or lack thereof—for brands).

Given buyers' changing preferences, the ineffective marketing strategy carried the ultimate risk of bankrupting many dot-coms, as their financial policy of relying on venture funds misaligned with another market trend, the changing flow of venture capital in late 2000. If the dot-coms' executives had identified the change in buyers' characteristics early on, they would have adopted more fitting policies, such as using direct mail, which costs a fraction of TV advertising. As a result they would have lowered their "burn rate" significantly and *might* have survived the cash crunch of 2001 despite the difficulties in raising new capital.

Prioritizing Risk

Identifying change early is a prerequisite for assessing the level of risk. But which change? Naturally, not all changes in the environment carry the same potential consequences for a company's performance. Determining the worst risk is based conceptually on the probability of a particular loss outcome, or what is known as *expected* loss.

The above is a standard concept used in economic theory to calculate events with known or estimated probabilities in an uncertain world. Translating it to the real world faced by strategic risk analysts, however, is far from simple. In real life, calculating the probability of a strategic change in market conditions is at best difficult. More often than not, assigning probabilities is a hypothetical exercise since events are unique and no history is available for drawing any kind of probability distribution. A more typical approach uses a subjective scale (say 1–5, 5 being the highest probability) or a three-grade scale (low, medium, and high probability), applied by an expert or a panel of experts (the so-called Delphi method). These methods are as good (or as bad) as the more "sophisticated" methods often concocted by consultants or academics.

Assessing expected damage is more straightforward. Logically, expected financial damage will be influenced by the gap between the existing strategy and the expected market development. The larger the gap, the higher the potential loss. For example, one company adopted a one-stop-shopping product strategy, offering buyers a wide range of products to satisfy many needs. Such a strategy was based on the assumption that buyers valued the convenience of shopping in one place, even if the price was not the lowest. The company's intelligence analysis predicted a change in the market with an influx of new customers. The gap between the above product strategy and this expected market scenario depended upon the exact nature of the new customers. The above strategy would be robust, i.e., would survive this expected change in buyers' mix, as long as enough new buyers preferred convenience to lower price due to real or perceived shopping cost. In this particular case, the gap between the strategy and the new market condition would have been relatively small. However, an influx of cost-conscious customers who tend to shop through the Internet (reduced shopping cost) would result in a significant gap between the company's strategy and the new market conditions.

A gap between strategy and market conditions must be translated into a potential impact on cost or revenue. Some market changes will have only a minor effect; some may lead to bankruptcy depending on what area in the company's operations they impact. A change in the supply chain that raises input prices on a relatively minor input will have less expected damage than a change in demand brought about by a merger of two major rivals, which significantly reduces the company's competitive space. For example, it was the potential impact of the proposed merger of GE and Honeywell on European competitors that prompted the European antitrust authorities to stop it (and caused Jack Welch his greatest failure of early warning).

While the concept of risk as a particular chance of a loss is hardly used consciously by CEW analysts, it drives one important point: An event with a small probability can still be classified as high risk if the expected loss is significant (the so-called worst-case scenario).

Say you are working for Palm, the largest producer of handheld computers, somewhere around 1998. You may assess the probability to be relatively small that Microsoft will decide to enter your market—the handheld devices market—*and* will succeed in changing the "rules of the game" with its enormous marketing muscle because it tried to do so twice prior to 1998 and failed miserably. Or, given Bill Gates's personal characteristics, you may deduce the opposite. Let's assume you chose the first option: If this event does transpire, the expected damage to your sales and even more to your profit is so large, given the almost certain price war that will ensue, that the risk is very high. A $200 million loss of sales with a probability of only 10 percent is still "worth" $20 million in risk level by the expected loss formula.

As a Palm analyst, you may actually calculate the expected damage, given a few simple assumptions about price and sales levels following Microsoft's entry, using a guesstimate of its market share during the first two years. You may even run simple spreadsheet scenarios of Palm's income statement and balance sheet under various assumptions regarding Microsoft's success (here the issue of probability comes through the back door again). *Or you may just subjectively assess this risk to be high.* In either case, you may want to sound the alarm and start taking steps to monitor for signs that this event is materializing, rather than wait until Microsoft inaugurates its new Pocket PC in a huge celebration at Grand Central Station in New York City. This is exactly what Palm did, and when it discovered the entry was imminent, it completely overhauled its marketing strategy to meet the challenge. For at least a year, it was able to blunt the effect of Microsoft's success, and it might have continued to succeed if not for a series of problems that plagued it during the introduction of its new M product line. Still, in most of 2002 it led the market with about 60 percent market share (down from 90 percent in 1999). An important lesson here: CEW is not a panacea, but it helps *control* strategic risks to the benefit of shareholders.

A qualitative method to prioritize risk is to use an impact matrix. There are several variations of this matrix. A popular one is to chart uncertainty on one axis and impact on another. Another is to chart time on one axis and impact on the other. An example of the first version is shown in Figure 5-5.

This method is a good tool when many scenarios are involved. Those that fall into the upper right side quadrant are the ones that an early warning system should monitor. There is no need for an early warning system to monitor a risky event that is certain to occur (unless exact timing is uncertain and is important to know). Instead, if a company knows an event is certain and carries high risk, it must prepare to confront it. An example of a certain event with high impact is shareholders' expectations based on past performance.

A final test I use extensively to prioritize risks is to assess a given change against Michael Porter's five forces. These forces, while exerting pressure on companies, "shield" the industry and its players from the *direct* influence of all other external factors. All environmental change drivers must work their way through the structural forces to actually affect an individual firm.

Testing trends and changes for their potential effect on an

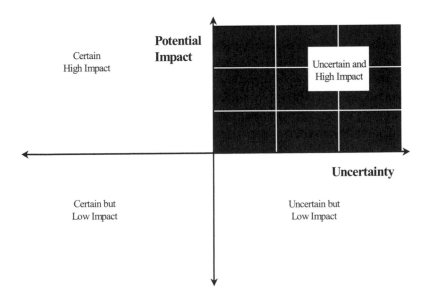

Figure 5-5: Impact matrix.

industry structure evolves from the idea that structural changes are the closest thing to what Tim Koogle of Yahoo! called *"tectonic"* changes. Figure 5-6 shows one blueprint for such testing using Porter's framework.

In my experience, a change driver that significantly affects any one of the forces in Figure 5-6 should be ranked at the highest level of risk. At times competitors react uniformly to a change driver, while other structural forces fail to change. For example, though fiber-optic capacity has increased in order of magnitude over the past decade, as its technology improves by leaps and bounds and competitors rushed to exploit it, buyers' preferences have not changed. The new technology adopted by telecommunications companies following a herd behavior had little effect on demand for voice or data transmission and the result was a horde of troubles for the industry.

Potential for entry
Uncertainty: Who intends to enter?
High risk: Potential entrants for whom the barriers are less prohibitive and who bring *new* capabilities

Bargaining power of suppliers
Uncertainty: Supply chain changes?
High risk: Suppliers planning vertical integration forward

Rivalry

Uncertainty: What new moves are planned?
High risk: Competitors' moves which set "new rules"

Bargaining power of buyers
Uncertainty: Will buyers pay high price for new products?
High risk: Demographic change increasing price sensitivity

Substitution
Uncertainty: What alternative technology emerges?
High risk: Substitutes' performance improving rapidly and/or experiencing price decline

Adapted with the permission of The Free Press, a Division of Simon & Schuster Adult Publishing Group, from *Competitive Strategy: Techniques for Analyzing Industries and Competitors* by Michael E. Porter, Copyright © 1980, 1998 by The Free Press.

Figure 5-6: Risk prioritization with Porter's model.

Naturally, there is considerable judgment involved in assessing potential effects on the forces. This is both a science and an art. It is based on economics, some psychology, and a lot of imagination. This combination requires analysts to have the right combination of background and talent and, above all, a keen sense of the evolutionary path of the industry.

Finally, an added aspect of prioritizing risk relates to competitors' posture toward it. As part of rivalry, companies may have different strategies to deal with the structural forces, and therefore change drivers that affect those forces may affect competitors differently.

For example, companies manage buyers' power differently, using various marketing and distribution strategies. In the consumer electronics industry, Sony's strategy for many years has been to be the leading innovator and to charge premiums for advanced technology features, while until very recently the Korean conglomerate LG competed mostly on price and offered more standard features. Companies employ different supply chain management philosophies to lower suppliers' power. In the portal industry, Yahoo! made search services a commodity, gaining reach and scale that attracted content providers and reduced their power, while Infoseek attempted to charge ten cents per search and limited its reach, thereby lowering its bargaining position vis-à-vis suppliers of content. As a result, the fees Yahoo! had to pay to content providers were the lowest in the industry and helped it gain market share at the expense of Infoseek (and others). Companies also invest substantially in raising different barriers to entry against new players. In the soft drink industry, both Pepsi and Coke invested in brand awareness, but Coke was early in acquiring its bottlers, making it difficult for others to use them as channels of entry, while for many years Pepsi's bottlers remained independent, and a few switched loyalties over the years. Finally, companies try to offer customers better value than substitutes in different ways. In the airline industry, Southwest Airlines was the first to fight trains and cars on shorter-haul routes by shortening the purchase-and-boarding process (with e-tickets, direct online purchasing of tickets, no assigned seats, etc.) *and* lowering its price, while others concentrated on making the trip at least comparable in service and comfort to other means of transportation while keeping prices higher.

The success of companies in countering the five forces determines their individual profitability within the constraints of the industry's overall profitability. Dell has traditionally been more profitable than Compaq or IBM in the relatively unattractive PC hardware industry because its direct-distribution made-to-order business model eliminated the power of distributors and retailers, substantially reducing its cost of inventory and channel support; its customization strategy lowered educated buyers' bargaining power compared to standard machines offered by competitors and allowed it to sell higher-priced PCs; its service strategy lowered bargaining power of corporate buyers who preferred stability and reliability to lower prices and brought in fat corporate contracts; and finally, its extremely efficient manufacturing and sales operations, honed over millions of orders, made it hard for new entrants to penetrate its competitive space.

The fact that competitors' strategies affect industry structure and are simultaneously affected differentially by changes to this structure should be taken into account in ranking risks. *One may want to consider that the highest risk is posed by those changes in the competitive arena for which competitors are better positioned.* I have used with considerable success the tool of war gaming to prioritize risks based on competitors' relative postures vis-à-vis change drivers. More on this in Chapter 6.

Summary: Identifying the Highest Risks

If a company waits until everyone is certain about the direction of change in its environment and its effect, it is a sure candidate for dissonance failure's Hall of Fame. Forces affecting a company and its industry must be monitored continuously to identify early signs of risk. This is a painstaking process that involves piecing together bits and pieces of intelligence data. The process flow is presented in Figure 5-7.

Figure 5-8 presents a particular risk identification process used at a large pharmaceutical firm. The whole process involved a core team of only six people, admittedly, though, exceptionally bright ones.

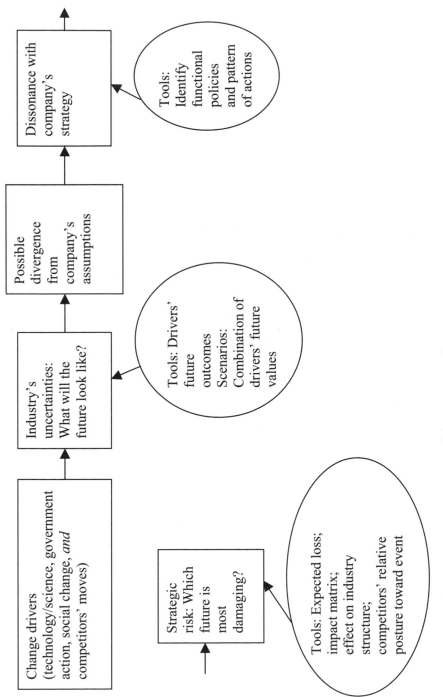

Figure 5-7: Identification and prioritization of dissonance risks.

Generate List of Trends, Environmental Factors, and Possible Discontinuities

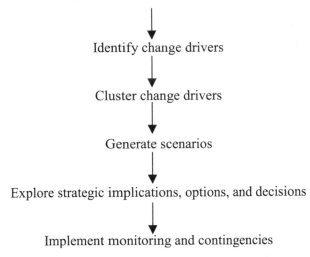

Identify change drivers

Cluster change drivers

Generate scenarios

Explore strategic implications, options, and decisions

Implement monitoring and contingencies

Figure 5-8: Risk identification flow chart, large pharmaceutical firm.

Notes

1. Elizabeth O. Teisberg, "Strategic Response to Uncertainty," Harvard Business School, note #9–391–192, 1991.
2. See also "Industry Transformation," by Michael E. Porter and Jan W. Rivkin, Harvard Business School, note # 9-701-008, 2000.
3. For more details about companies' strategic options in the face of an uncertain future, the reader is referred to Elizabeth O. Teisberg, "Strategic Response to Uncertainty," op. cit.
4. Jasper H. Arnold III, "Assessing Capital Risk: You Can't Be Too Conservative." *Harvard Business Review*, Sept.–Oct. 1986.

CHAPTER 6

Step 1, Continued: War Gaming

"Frankly, I'd like to see the government get out of war
altogether and leave the whole field to private industry."

—*Joseph Heller*

One of the hottest and most effective managerial tools for assessing competitors' responses to a changing industry landscape is the war game. In Chapter 5, war games were mentioned as one of the most effective and sophisticated ways to prioritize strategic risks (and opportunities). Whether the industry's future landscape is drawn using scenarios or just by imagining the evolution of significant changes in one's industry, a war game brings order and discipline to the process and practicality to the outcomes. Without a serious attempt to assess competitors' most likely moves in light of changes in the industry, one is left with interesting hypotheses but misses out on the force that makes it all happen—competitors' moves. *The future industry landscape will be determined by competitors' (and potential competitors'—new entrants') actions and interactions.*

Moreover, the degree of risk a company faces is correlated directly with the relative posture of its competitors vis-à-vis the event underlying the risk. If competitors are better prepared to face a changed industry structure, the company confronts an increased risk. The reverse is true for changes against which competitors are less likely to have a good defense. For example, as consumers grew more sophisticated and knowledgeable in using PCs, Dell became a bigger and bigger risk to IBM, Compaq, and HP, since its lower-cost model was based on direct marketing, while the others used costly distribution channels. Knowledgeable users needed less support and therefore relied less on distributors. Apple, on the other hand, was less threatened by Dell because, first, its Mac buyers had always been more sophisticated and knowledgeable, and second, they cared less about the price and more about features and design.

A war game allows a company to distinguish likely from unlikely futures and risky from less risky developments. Remember that a handful of change drivers can mushroom into hundreds of scenarios based on different combinations of their values. A war game is the quickest, most elegant, and most practical way of bringing the number of relevant scenarios down to a manageable quantity and getting a quick buy-in from management to one's prioritizing scheme.

By way of introducing war gaming to my corporate clients, I start by telling my audience that a war game is:

1. Not a war, and

2. Not a game

That leaves little meaning or rationale for the name *war game*. Indeed, the name is an unfortunate "translation" from the military, which uses war gaming to play out its moves in a future battlefield. Though I fully understand corporate cowboys who regard competition as a sort of a battle and opt to rally their "troops" using military metaphors, as a former business professor *and* a former military officer, I regard competition as a bit more civilized. Besides, in today's environment, many of one's competitors may become partners or suppliers. Looking at them as the enemy is therefore of dubious validity. Finally, war metaphors make it hard to get into competitors' shoes. One does not identify easily with an "enemy." Fostering animosity to competitors can only reduce the ability of managers to understand their potential moves. For these and other reasons, it is probably better to name war games "competitive role-playing exercise" or "competitive simulation," but naturally, war gaming is a sexier title even if it is inaccurate, and who am I to stand in the way of a good marketing buzzword?

A war game is a method of role-playing in which *both* the host team and its competitors move into a prespecified future horizon. It is the most effective form of preparing for major initiatives, testing them against potential response. Yet, only 5 percent of our sampled managers reported their companies used it regularly. Why is that? One answer is the unfortunate path war gaming took during the prosperous 1980s. In those years, war games evolved in much the same way as did scenario development exercises. From simple, human-based, insight-driven team thinking, war games became a playground of large consulting firms, gained large-scale computer simulations for "stochastic variable generation" and a hefty price tag (in the $1 million to $2 million range!), and lost all value to managers.

These are not the war games I am talking about. Costly war games are worthless. In a human-based, insight-driven team-thinking war game, four or five teams of up to seven managers, executives, and field people use structured frameworks to predict competitors' moves, the resulting industry structure, and the host's best-course actions given these played-out circumstances. These games are purely human—a focused effort to get into other people's states of mind. They last one to two days at most. No computer simulations are involved, and there is no million-dollar "preparatory work" by fancy teams from the major consultancies. These games are worth their weight in gold.

Consultants Out, Discipline In

The best war games are played by a company's own managers and employees without using outside analysis (but definitely using data from outside agencies if intelligence is not available from inside sources). The cumulative analytical power and industry knowledge of the right group of employees far exceeds anything a group of outside experts can ever deliver. However, the value of this accumulated internal knowledge depends on using the right amount of discipline in the war game. For that, it is highly recommended that the company running a game use an experienced external *facilitator* (as opposed to an industry "consultant") or a trained internal facilitator.

The importance of using rigorous analytical frameworks in a good war game cannot be overemphasized. Without them, a Red Team–Blue Team format can easily deteriorate into a mirror of internal biases, obsolete beliefs, or downright imposition of how things are done at the host's organization. To prevent that, discipline must be imposed on the way predictions are made. The frameworks I have used with great success in the past are those of Michael Porter, Jan Rivkin and Pankaj Ghemawat, Elizabeth Teisberg, and myself.[1] Different games naturally call for different frameworks, and care should be exercised in making sure the objectives of the game match the frameworks selected for it. The art of aligning goals and deliverables with the right methodology is as important as using the frameworks themselves.

A fundamental assumption behind a good war game is that it is possible for managers and analysts of one company to think like a competitor. If that is not the case, there is no point in role-playing a competitor as one would easily fall into the trap of duplicating one's own assumptions. There are additional reasons why a war game should *not* be played:

- ▶ The company has no intelligence capability and therefore no real data on competitors. Armchair reasoning was good for the jolly 1960s.

- ▶ The company's culture is so intense that any attempt to "think like competitors" will be perceived as treason ("sleeping with the enemy").

- ▶ Management is so defensive that any attempt to question the company's strategy in light of competitors' capabilities or intentions is politically dangerous.

I once ran a war game at a division of a leading American consumer-product company. The brands produced by this division can be found in almost every home in the United States and Europe, but its performance had been lackluster for several years as more aggressive and creative competitors were gaining on it. Halfway through the game, a senior executive accused two young managers of being ignorant of senior management's plans. He further implied that their careers might be in jeopardy if they continued with their line of reasoning. That was the end of this game, even though it continued for four more hours. Not surprisingly, most of this division's senior leadership was eventually either kicked out or pushed out as its performance continued to stagnate. Not surprisingly, I was not called in again. One could have predicted this by just observing the defensive behavior of this group of senior managers.

In another case, in a war game at a leading high-tech company on the West Coast, the teams were making excellent progress on analyzing a major rival. They also reckoned, based on their predictions of the rival's next moves and changing customer profiles in the market (an industry change driver), that their company needed some significant strategic initiatives and a series of proactive investments to counter the rival's build-up threat over the longer run. There was a consensus around several strategic implications and there were recommendations for actions.

Then the chief marketing officer walked into the room. In a fifteen-minute speech he turned all their findings on their heads. Instead of the long run, he wanted them to look a quarter ahead. Instead of addressing strategic future threats, he wanted them to come up with marketing communication blurbs to bash the competitor's advertising. In short, the company's top management culture was so short-term focused and so sure of its technological superiority that any attempt to seriously look beyond the immediate marketing tactics was doomed. These are examples of companies that should not play war games.

Choosing the Right Type of War Game

A war game's structure differs depending on its goals. There are several types of war games, but two are the most effective: the competitor's response war game and the strategy war game.

The competitor's response game is a decision-specific game. It is run when a major decision about a new product introduction, market entry, merger/acquisition bid, or a new technology adoption is to be taken. The host's goal is to test best-course options and prepare contingency plans in light of expected competitors' responses to its intended move. This game makes the outrageous assumptions that competitors, rather than rolling over on their collective backs and playing dead, will respond to the company's actions (unless these actions are so ridiculous that they just sit it out laughing . . .). One sector where this form of war game is very popular is the pharmaceutical industry. Given the enormous cost of launching a new drug, which involves thousands of "detailers" who make sales calls on physicians and hospitals, and the dire consequences of failure to companies that thrive on a few megabrands, assessing the market response to a new drug introduction is a very smart and *very* cheap way to save millions of dollars.

However, the war game relevant to the subject of this book, early warning, is not a decision-specific game. It is a broader, strategy war game. It is run for the sake of formulating and testing overall strategic options for a division, a business unit, or a corporation.

Since the objective of the strategy war game is to investigate strategic options, a detailed examination of areas of greatest uncertainty is a necessary step, and the result is the identification of strategic risks. A strategy war game that does not involve mapping uncertainty and identifying specific risks is worthless as a "war game" since its conclusions are bound to be overly optimistic.

Elizabeth Teisberg recommends charting uncertainty around Porter's industry forces.[2] Whether this methodology or some other structured approach to delineating future uncertainties is used, a war game allows the participants to "get into their competitors' heads" for one day, and try to think about what competitors are likely to do in response to a specific uncertainty. Out of competitors' likely moves participants can identify the high-risk environments for which a monitoring effort should be deployed. This is the most effective methodology known today for minimizing nasty surprises.

Competitors' likely moves are a subset of competitors' potential moves. Herein lies one of war gaming's biggest secrets. Many companies end up playing the role of competitors' "doctors." They "prescribe" solutions to competitors' needs. They look at the environment and ask: "If I were in the competitor's shoes, what would *I* do? What makes most sense?" While this variant on the "rational expectation" theory can result in a lot of good predictions, its greatest shortfall is that it misses out on the most crucial ones. Since it does not make use of real competitor intelligence, it can only stay "rational." Competitors may indeed be better off if moved in a prescribed direction (because it makes economic sense), but internal constraints can hamper the formulation or implementation of such "rational" strategies. Constraints include political infighting, resource shortfalls, lack of capabilities, weak management, the influence of particular consulting firms and their latest paradigms, and—last but not least—*blindspots*.

In many cases, companies have little good intelligence analysis on their competitors. The responses to the survey question about predicting competitive shifts in Table 5-1 show that only about 16 percent of the respondents felt their companies had a good systematic approach to predicting competitors' future moves. Fully 20 percent replied that their companies knew very little about their competitors. Thirty percent reported that informal discussions were the main method of analyzing competitors. About 22 percent discussed competitors once a year in their annual meeting without the help of any structured intelligence analysis, and 13 percent reported their companies did not view competitors as a strategic threat at all (aren't they lucky!).

When there is no intelligence, companies have little choice but to opt for simplistic predictions of future moves: "This is what I would do, so they must do the same." With real intelligence analysis, managers can do much better. Knowing thy enemy, and knowing thyself, as Sun Tzu said, they can actually predict *likely moves*. And I am sorry, I promised myself not to quote Sun Tzu—I am tired of reading the same overused Sun Tzu quotes in every book on strategy—but I succumbed.

The prediction of competitors' likely moves in the face of the evolution of the industry leads to the identification of highest risk environments. The future bearing the highest risk will depend on competitors' capabilities and intentions and on the host's capabilities and future plans. A company with weaknesses in specific areas will identify high risk differently than a company with strengths. This is rather obvious, but it also assumes that a company knows its own limitations. Alas, identifying one's own vulnerabilities is not a simple task.

Weaknesses or vulnerabilities emanate from strategic choices made by the company, such as breadth and quality of the product line, its price positioning, service offering, efficiency of manufacturing processes, technological lead, etc. Weaknesses can be identified globally or as they pertain to specific locations ("our product offering is weak in Asia"). One should be aware that while low market share, low profitability, or lack of capabilities in certain areas are often thought of as vulnerabilities, these are the *outcomes* of making particular strategic choices in particular locations, and the real question is which choices are the ones falling short of competitors' choices. Vulnerabilities are always relative—and so are strengths. A company is vulnerable only where competitors are stronger, on specific dimensions in certain locations.

Competitors' intended moves in the face of change drivers will then be measured against the company's relative vulnerabilities, as in the following hypothetical intelligence report for a high-tech diagnostic equipment manufacturer in the semiconductor business: "In the face of buyers demanding more accurate testing for defects in the production process of _____, we estimate that competitor X will accelerate the development of technology Y and introduce it first in region Z, where it has access to several plants. Our competing testing technology is at too early a stage in development to yield a strong defense; our sales force in region Z will therefore need some intermediate solution to fight against this intended move." The logical next step will be to watch for signs of competitor X's accelerating its R&D in this technological area, and for signs of competitor X's doing a market study in region Z. In this case the vulnerability was clearcut—a shortfall in technology/product and a specific region where competitors seemed to have the upper hand. I will claim, however, that this is not always so straightforward.

The Curse of the SWOT

In many Western companies, vulnerabilities are identified using the widely popular SWOT exercise. SWOT stands for Strengths,

Weaknesses, Opportunities, and Threats. It should stand for Silly Ways Of Thinking. While it sounds as if this is definitely a worthwhile exercise and while it ties logically into the war gaming and CEW methodology described above, most SWOT analyses I've seen were more surreal than real. There were several reasons for that.

❏ Most managers tend to exaggerate in their assessment of competitors. The most common tendency I have witnessed again and again in numerous Fortune 500 companies is to see competitors as either "all mighty" (AM) or "poor and miserable" (PM). Employees who lament that their company must be faster, more proactive, and more innovative share the AM opinion. For them, the competitors, especially if they are market leaders, always do things better. The fact that there are as many employees at the market-leading company who lament that *their* lead is about to disappear if senior management does not move faster, become more proactive and innovative, etc., etc., is naturally irrelevant.

Employees who are fiercely loyal and proud of their company, or who have gone through too many motivational seminars, or who drink too much too early in the day adopt the PM approach. For them, competitors are a bunch of incompetent amateurs who can never do anything that will amount to a strategic surprise. Naturally, both camps use phrases such as "We've known them for decades" or "We're pretty confident we know where they're going." Only a select few hold the realistic view, which reflects true competitive intelligence and an in-depth understanding of competitors' motivation. For some strange reason, those few usually do not participate in my SWOT exercises.

❏ SWOT requires a relativistic approach. What is strength? This is not a philosophical new-age question about inner peace. Strength is hard to measure objectively. For example, many pharmaceutical firms measure strength in R&D or in sales by counting the number of bodies thrown at these functions: 3,500 researchers, 16,000 salespeople—these are strong capabilities. Yet, if five brilliant biotech researchers in a garage lab in California can come out with a better molecule at a fraction of the cost, should the number of researchers matter? And if a company utilizes its smaller sales force more creatively by tying in physicians and "thought leaders" in a given field with "soft money," is the number of salespeople the only indicator of strength?

❐ Finally, SWOT requires companies to objectively identify and admit to weaknesses. How many of the readers expect during their lifetime to hear a vice president admitting *his* function is weak and *his* strategy is not working?

If the traditional SWOT analysis is often ineffective, how can companies identify vulnerabilities so they can prioritize strategic risks? One tool is to use the blindspots version of a war game.

The Blindspots Identification Methodology (BIM)

The blindspots war game is a variant on the strategy war game discussed above. Its objective is to air blindspots inside the host company, while at the same time identifying competitors' blindspots. It is the promise of uncovering competitors' blinders that makes this version of the game palatable to senior management, which is usually less than eager to have its own blinders exposed in front of middle management.

The Blindspots Identification Methodology, or BIM, for lovers of corporate acronyms, used in a blindspot war game is based on the implicit assumption that middle management is better suited to see what senior management no longer can. In other words, middle managers, especially those who serve in "sensory units"—units that come in direct contact with the outside environment, such as sales, marketing, service, purchasing, and, naturally, intelligence personnel—can view the industry through more objective eyes than senior executives can. The reason is what psychologists investigating the phenomenon of cognitive dissonance call "ego involvement."[3]

Ego involvement signifies a bias in judgment based on personal involvement in the decision or issue at hand. In terms of industry analysis, ego involvement means a senior executive is less capable of seeing reality for what it is because of her stake in the outcome, her involvement in creating strategies based on her beliefs about the industry's direction, and at times her very public position regarding the industry's future (think Scott Mc-Nealy of Sun Microsystems and his strong statements about Windows NT).

Because executives have significant ego involvement in their industry, their assumptions regarding the nature of the structural forces and the direction they are taking are bound to be colored by wishful thinking as well as predetermined beliefs and a strong need to defend both. On the other hand, a middle manager, be it a field sales manager or a brand associate director, looking at the same industry and trying to chart the direction of the same forces, will come out with several conclusions not shared by the top. This is especially true of well-trained competitive intelligence professionals. I guarantee it or your money back. In my twenty-year career of running BIM exercises, it has never been the case that middle management was not able to point out top management's blinders within the first twenty minutes of the exercise, no matter what industry I was involved with at the time. The only obstacle to doing so was top management's presence in the room.

I am not saying that middle managers are smarter or that they possess better analytical skills than top executives. As cynical as I may be regarding the *personal* qualities of some of the top executives I have encountered, they are quite capable people and quite knowledgeable (aside from those who *prefer* not to know). Moreover, their views are broader and encompass many more factors and facts than those of their middle managers, many of whom are "siloed" into a tiny part of the market by the nature of specialization required in corporate work. Yet executives cannot for the life of them be objective. Their broad perspective is susceptible to strong personal biases and severe blindspots aggravated significantly by the effect of influence peddlers (investment bankers, consultants, etc.). Their self-interest *should* be to let other less involved managers and especially trained competitive intelligence managers examine the same "facts and factors."

Not all executives are alike, and some are very tuned to what's going on around them. But "paranoid" executives such as Andy Grove of Intel, or humble executives such as Tim Koogle of Yahoo! (see Chapter 2) and Lars von Kantzow of Pergo (see Chapter 9) are a rarity, and even they could not always control their strong prior beliefs in looking at their industry. Their wisdom was in their willingness to dialogue openly and freely with a wide range of middle managers (and not just the core of favorite protégés), because middle managers just don't carry the same burden of blinders. A simple question such as "Are we still doing the right things?" leads inevitably to fostering such an open dialogue.

Given the *general* validity of this implicit observation about the better reality check at lower levels (and exceptions are always possible), BIM involves a sophisticated comparison of management assumptions and intelligence evidence. Characterizing accurately the structure of an industry using intelligence and then comparing this "industry map" with top management's assumptions yields a quick diagnosis of the reality check at the top. Any gap between assumptions and reality (or evolving reality) indicates a potential blindspot.

The most useful application of BIM is to one's own company. If management can follow this straightforward process, blindspots *will be* exposed:

1. List top management's assumptions about the nature of buyers' preferences, the conventional wisdom about supply chain rules, the fundamental nature of competition (e.g., the famous "success factors"), the barriers to entry and who can overcome them, and finally, the threat appeal of substitutes to your customers. If needed, add industry-specific factors such as the direction of technology, the role of government agencies, and the rules of globalization employed by the various players.

2. Using competitive intelligence, analyze these industry-wide forces again, this time without regard to top management's assumptions. The order of steps 1 and 2 does not matter as long as one can pull together a team capable of doing both with integrity (or use separate teams).

3. Compare the results of 1 and 2 above. Any gap is a potential blindspot.

4. Now repeat the same process, only this time, list *compet-itors'* top management assumptions.[4]

Obviously, identifying competitors' blinders is as much an art as a science. But it is feasible, and furthermore, it is an ac-quired corporate skill.

What Does It Take to Uncover Competitors' Blinders?

First, it requires a serious intelligence capability. This is not equivalent to having a large information center or one of those "knowledge sharing" projects, the new pet toys of the large Knowledge Management "practices."* It is neither tantamount to nor derived from market research capability; the two disci-plines, market research and competitive intelligence, differ widely. For a company to be able to get into its competitors' blindspots, it needs real intelligence *expertise.*

Intelligence expertise does not grow on trees and is not cre-ated by searching the Internet or compiling internal "competitive newsletters," a favorite form of semi-intelligent activities at some large Fortune 100 firms. Intelligence expertise is built over time. It takes patience and an ability to retain the experts. Most U.S. firms have little understanding of the career path of their competitive intelligence professionals or of the qualities needed to select the few who will become experts on competitors. While intelligence services worldwide spend a fortune recruiting, train-ing, and retaining their best analysts, most corporations throw the first available marketing services person or information "specialist" (read: human search engine) at the job and demoti-vate them quickly as they swamp them with random requests for tactical data, mostly historical public statistics (competitors' prices, market shares, sales figures, etc). The turnover of "com-petitive intelligence professionals," as these people are misla-beled, is extremely high. A more detailed account of what it takes

---

* One can only wonder: Do these practices teach what they practice or practice what they teach?

to be an intelligence professional/competitor expert in a firm will be presented in Chapter 10.

Once a company recruits, trains, and motivates a competitor expert, the task of delineating competitors' assumptions can begin in earnest. This task involves two methods: direct uncovering and indirect inference.

The direct method culls published sources for speeches and documents written and delivered by the competitor's top management (corporate or business unit, depending on one's needs). While most published corporate documents and most public speeches are carefully orchestrated and *castrated* by corporate communication and investor relations departments, and some top executives have not written their own words in years, perhaps to the betterment of their audience, these documents can still give a frame for the executives' thoughts and vision for the industry. As long as one reads them with a skeptical eye, and sifts through their propaganda, there is a method of gaining value from them. Just separate the constant from the transitory. The common theme of, for example, letters to shareholders published in annual reports and 10K reports and signed by the chairman or CEO shows the consistent concerns or strategic directions adopted by the executive in question. The transitory statements in 10Ks reflect fewer of the deep-rooted assumptions about the industry's structure and more of the pressing, immediate issues influenced by tactical pressures and internal political concerns.

Published speeches and letters, as well as biographical notes, especially unauthorized ones, are just the beginning. Press conferences and security analysts' conferences are the next step. The trick is to look for comments and statements made without the aid of a prior script. Answers in response to analysts' questions, especially questions that irk the executives, are invaluable as they reveal true thought pattern rather than window-dressing communication. Following the passage of a regulation requiring equal dissemination of information to analysts and the public, services emerged that offer online access to the transcripts of security analysts' conferences with companies' executives. Business publications such as the *Wall Street Journal* and *Business Week* are notable for their relatively unbiased interviews and tough questions. I personally try to read everything that is written by Carol Loomis of *Fortune* magazine, as she delivers candid and penetrating portraits of corporate executives without the hype. The expert must watch out for business publications that traditionally suffer from too much corporate cheerleading syndrome. Their value as intelligence sources on executive thinking is nil.

It is not always possible, however, to gain a direct window into competing executives' mindsets. Sometime, when the competitors are private companies or small upstarts or just secretive, no published information is available. In these cases, an indirect approach is still available. This approach *infers* assumptions from observed behavior.

The indirect inference method calls for asking a simple question in regard to competitors' strategic moves: "*Why* are they doing this?" This question is a gate to a wealth of possible explanations.

To start the analysis rolling, the answer should start with the words "They *must* assume that. . . ."

As simple as this method sounds, I have seen its power in uncovering competitors' assumptions about the industry structure and its future. Certain behaviors, especially those that make little sense or cost a lot of money, or both, reflect strong beliefs about the market, its characteristics, and its future evolution. Often, they also reveal strong blindspots in action. For example, spectacular mergers and takeovers often follow this route. The only way to answer a question such as why Daimler-Benz bought Chrysler at a price that reflected an enormous premium over Chrysler's real value is to infer that Daimler's top management, especially Jürgen Schrempp, its all-powerful chairman and CEO, held strong beliefs about the importance of economies of scale, the need for a broad product line, the significance of a global rather than regional dominance, and the value that buyers, especially Americans, will place on German quality in a U.S. car. The validity of these beliefs is completely unrelated to Daimler's horrendous messing up of the implementation of the takeover. Even if the takeover had been executed flawlessly, and all the commonly hailed "synergies" been achieved, probing the validity of the assumptions might have revealed significant blindspots underneath several of them.[5]

Inferring assumptions from behaviors is an old trick. It uses the logic that people act based on their assumptions. This is economists' oldest theory of utility maximization. People (and companies) act in self-interest and with the hope of achieving their goals. Their assumptions about cause and effect will guide them toward certain choices. These choices may only look irrational to other people because they hold different *assumptions*.

Identifying competitors' blindspots is a powerful weapon. It allows a company to execute actions with a significantly reduced risk of retaliation. It is especially compelling in identifying opportunities for first-move advantage, before competitors can see them. The story of how the famous Xerox's Park Laboratory invented some of the most popular technologies—the mouse, the graphic interface used in Apple's and later Microsoft's operating systems, and desktop home printers—and never realized their potential is a classic example of how blindspots can yield powerful benefits to those who uncover them.

War Gaming and Risk Prioritizing

Putting all the elements together, the process depicted in Figure 6-1 summarizes how companies can use war games to determine the most risky future developments in their environment, and prepare the stage for the next step in the early warning cycle—monitoring these risks. Figure 6-1 is an elaboration on Figure 5-7, incorporating the war game tool into the company's analytical arsenal.

A Sample War Game Agenda

The following agendas are taken from real war games used in various companies in a wide-spectrum of industries (service, high-tech, pharmaceutical, consumer, industrial, and financial).

A Two-Day Strategic Risks, Strategic Options Exercise

Day 1: Frameworks and first-round analyses

08:00–10:00 Analytical frameworks to be used (facilitator)
10:00–10:15 Break

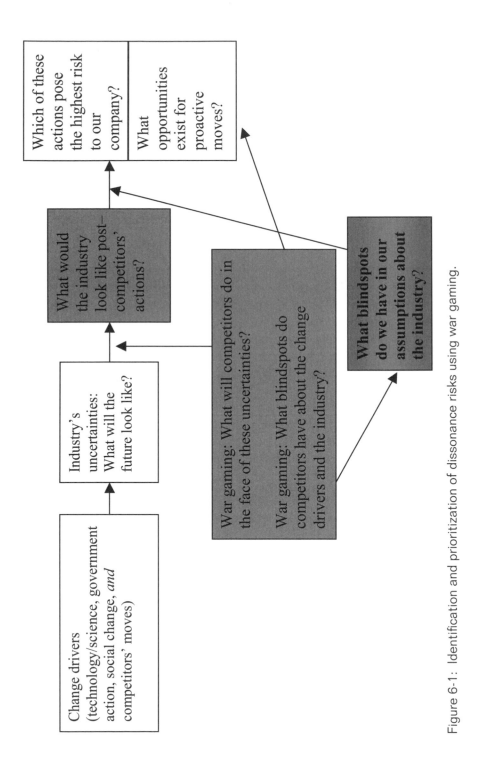

Figure 6-1: Identification and prioritization of dissonance risks using war gaming.

10:15–12:00 Analysis of the industry structure and delineation of uncertainties around them (in teams)

12:00–13:00 Working lunch (teams continue to work together)

13:00–14:30 Teams' presentations and debate

14:30–14:45 Break

14:45–16:00 What will competitors do in the face of industry scenarios? (in teams, by prior assignment)

16:00–17:30 Teams' presentations and debate

17:30–18:00 Instructions for next day round

Day 2: Second-round analyses

08:00–09:45 Synthesis: Industry scenarios in light of competitors' actions and interactions (group exercise)

09:45–10:00 Break

10:00–12:00 Host's best-course options in light of industry scenarios (in teams)

12:00–13:00 Working lunch

13:00–14:30 Teams' presentations and debate

14:30–15:00 Summary: strategic options (facilitator)

15:00–15:15 Break

15:15–16:00 Strategic risk targets for EW monitoring based on scenarios (group exercise)

16:00 End

A One-Day Strategic Risks Identification Exercise

08:00–09:30 Analytical frameworks to be used (facilitator)

09:30–09:45 Break

09:45–11:00 Analysis of the industry structure and delineation of uncertainties around them (in teams)

11:00–12:00 Teams' presentations and debate

12:00–13:00 Teams' presentations continue through working lunch

13:00–14:30 What will competitors do in the face of industry changes? (in teams, by prior assignment)

14:30–16:00 Teams' presentations and debate

16:00–16:15 Break

16:15–17:00 Synthesis: Industry scenarios in light of competitors' actions and interactions (group exercise)

17:00–18:00   Strategic risk targets for EW monitoring based on scenarios (group exercise)

18:00   End

A Two-Day Blindspots Identification Methodology (BIM) Exercise

Day 1: Practice

08:00–10:00   Analytical frameworks to be used (facilitator)

10:00–10:15   Break

10:15–15:00   Practice case on using BIM (facilitator)

15:00– 17:00 Analysis of industry structure (in teams)

Day 2: Application

08:00–10:00   Teams' presentations and debate

10:00–12:00   Analysis of host and competitors' assumptions, identification of blindspots (in teams, by prior assignment)

12:00–13:00   Lunch

13:00–15:00   Teams' presentations and debate

16:00–16:15   Break

16:15–17:00   Which host's strategies should be changed? (in teams)

17:00–18:30   Teams' presentations and debate

18:30–19:00   Action plan (facilitator)

A One-Day Blindspots Identification Methodology (BIM) Exercise

08:00–10:00   Analytical frameworks to be used (facilitator)

10:00–10:15   Break

10:15–11:00   Analysis of industry structure (in teams)

11:00–12:00   Teams' presentations and debate

12:00–13:00   Lunch

13:00–14:30   Analysis of host and competitors' assumptions, identification of blindspots (in teams, by prior assignment)

14:30–16:00   Teams' presentations and debate

16:00–16:15   Break

16:15–17:00   Which host's strategies should be changed? (in teams)

17:00–18:30 Teams' presentations and debate

18:30–19:00 Action plan (facilitator)

Notes

1. Those included Competitor Response Profile and Strategic Mapping from Michael E. Porter, *Competitive Strategy* (New York: Free Press, 1980), Pankaj Ghemawat and Jan Rivkin's competitive advantage analysis from "Creating Competitive Advantage" (Harvard Business School, note #9-798-062, 1998), Elizabeth O. Teisberg's uncertainty scenarios from "Strategic Response to Uncertainty" (Harvard Business School, note #9-391-192, 1991), and blindspots identification methodology from Benjamin Gilad, *Business Blindspots* (Infonortics, 1998).
2. See Elizabeth O. Teisberg, "Strategic Response to Uncertainty," Harvard Business School, note #9-391-192, 1991.
3. See Benjamin Gilad, Stanley Kaish, and Peter D. Loeb, "A Theory of Surprise and Business Failure," *Journal of Behavioral Economics* 14 (Winter 1985): 35–55 for an application of this term to business decisions.
4. If one is interested in a more technical discussion of this process, see Benjamin Gilad, George Gordon, and Ephraim Sudit, "Identifying Gaps and Blindspots in Competitive Intelligence," *Long Range Planning* 26, no. 6 (1993): 107–113, and Craig Fleisher and Babbette Bensoussan, *Strategic and Competitive Analysis: Methods and Techniques for Analyzing Business Competition* (Upper Saddle River, N.J.: Prentice-Hall, 2003), Chapter 10.
5. Most synergies are illusionary, anyway. See Michael E. Porter's lucid and skeptical analysis in "From Competitive Advantage to Corporate Strategy," *Harvard Business Review*, May–June 1987, pp. 43–59.

CHAPTER 7

Step 2: Intelligence Monitoring

"For example, you have frequently seen the steps which lead up from the hall to this room."

"Frequently."

"How often?"

"Well, some hundreds of times."

"Then how many are there?"

"How many? I don't know."

"Quite so! You have not observed. And yet you have seen. That is just my point. Now, I know that there are seventeen steps, because I have both seen and observed."

—*Sherlock Holmes and Watson, in "A Scandal in Bohemia"*

Assuming a company gets itself a capable risk identification and prioritization process, a competent war game team, and a list of most significant risky developments in its environment in the next one to three years—the most relevant planning horizon for most companies in a fast changing arena—what next?

As Chapter 4 showed, companies that stop at the analytical step are not going to enjoy the protection of an early warning system. American companies are especially vulnerable to this problem. They hire many MBAs and tend to engage in a signifi-

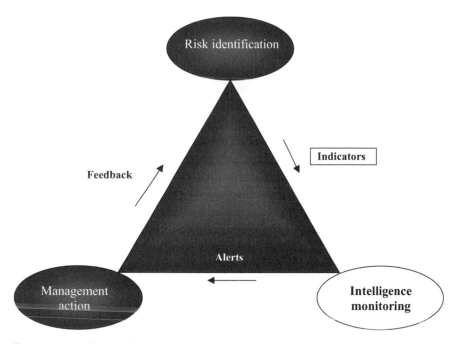

Figure 7-1: CEW's Step 2—Monitoring risks.

cant amount of analytical work that leads to no action. Close to 20 percent of the respondents in the survey by the Academy of Competitive Intelligence claimed their companies are "paralyzed by analysis." This is especially obvious in Fortune 100 companies. Size has the effect of allowing a company to engage in many unproductive activities without facing imminent bankruptcy. But analysis without action leads to a downfall sooner or later. That should not be interpreted, however, to mean that action without analysis is beneficial. Many Japanese companies lack capabilities of intelligence analysis. Instead, they collect enormous amount of *data*. The lack of analytical prowess means they actually use very little of the data for good decisions, which may account for many of the failures in Japan in recent years. It is clear there must be a balance between these two extremes.

The central objective of early warning systems is to prevent surprises. In other words, the strategic risks identified in the analytical step should not be allowed to materialize without the company's taking preemptive action, or at least reacting as quickly as possible. This is where monitoring the risks becomes crucial, as illustrated in Figure 7-1, above.

Monitoring risks is a collective effort. One person, no matter how knowledgeable or how senior, cannot do it. At the same time, monitoring risks is not a random activity. It needs coordination to be effective. The need to coordinate the efforts of a group of people monitoring significant risks means that some organizational investment must be expanded on the issue. Alas, this is where most large Western firms fall flat on their faces. The reason? Their CEOs have no idea what to do.

This is a harsh accusation. CEOs are smart and knowledgeable people (a few crooks notwithstanding) with enormous power at their fingertips. If they want to move mountains, they move mountains. How come they cannot organize their companies to watch out for risks that can wreck their careers, their alimony checks, their employees' livelihood, and, most significantly, their shareholders' wealth?

The explanation lies in a quirky paradox. In a survey carried out by Accenture and the Conference Board in 2001 and cited in the Society of Competitive Intelligence Professionals' official publication, *CI Magazine*, 506 CEOs from North America, Europe, and the Pacific Rim responded to a question about their strategic concerns. Below are the three highest ranked concerns and the percent of executives who listed them:[1]

First Place: 41 percent were concerned most about challenges in the type and level of competition.

Second Place: 38 percent were concerned most about the impact of the Internet.

Third Place: 37 percent were concerned most about industry consolidation.

If we take the top three challenges above and classify them according to the strategic risk they represent, CEOs are quite aware of the major sources of their future problems, or what I called industry change drivers earlier in this book. Recall that four major change drivers were noted: (1) technology, (2) regulatory, (3) social/demographic, and (4) competitive action. These change drivers are responsible for the most profound changes in one's industry, those termed structural changes (changes in the underlying structure of the industry).

CEOs' number-one concern, a change in the type and level of competition, falls within the realm of "competitive action." It comes mainly from new entrants into their markets, by way of mergers, acquisitions, or internal development. This is not typically a fear of the familiar competitors but of a new level of competition. It is definitely a change driver worth watching.

CEOs' second-ranking concern, the impact of the Internet, may look a little more tactical, but it is not. Though the Internet has been hyped beyond reason, it is one technology driver that has affected buyers. The ability to shop around with the click of a mouse increased buyers' power significantly in certain industries, especially those whose products are easily translated into e-commerce.

The final issue mentioned by the CEOs—consolidation—falls well within the domain of the competitive change driver. Consolidation brings about changes in the nature of rivalry, one of the major forces in the industry structure. In short, CEOs are concerned about industry change drivers that history has shown have been the source of profound industry transformations. Figure 7-2 sums up this relationship between CEOs' concerns and industry forces. So how come the majority of these executives don't have an effective system to monitor these risks and are surprised *again and again* by developments about which they are supposedly worried?

The next findings explain the paradox. In a separate survey, by the research firm Knowledge Systems and Research, Inc. (KSR), 500 senior executives were queried about their strategic intelligence needs and what they considered competitive intelligence's challenges. Consider their response:

- Eighty-seven percent reported that their major intelligence-related problem was rapidly gathering intelligence to support critical decisions.

- Seventy-seven percent reported that they regarded intelligence that supports and improves sales and marketing efforts as most valuable.

- Sixty-eight percent felt that the key intelligence-related issue for executives was getting 24/7 competitive intelligence alerts distributed to appropriate end point users.[2]

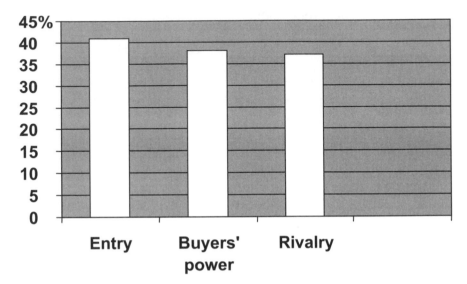

Figure 7-2: CEOs' strategic concerns and the structural force to which they relate.

Consider what the responses truly mean. Why would exec-utives demand *rapid* gathering of intelligence for critical deci-sions? Critical decisions take weeks, months, and sometime years to work out. Strategic moves should not be hasty, last-minute shots from the hip, should they? An exception may be a snatch-ing of an acquisition from someone else's jaws in a hot market, but most strategic moves do not happen after twenty-four-hour deliberations. They have to evolve and mature, and they go through rounds of discussions before the final decision is made. Any executive describing his business environment as "fast-moving, dynamic, requiring split-second decisions" is actually admitting he has no early warning capability in his organiza-tion. So why would executives insist on *rapid* gathering of intel-ligence? The only reason executives need quick intelligence is because they have already made up their minds, and as the time to act gets closer, they want *confirmatory* intelligence to push the decision through.

Confirmatory intelligence is a well-known phenomenon to many professional intelligence officers, both in government and in business. Decision makers want evidence to support their pre-determined beliefs and allow them to push for the decisions they favor. Confirmatory intelligence is not gathered slowly and methodically over a long stretch of time. It does not grow out of an unbiased monitoring of the competitive environment. It is gathered from one day to another as backing for one political party or another in the organization, and as a last-minute insert into a PowerPoint slide presentation. All competitive intelligence professionals in major companies know these demands. They can smell them from miles away. "The division head wants evidence on the growing opportunities in the telecom business in China, and she wants it by 4 P.M. today," the CI manager is informed. What the big boss does not disclose is the reason for the last-minute request, which is typically a desire to push for a particular move, in this case, into China. Negative evidence on the lack of opportunities or growth will *not* be welcomed.

If rapid intelligence signifies lack of strategic planning, the view that intelligence is most valuable in improving sales and marketing signifies a complete disregard of executives' own strategic concerns. It is not that sales intelligence is immaterial. Obtaining and using intelligence on new accounts, competitors' product offerings, or as a benchmark of sales organizations' compensation practices can be essential in improving a company's sales pitch vis-à-vis its competitors. Similarly, intelligence on competitors' planned marketing campaigns or upcoming price changes is exceedingly useful. But all of this intelligence in support of sales and marketing is mostly tactical. It is short term, and its goal is immediate results. It is a very different creature from strategic intelligence on industry change drivers and the risks they entail to the company's long-term survival. Telecommuications companies such as Qwest, SBC, Nynex, and WorldCom have been notable for the tactical (mostly product and pricing) intelligence support they provide to their product teams. It is the long-term strategic risks they ignored. Tactical sales and marketing intelligence comes from different sources than strategic intelligence, requires different channels to communicate, and is created by very different organizational mechanisms. To put it bluntly: An executive who cherishes a tip that improves sales calls but ignores signs that substitute technology may render the company's whole line of products and services obsolete in three years is stupid. He will face a very nasty surprise down the road, exactly the type of surprise he was, supposedly, worried about in Accenture/CB's survey!

Finally, the last issue raised in the KSR survey seems perfectly consistent with executives' strategic concerns. Sixty-eight percent of the respondents said a key issue was getting intelligence alerts distributed to the appropriate end users. This seems very reasonable and consistent with the approach I am taking in this book. The staunchest advocate of competitive early warning systems could not say it better. So, where is the catch?

The catch is in defining end users. In my experience, the vast majority of senior executives do not see themselves as the end users of intelligence. They applaud any effort to get (tactical) intelligence into the hands of their subordinates, especially salespeople, marketing managers, and project teams. In their opinion, however, they themselves do not need it. Indeed, why would they? If most executives believe that competitive intelligence is mostly about marketing and sales leads, it really has little relevance to their job. This ingrained misconception is reflected in the Fortune 500's approach to the use of competitive intelligence resources. The overwhelming majority of intelligence units that operate today in Fortune 500 companies do not have a direct reporting line to executives. They do not brief executives on a regular basis. Many executives do not even know they have a CI unit somewhere in their organization or who is in charge of defending their company's future. Executives may be on a distribution list of CI reports, but their contribution to and use of these reports is so minimal that CI professionals are happy to receive back a copy of a report a few months later with an unintelligible comment scribbled on its side showing the executive read (part) of it. Figure 7-3 sums up what executives want from their organizational competitive intelligence activities, as evidenced in the KSR survey results.

So, executives are concerned about long-term change drivers, but they use their intelligence resources to chase sales leads or collect competitors' price sheets. They lose sleep over new competitive bases but want quick, last-minute answers to confirm their prior beliefs. They are very supportive of intelligence for *others* in the organization. If one solves this contradiction, corporate management will improve several magnitudes. Vivendi Universal, WorldCom, Budget Rent A Car, Xerox, and others like them could benefit greatly. Perhaps the greatest change Louis Gerstner instituted at IBM was to change the focus of its

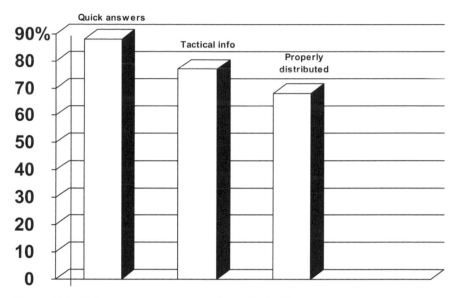

Figure 7-3: What executives want from their CI.

executive team from having state-of-the-art product intelligence in the hands of its salespeople to having competitive (read: strategic) intelligence at the top. His predecessor's neglect of strategic intelligence cost IBM's shareholders billions of dollars. One can only hope his successor keeps the pressure on.

From Risk Identification to Risk Monitoring

An effective monitoring system that provides top management with 24/7 monitoring of significant threats and opportunities requires careful planning and even more careful maintenance. While Far Eastern companies, mainly Korean and Japanese, built up sizable capabilities in collection of the bits and pieces of competitive data needed to assemble a picture of the competitive environment, Western companies have done a poor job. The Eastern capability was based on an extremely loyal workforce who followed directives with little need for a continuous investment in motivation and awareness. For many years, Japanese workers and managers collected every bit of information that could help their corporation. Intelligence gathering in Japan is "part of everyone's job. Anyone visiting a trade show will spend time analyzing their competitors' new product features and pricing, even if it is outside their own area of responsibility."[3] It was not unusual for employees of Japanese companies who came across competitive intelligence to file a detailed report and share it with the entire company. While this may have changed in recent years as Japanese companies have started laying off managers and internal loyalty has been eroding, Western companies have never enjoyed such tacit understanding of duties and responsibilities from their employees or such loyalty from their managers. A process of clear assignments, rational tasking, and planned incentives has to replace intrinsic and implicit expectations in many Western firms. Such a rational process, however, does not exist in most of them.

Clear Assignments: What is to be monitored? The choice is between a broad directive—"monitor and report whatever is relevant to the competitive position of the company"—and specific assignments derived from a clear conceptual frame. My choice is clearly the latter. The method can be to derive indicators from scenarios or to derive indicators from clearly identified change drivers in the marketplace.

Indicators: Also known as signposts, indicators are specific questions or targets for collection, assigned to specific employees identified as gateways to this information, that signify a particular scenario is emerging. Indicators can be quantitative or qualitative.

Here is a hypothetical example based on a real but disguised case: The Bold and Beautiful Company markets most of its products through mass merchandisers. The early warning team in the H division constructs a scenario in which hair-care products' distribution share of mass merchandisers declines and new outlets' share increases as the result of both a shift in consumer preferences for distribution channels and a competitor's action reinforcing a low image of the mass merchandise channel. The change driver, changing buyers' preferences for where they shop for their hair-care products, represents a risky development for the division. In order to monitor a possible shift in the buyers' preferences, the team can select several indicators that will provide evidence if and when this shift is taking place, how fast it is emerging, and how severe change is. One clear indicator can be the share of all hair-product purchases made in the new outlets, another, the percent of high-end products purchased in mass merchandisers. Both are the end result, though, and one may want to also accumulate evidence for the underlying processes as earlier signposts. A qualitative indicator can be the emergence of competitive advertising reinforcing the quality image of buying through the new outlets, publications of articles in specific prestigious magazines discussing where to purchase high-end hair-care products, interviews with celebrities about using the new outlets for buying hair products, and, naturally, any data from the market about competitors' plans to bolster alternative channels. While these developments are not indicators of the shift in consumer preferences itself, they are indicators of a push against the preference that may cause it to shift.

Another example: Sun Microsystems sells servers loaded with the Unix operating system. Microsoft sells Windows servers. And then there is Linux, and Linux-based servers. A Unix-based server costs on average $50,000. A Linux server costs $3,000, and the operating system is free. Linux is an open-source operating system, where anyone can add and improve the code. Unix and Windows are proprietary.

Linus Torvald, a University of Helsinki graduate student, created Linux in 1990. At first it could be downloaded free from a Web site. For the first years, Linux was regarded as a peripheral phenomenon, used by software "purists" to drive Web pages and e-mail systems. These days, distributors like Red Hat, SuSE, and Mandrake, who tailor it to specific applications, also sell it.

Sun and Microsoft managements have been deriding Linux from its start. Their public posture has been that Linux is incapable of complex corporate tasks. However, if I were Bill Gates or Scott McNealy , I would have made sure that my early warning system placed Linux on the scope back in 1990—OK, *1991*. Being a target of a CEW means people would have been watching for the following indicators or signs of an emerging scenario:

1. Who was adopting Linux and why? Specifically: Has any company with complicated tasks (banks, hospitals, etc.) been trying Linux? What was their experience?

2. What corporate backers have joined the race? Who sells Linux and how is their performance?

3. What software developers and producers are joining the Linux community?

If Sun or Microsoft had a systematic and professional CEW, they would have picked up the following signposts—and probably much earlier signs as well:[4]

❑ An investment bank in Germany, Dresdner Kleinwort Wasserstein, switched from Unix to Linux in 1999. The Linux servers proved faster. In 2002, Merrill Lynch, Morgan Stanley, and Credit Suisse First Boston operated Linux projects. Reuters is using Linux to provide news and data to Wall Street traders. Disney, DreamWorks, Pixar, and other Hollywood studios have replaced Unix with Linux for complex animation tasks. Military and intelligence agencies in the United States, Canada, France, and the United Kingdom are using Linux. The German government has begun standardizing public administration operations on Linux.

❑ IBM was an early adopter of Linux and is its biggest backer. It has 300 customers, and it is pushing it to the financial community. HP is pushing it in Hollywood. Red Hat has seen business jump from nothing to a "hurricane."

❑ Oracle joined Dell and Red Hat in offering Linux servers equipped with Oracle database to replace Unix servers. The tasks pitched by Oracle include data storage, accounting, and customer service functions—all the corporate tasks Microsoft and Sun claim Linux cannot do as well as their systems. SAP, J. D. Edwards, PeopleSoft, and Borland now offer Linux versions for their programs.

Will Linux replace Windows or Unix? Will it offer a tough competition in the longer run? Hard to tell. One thing is clear. The spirit of Microsoft's reaction that "all the noise and optimism of the early adopters doesn't in any way guarantee Linux will cross into the mainstream" and Sun's statement that Linux is a "bathtub of code" that is bound to fragment into incompatible versions both look eerily familiar.[5] The same dismissive responses were made by the traditional airlines when Southwest Airline showed up with its low-cost strategy and open seating and the efficient structure to support it. Today US Airways is bankrupt and United is bankrupt, but Southwest prospers.

A reaction of companies with serious, systematic, and honest early warning systems would have been "we are watching carefully." But watching carefully was never the culture at Sun or Microsoft. And don't be misled by statements from executives that their companies are taking all the necessary steps to stay on top of things. Once you go inside, you realize there is no central coordination of the monitoring for early signals; even less effort is invested in systematizing the analysis, debate, and action based on early signals. At annual retreats, the name Linux may pop up occasionally and is probably dismissed as quickly. There may be moments of a heated debate, if someone dares to debate the topic. That's about it. It is just not in the culture of dominant, proud organizations to implement a serious early warning paradigm and a continuous serious watch of the threat. As the Roman Empire showed, it is just a matter of time until this intrinsic flaw catches up with the leader.

But why use specific targeted indicators as a basis for early warning monitoring? Why not ask each and every employee and manager to watch out for developments that can be critical to the future of the company? The reason is that the latter approach has failed miserably in most American and European firms.

Many corporations have attempted to develop intelligence "networks" over the past decade as competitive intelligence became an accepted corporate practice. I myself was an early advocate of those internal networks.[6] Those early networks were more or less random collections of people who were willing to send competitive data to a central place—a CI "unit" compiling and maintaining a competitor database. No serious attempt has been made to understand the motivation behind the participation in those networks. My experience suggests a mixture of personal and professional reasons. Some people, especially experts in specific areas or on specific competitors, like to be asked about their knowledge. Examples are former employees of a competitor, scientists with esoteric specializations, etc. They will share freely and profusely. Others do it because the CI collector is a friend. Many do it to genuinely help the company.

The problems with those early networks were twofold: First, few employees joined them—back in the 1980s, AT&T's corporate CI unit boasted that its CI network encompassed 800 active participants. Sounds good, but keep in mind that AT&T at that time had 300,000 employees. That's 0.2 of one percent. Second, the networks did not last. Management never paid serious attention to them, and participants had little incentive to join. Some companies offered mugs and T-shirts to those who joined. Others offered a free subscription to an internal competitive newsletter or an internal expert "yellow pages." As tempting as these offers were, they failed to attract high-level or long-lasting participation. After all, how many mugs does one need?

With the advent of IT technology, the Internet, and Knowledge Management tools, modern internal networks have "evolved" into information-sharing projects. Rather than a network dedicated to gathering intelligence, these networks have become a forum provided for employees to exchange all kind of useful information, internal or external. CI analysts interested in using the network for a specific assignment post "intelligence queries" on the internal cyberboard and hope for the best. At Royal Dutch/Shell, they do get answers. Shell Exploration and Production, Shell's largest division, has a unique network of more than a thousand participants, mostly technical personnel. The network is run from The Hague in the Netherlands and coordinated by a very popular CI manager whose personality is one of the main reasons it has held together. In most other companies, the networks are much smaller and less well motivated.

The idea behind internal intelligence networks is that most of the intelligence about the external environment already exists inside the company. Some estimates put it at 80 to 90 percent. While this might be true—or not—no one has ever measured it, this concept suffers from several shortcomings that have become obvious with the experience accumulated in numerous U.S. firms. These problems do not change whether the network is organized as a fancy virtual community or as an old-fashioned, inexpensive phone-in network.

First, people who join the internal networks are not necessarily those with the best access to the information about the external world. Often, gatekeepers to industry knowledge are too busy, too "siloed," or too senior to partake in network exchanges. If they belong to a division or a strategic business unit (SBU), they may share their information with their division only. If they are senior enough, they may feel their information is on a "need to know" basis. If they are uniquely qualified on a given external aspect (e.g., specific technology), they may be tapped by so many functions in the company that intelligence needs may not come with a high priority for them, even though such needs might have the highest priority for the company as a whole.

Second, collecting external information by internal employees is haphazard. They see what they see, hear what they hear, and it may or may not be what the company's intelligence needs are. Seeing is not observing, noted Sherlock Holmes. Without guidance, they don't really know what to look for.

Third, and most important, internal networks don't last. The problem of motivating volunteers is huge. Most participants in internal knowledge networks contribute actively for about six months and then drop out or chip in infrequently. Active participation is almost impossible to maintain over a long stretch of time. Over the years, companies attempted the following incentives, with uneven success:

- Including intelligence collection as part of a job description failed.
- Offering cash incentives to salespeople to report competitive activity failed miserably.
- Offering information exchange—give me and I'll give you—succeeded as long as the CI analyst had something of value to share.
- Recognition—from peers and/or superiors—succeeded if taken seriously by management.

This last point deserves an explanation. Recognition is probably the most powerful incentive for knowledge sharing. For scientists and engineers, recognition from peers is a significant motivator. For managers and professionals, recognition from senior executives carries significant weight. Recognition sounds like an easy incentive to implement, but the reality is different. Top executives' recognition is very hard to obtain and even harder to sustain given the demands on their time, while peers' recognition is not necessarily related to expertise that is relevant to the intelligence needs of the company.

Government intelligence agencies reward a good source with money, respect, and, sometimes, a meeting with a high-ranking official, who may debrief the source herself. In business, an employee with good insight into a competitive development—such as a service engineer who observes competitors' products while on tour at a customer's facility—will be lucky to receive an acknowledgement from his busy district manager. There is not a chance the CEO will call him to say, "Thanks, Bob, you've been very helpful to the company."

The early warning's monitoring network solves several, but by no means all, of the above-mentioned problems. It does not replace spontaneous reporting by field personnel of valuable competitor or customer intelligence. Instead, the network works more like a continuous task force, and the monitoring process is fully integrated into the planning process.

The Monitoring Network: Who Watches What?

The basic philosophy underlying the monitoring network is that strategic collection should be planned. Unlike the ongoing tactical competitor intelligence collection, whereby management hopes that any kind of competitive development will be reported in time by whoever got word of it, the monitoring for early warning (MEW for collectors of corporate acronyms) should be premeditated to prevent disastrous surprises.

That said, it should also be clear what I am *not* saying. I am not saying that the ongoing collection of competitors' data should stop. The activities of collecting and distributing tactical, mostly marketing information should continue unabated in every company that faces competitors in the marketplace and needs to react quickly to tactical moves. In the vast majority of companies, salespeople and marketing managers, and sometimes information professionals, go about their business reporting (or not) random bits and pieces about competitors as they see fit or as the culture calls for as part of their daily business. Unless the culture and management are completely self-absorbed, some windows on the outside world are routinely kept open. That has little to do, though, with monitoring for strategic risks.

Monitoring for strategic risks cannot rely on haphazard goodwill because the consequences can be the survival of the company as an independent entity. Planned monitoring is therefore required. This is not as difficult as it sounds. The premeditated part of monitoring for strategic risks (and opportunities) comes from the fact that the issues—industry uncertainties and their associated strategic risks—have been identified and prioritized in the previous step of the early warning cycle. It is therefore possible to derive a list of topics and questions and to have the responsibility for them assigned to particular individuals. As shown below, the difference from random collection can be quite substantial.

Say you are a sales manager in a large division of a Fortune 500 company. A colleague knocks on your door (if you have a door) and the conversation goes as follows:

Colleague: Hi, Bob. (You are Bob. In my experience, 99.98 percent of all middle managers in the Fortune 500 are Bob.) Listen, would you do us a favor and watch what Company X is doing? We think it is going to be a problem for us in the next few years. If you see or hear anything interesting, let us know.

You: Sure, Bob (He is Bob too. See stats above). No problem.

Now let's look at a different conversation. Same Bob. Same place. Same lousy coffee.

Colleague: Hi, Bob. Listen, we've identified Company X as a strategic risk to the division. We think that in the next two years it will be going aggressively after broadband customers with an offering of financial content and new online communities that will be at least as attractive as what we offer. We suspect it will begin by entering our traditional customer base in the Midwest. You have the best access to their activities regarding new content and new markets. We would like to hand you an intelligence assignment that requires little work on your part. All we need are answers to three questions: What would their new offering in finance be? What new online communities do they plan to come out with? And are there any signs that they are actually rolling out in the Midwest region? We wrote these three questions on this plastic card, which we would like to place on your desk. It also has a nice Dilbert cartoon on the side about a company going out of business. Is it OK with you if we ask you to become our content expert on Company X?

You: Sure, Bob. No problem. I actually know whom to call in Chicago to get some leads on the last question. I'll call today. Nice cartoon. Quite inspiring.

The outcome of the first conversation depends on the judgment of the employee regarding what is and what is not an important development to report. While it has the advantage of picking up intelligence data that might have not been identified as significant by the risk analysts, it also has the disadvantage of leaving on the table bits and pieces of strategic importance because the employee never thought these are worth reporting.

A second difference is that the first approach leaves it up to the employee to figure out why Bob was interested in company X. The second approach—using specific indicators—puts the issue in perspective, giving the employee a context in which to remember the assignment. It is not an amorphous "danger" from a competitor, but a specific risk facing his company. The latter, in my experience, is more motivating. I remember once standing up in front of a tough crowd of union workers in a food processing plant in the middle of America and talking about competitive threats to their company. I was warned I might not come out in one piece from this meeting, as the union and management had been at odds for many years, and union members did not trust management at all. Yet when the company's young competitive intelligence manager explained, using graphs and charts, the competitive risk looming from a specific competitor and why its actions were strategically threatening, the audience was extremely receptive. At the end, they asked numerous questions, many more intelligent than those asked by other, more professional audiences. The questions were definitely more intelligent than the questions *not* asked by the board of this famous company.

In addition to being planned, monitoring strategic risk factors should be integrated into the planning process. There are two reasons for this simple—yet far from trivial—requirement:

1. Sanctioning the monitoring network as part of the planning process guarantees some measure of reality check to the planning process itself.

2. The integration acts as a clear motivator for the monitors.

The first point is (almost) self-explanatory. As noted extensively in Chapter 3, strategic planning processes in large Western firms are rather outdated. Yet even worse is the fact that once the strategy document is published, it is not changed until the next cycle ends. Assuming the strategy document is not meant merely as a decoration on the shelf, management should be interested in a tool that allows it to know which of many scenarios are actually taking shape outside their office windows. This is the role of an effective monitoring network. Once management gets a clear idea of the evolving scenario, refinements to the strategic plans do not have to wait till the next retreat.

The inclusion of a wide-reaching network of experts following specific critical issues makes the strategic planning process so much more viable to top management. A good monitoring network involves many more people in the planning process, a goal that management should strive to achieve.

The second point is not as obvious, but then motivating the network is the number-one problem facing the intelligence operations of any typical Western company. Actually, motivation in general is not the strong suit of corporate cultures. It would be pretentious of me to suggest the answer to this issue, but I do believe that Figure 7-4 sums up nicely what a monitoring network member should *not* be.

Tying the monitoring network firmly to the strategic planning process gives the monitors a sense that their work is appreciated and *used*. While there is just not enough hard research to pinpoint exactly what incentives monitors react to, it is my experience that they react well to the fact that their information is actually valuable (and then even better if someone says,

Figure 7-4: Not a good member of a monitoring network.

"Thanks, we had great use for it . . .". If monitors perceive that
the information goes into a black hole, they stop producing. If
they see results, in the form of a planning document or company
action, their contribution continues. That may not be a scientific
observation, but it is not a bad start.

So Who Is a *Good* Monitor?

Figure 7–4 described the bad monitor. So who is a good monitor?
There are several commonsense generalizations.

❐ *Access:* The monitor has potential access to the topics/issues
he or she is asked to monitor. In competitive intelligence jargon that means that the monitor is a "gatekeeper" (not as
bad a position as may be implied from the *Ghostbusters*
movie . . .). Access can stem from expertise, position, profession, or education. Sometime it is as simple as physical location. Example: If the EW analyst needs someone to watch
capacity expansion, and an employee drives by the competitor's plant on his way to work every morning and on his
way back every evening, that's access. (This is not a hypothetical example, incidentally.)

❑ *Ease:* Related to access but not synonymous with it. Ease refers to the monitor's ability to access the target as part of his or her routine work. In other words, no point in asking an R&D scientist to monitor a marketing question even if he may have an access to this information by the virtue of being married to her. The ideal assignment should be a part of what the monitor does in his daily routines. Example: If the early warning question involves lobbying efforts in Washington, a monitor in the regulatory or legal department who is positioned in Washington or flies there frequently will have an easier time keeping a watch on the target.

❑ *Expertise:* Access does not necessarily mean the monitor can comprehend the data glimpsed. A mailroom clerk may have access to the trade journals, but he may not understand their content.

A group of employees with relatively easy access and sufficient expertise to monitor a change driver is sometime called a "shadow team." They are assigned to "shadow" specific developments in the change driver and report on them. Shadow teams may meet periodically to compare notes and write up a report, or they may be called upon to make presentations to management on their specific change driver. The problem with shadow teams is that they are high maintenance, and in the typical overload conditions of large companies, employees find it hard to sustain their involvement in them over a long period of time. A high-charging CI manager is required to keep them alive and kicking.

An Internal or an External Network?

Monitoring is a neglected art. In the early 1960s, "environmental scanning" was a buzzword, and its implementation in large, resource-laden companies meant the assignment of a few strategic planning staffers to read business magazines. Today, the buzzword is "information sharing," and internal Web-based networks connect employees from all the corners of the globe. In both cases the goal was admirable: Shift management's focus from internal to external. To judge by concrete achievements, this goal remains as unattainable today for many Fortune 500 companies as it was in the 1960s, expensive Knowledge Management projects notwithstanding.

As a clear example of internal focus, examine the working of the music industry. Since the emergence of the Internet and online file-sharing networks such as Napster, Audiogalaxy, and KaZaA, which allowed music lovers to download free songs, the industry has been mired in internal struggles between the major players—music labels, distributors, retailers, and online music services. The players are fighting for control of the customers, and in the process have alienated millions of music fans, especially in the critical age group of eighteen and under. Industry experts agree that the future inevitably will be a mix of physical and digital delivery of music, e.g., prerecorded CDs and computer downloaded music, but the industry players have failed to execute a consistent strategy that will lead to this future with maximum profitability. Until the late 1990s, the major labels—Sony, Universal, Warner Bros., BMG, and EMI—focused on court battles against the free sharing networks through their association, the Recording Industry Association of America (RIAA). By the time they came around to cooperating with paid online music services such as Rhapsody in 2002, the sales of CDs had fallen by more than 20 percent after having declined another 10 percent in 2001. And even then, a move by Sony, Universal, and Warner Music to make thousands of songs available for download over the Internet for 99 cents each met with resistance from retailers and distribution wholesalers, each for its own reasons.[7] That's a classic example of a common mentality of internal focus.

One major reason corporations find it hard to truly shift focus from internal to external is the lack of external perspective. If intelligence networks monitoring external events are composed solely of employees, the culture, perspective, conventional wisdom, and implicit assumptions of the organization will hinder the ability to see new things and will color the interpretation given to external events.

It is definitely true that companies hardly tap the full external knowledge possessed by their employees. In numerous cases, I have encountered expertise needed by management that was already inside the firm, just waiting to be tapped. One of old AT&T's most cherished prizes was the internal "Yellow Pages" published by the CI department in which employees in need of expertise on external entities (competitors, projects, technology) could find just the right person inside AT&T who possessed that expertise. Without access to available experience, many employees at AT&T were reinventing the wheel not knowing others inside AT&T had already been there. The internal expertise "Yellow Pages" were therefore of great use.

It is also quite obvious that companies invest substantial resources in employees whose role is to keep tabs on some aspects of the external environment: market researchers, brand managers, technology watchers, librarians and information specialists, and so on. It is as obvious that there are many functions in the organization that deal with the outside world on a regular basis: purchasing managers, service engineers, customer center reps, economists, etc. The total knowledge of these workers exceeds by far anything a consulting firm can bring to the company and anything a few senior executives can gather from their sources. Tapping it should be high priority.

That said, there is an element of myth in the absolute, uncritical praise for the internal network. Even if it is true that "90 percent of all information is already inside the company," as some claim, what about the remaining 10 percent? Is that 10 percent equally important as the 90 percent available inside?

Think of the following example. The fast-food industry has been going through some earthshaking structural changes, most driven by changes in consumer preferences and the reaction of entrepreneurial companies to these trends. In 2002, Subway, the fast-food chain that does not sell burgers, surpassed McDonald's to become the largest chain in the United States, with 14,000 outlets, as opposed to McDonald's 13,000 outlets. More impressively, same-store sales are much stronger for Subway than for McDonald's or Burger King. The reasons for Subway's success include the fact that it takes only a $65,000 investment to open a Subway franchise. Subway stores are smaller and located in already existing commercial environments such as gas stations, convenience stores, and even schools. However, the real engine under Subway's growth was a trend for weight watching. Subway's focus on fresh, low-fat sandwiches and baked chips replaced French fries and fatty meats for many U.S. customers.[8]

Does it surprise you? The trend against obesity has been in the making for years. American Medical Association recommendations, national campaigns by the federal government, the rise in heart diseases, and the growing number of aging baby boomers have been known for years. Has this information passed by the managers at the burger companies? Probably not. But the franchisers and employees of McDonald's and Burger King are heavily invested in their current offerings. Looking at warning signs that go completely against the corporate raison d'être is tough. Internal networks can go only so far when it comes to questioning the fundamentals of the business. An outside perspective may be an added defense against stagnating cultures and strategic thinking even if it is not a panacea.

Who should be included in an external network of monitors for early warning? It depends on the industry and the company. In some cases, industry associations are strong and influential. They often serve as a substitute for a true outside network. Managers and executives meet and mingle at industry events and engage in a lively exchange of opinions through debates, keynote speeches by industry captains, presentations, and trade shows. However, industry meetings suffer from the tendency for industry players to converge into a common "conventional wisdom," and the access to presentations and talks is open and therefore confers no unique advantage. The essence of a powerful outside network is that it offers a unique perspective to the company that is unavailable to its competitors.

An external network, therefore, cannot be solely based on open sources. It has to include unique sources working on an exclusive basis. That does not mean these monitors should be full-time employees, but it does mean that the reports they write for the company must be proprietary, and they should not share them freely with every paying customer. Academics, financial analysts, freelance reporters, small (industry-specialized) consulting firms, technology experts, industry critics—these are all possible sources in an outside network. The test of such a network is not in the prestigious names that are included in it but in its ability to draw on critical thinkers and trendspotters. Just as fashion companies employ "style checkers," all companies should recruit "trend checkers" for their industry if their future is important to them. These external experts should provide unique perspectives on the early emergence of significant trends, years before these trends manifest themselves clearly in market statistics available to everyone through commercial databases.

The Disaster of Executives' Networks

A problem related to relying on industry groups for external information is the tendency of high-level executives to rely on a small circle of trusted advisers as their network of outside information. This practice, long accepted as the normal way to do business, is probably one of the greatest risks to a company's future. Just as the Securities and Exchange Commission's inquiries in 2002 revealed inappropriate relationships between companies and stock analysts that rendered the latter's work irrelevant, CEOs and their lieutenants are notorious for asking advice from highly paid investment bankers, M&A experts, and large consulting firms' partners, all of which have their own agendas to pursue, their own deals to make, and their own fees to earn. Closing the walls around the executives is the most significant reason CEOs fail. The executives and their trusted high-powered advisers move in the same circles, dine in the same restaurants, and read the same publications (if and when they read at all). A well-run external network brings into the early warning process opinions of people CEOs don't usually converse with. They might not pay attention to their opinions, but then they can blame only themselves when the sky caves in.

When it comes to monitoring indicators related to competitors' activities, the external network becomes a bit problematic. Issues of legality and ethics have greatly hampered the resolve of U.S. companies to track competitors with human sources. Most competitive intelligence managers in Fortune 500 companies have simply concluded that it is too risky and have retreated to the safety of Internet and database searches. While these are important sources, they cannot replace a good human observer, and they provide the same information to everyone (though it is true that the interpretation of that information might still differ greatly).

How does one deploy a human source network without running into legal questions? The answer is: carefully, with the collaboration of the legal department. The best guarantee against unethical collection is the use of specific indicators that are derived from an analytical risk identification process. The second best guarantee is the clear understanding that early warning does *not* deal with tactical details or secretive marketing moves that are time sensitive and may require an immediate response. Strategic early warning is based on the patient assembly of early signals. These early signals require an insightful observer, not a spy. One did not have to hire the CIA to observe that the grandiose scheme of the (former) Vivendi CEO Jean-Marie Messier, who was piling up debt trying to create the ultimate media company and change the entertainment industry's structure, was actually a failure, and one did not have to wait until 2002 when the company almost collapsed to see that. The early signs that the strategy was wishful thinking were already there in 2000 and led the brokerage firm Collins Stewart to issue a report calling Vivendi "dangerous Eurotrash."[9] These early signs were not hard to detect. If a competitor (or an investor) wanted to predict where Vivendi was going, it did not require unethical collection. It did require smart human sources: those who did not fall for Wall Street's obsession with size or for Messier's flamboyant personality. This is where professional competitive intelligence shines, but this is not how large companies customarily use it.

The High Reliability Organization (HRO)

To sum up this section on the early warning monitoring network, it is enlightening to compare the observations above to the conclusions reached by a highly respected researcher of corporate cultures, Karl Weick. Weick and his coauthor Kathleen Sutcliffe studied the culture of high reliability organizations (HROs)—e.g., firefighters, nuclear power plants, aircraft carriers, etc., where high and consistent performance in a complex and changing environment is a must.[10] Their conclusion was that HROs build an infrastructure that allows them to spot the unexpected early on and then adapt quickly to the new challenge. Among the five habits of HROs (no one can escape the five habits routine nowadays), are these:

▶ Don't be tricked by success. This is the old blindspot warning.

▶ Defer to your experts in the field. According to Weick and Sutcliffe, top executives think they have the big picture, but the truth is that they have only a partial picture, which is often different and less relevant than the pictures those on the front line have.

▶ Anticipate beyond budgets, plans, etc. HROs add two dimensions: They update strategy more frequently, and they focus attention on key mistakes they want to avoid. This is exactly the modus operandi of the CEW proposed here with its worst-case scenario.

Weick and Sutcliffe recommend that decisions be allowed to migrate to the front line because people at the front see more opportunities for bolder actions than those at the top. This is the topic of Chapter 8—Management Action.

Notes

1. "The CEO Challenge: Top Marketplace and Management Issues. Accenture/CB. 1st Q, 2001." Cited in "Competitive Challenges Top CEOs Concern, Says Global Survey," CI Newswatch, *Competitive Intellligence Magazine*, Sept.–Oct. 2001, p. 8.
2. A survey by Knowledge Systems and Research, Inc., Nov. 2000. Cited in "Executives Lack Competitive Info, Market Study Reiterates," CI Newswatch, *Competitive Intelligence Magazine*, Sept.–Oct. 2001, p. 8.
3. Nozomu Ikeya and Katsumi Ishikawa, "The Japanese Intelligence Culture," *Competitive Intelligence Review*, 4th Quarter, 2001.
4. The following data are based on the reporting by Byron Acohido, "Linux Waddles from Obscurity to the Big Time," *USA Today*, 5 Aug. 2002.
5. Ibid.
6. See Benjamin Gilad and Tamar Gilad, *The Business Intelligence System: A New Tool for Competitive Advantage* (New York: AMACOM, 1988), Chapter 5.
7. Jane Blake, "The Labels Start Turning up the Volume," *BusinessWeek Online*, 12 Aug. 2002.
8. Diane Brady, "Why Subway Is on a Roll," *BusinessWeek Online*, 19 Aug. 2002.
9. Stanley Reed, "When Terry Smith Growls, the Markets Listen," *BusinessWeek Online*, 26 Aug. 2002.
10. Karl E. Weick and Kathleen M. Sutcliffe, *Managing the Unexpected: Assuring High Performance in an Age of Complexity* (San Francisco: Jossey-Bass, 2001). I am grateful to Babette Bensoussan for bringing this study to my attention. Her summary of the findings can be found in *Mindshifts Matters*, a publication of the Mindshifts Group Pty. Limited, Aug. 2002 (Australia).

CHAPTER 8

Step 3: Management Action

"It is not only for what we do that we are held responsible, but also for what we do not do."

—*Moliere*

Getting management to act is always the most delicate and problematic issue for any organizational process, and the CEW is no exception. Karl Weick and Kathleen Sutcliffe suggest that management of highly reliable organizations distribute decisions to frontline people, exactly because these employees are better able to see opportunities to act than top management. But the type of decisions and actions involved in a CEW cannot be migrated to the "front line." Any way one looks at it, it is top management that must ultimately decide on the direction the organization takes in light of the looming risks and opportunities of industry evolution.

I personally regard top executives who surrender their role of formulating strategy to the large strategy-consulting firms (without, in turn, reducing their own compensation, of course) as weak on integrity and low on productivity. However, even these questionable leaders must from time to time involve themselves in strategic decisions, especially those involving serious risks to their companies. This is where the third step of the CEW comes into play, as shown in Figure 8-1. An effective CEW must

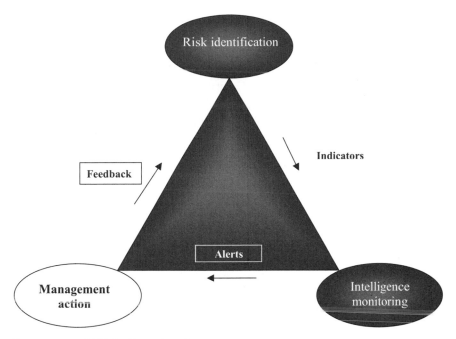

Figure 8-1: CEW's Step 3—Getting management to act.

grapple with the issue of inducing management to act. The accepted wisdom is that the triangle cannot be complete unless it produces actionable intelligence (so-called "management alerts"). Unless management *does* something about the risks and opportunities uncovered by the CEW process, all the warnings in the world and all the reading of early or weak signals are worthless. *Or are they?*

This is an old controversy among intelligence professionals and scholars. The dilemma of management action is simple enough: If the top executives—or politicians—do not act, or act slowly, is it the early warning's fault? Is the test of the value of intelligence in the action it promotes? Unless we can answer this question, there will be little we can do about measuring the value of the CEW process, and even less we can do about structuring the program to achieve maximum effectiveness.

Management Action Failures

To sharpen the dilemma for intelligence researchers, not all management action failures are alike. There are three kinds of action

failures when it comes to management. I will label them according to their most prominent characteristic:

> ▶ *Snail Pace Management Style (SPMS)*. Management chroni-
> cally acts too slowly. Thirty-eight percent of the respon-
> dents in our survey described their management style as
> too slow on action (Table 3-1). Should CEW take respon-
> sibility for too slow an action?

> ▶ *Maginot Line Management Style (MLMS)*. Management
> acts, but its action is not sufficient to either stem the risk
> or take advantage of the opportunity. This is named after
> the infamous French massive defense line that failed to
> stop the German invasion of France in World War II. Was
> the Maginot Line a failure of intelligence?

> ▶ *Black Hole Management Style (BHMS)*. Management just
> does not act at all. About 36 percent of our respondents
> worked in companies where "paralysis by analysis" or no
> management response at all was the dominant character-
> istic of management's action style. This should be an easy
> case—surely if management did not act, CEW failed.
> Right?

Well, that depends on the definition of the role of CEW. Note
that I defined its role as prevention of surprises. *Accordingly, the
test of the effectiveness of CEW is "zero surprises," not management
action*. However, one may see the validity of an argument, such
as that advanced by my partner Jan Herring, a leading authority
on business intelligence, that lack of management action may
signal lack of actionable information: "The business intelligence
manager's number 1 job is producing actionable intelligence.
The production of intelligence that is understandable, credible,
and *compelling* is the manager's principal objective and responsibility"[1] (italics added). In other words, if the CEW team had been
convincing enough, management would have acted.

The argument will not be decided here. Moreover, each case
may represent unique circumstances. It is hard to imagine blam-
ing a CI manager who is too junior to get an audience with a VP,
let alone the CEO, for her company's lack of action. If the CI
manager does not reach an influential position, how can one expect her to influence action? No matter how good the CEW alerts

are, if top executives never get to see them (at least without their having been thoroughly "massaged" on the way to the top)—can we blame the CEW analyst?

On the other hand, my experience shows that bright, bold analysts with integrity and guts do rise to an influential position. It may take time and patience, it certainly takes drive, but excellent analytical work more often than not catches the attention of superiors. In most companies, short of the most political ones, senior executives are on the lookout for talent. Producing insights is a sure way to be recognized.

The difference between snail and Maginot style management on the one hand, and black hole on the other is that the first two represent a failure of assessment while the last represents a failure of attention. Management that acts slowly when it should act fast reflects an assessment that the situation is not as risky or the opportunity not as large as the CEW team thinks. Management that acts in a way that is insufficient to address the issue represents a failure to correctly assess the options available to it. Assuming that insightful intelligence was available to management, in both cases it failed to incorporate it optimally into its decision process. An effectively designed CEW can address SPMS and MLMS with the various organizational tricks described below. The solution may not be perfect, but then the role of CEW is not to cause a specific action at a specific time. That role is reserved to management, as incompetent or indecisive it may be.

A black hole management style is a different kind of animal all together. Management that does not do anything with the intelligence available to it will ignore all early warnings. This failure of attention cannot be remedied by stronger warnings or more actionable ones. It may not be remedied at all. The 20 percent of our respondents who work in companies with such a culture may very well send their résumé around but skip Fiat, EDS, or Boeing. . . .

A Test Case

To test the reader's understanding of the distinction between SPMS, MLMS, and BHMS, let me suggest the following classic case of the U.S. automobile industry.[2]

In 1962, General Motors had 50 percent of the U.S. market in cars and trucks. The U.S. government might have considered

it a candidate for a breakup as it did with AT&T and as it attempted to do with Microsoft. In 2002, GM had only 28 percent
market share.

This in itself is no big surprise to anyone following the ups
and downs of Detroit. The story is well known: The onslaught
of the Japanese and European car manufacturers started in1982
when Honda built its first plant in Ohio. The attack by Toyota,
Nissan, BMW, and Mercedes on the U.S. market succeeded in
bringing the Big Three—General Motors, Ford, and Chrysler—to
the brink of bankruptcy, with huge losses and continually eroding market share. Detroit reacted exceedingly slowly. First, it
ceded the small car market and, later on, the market for compact
cars to Toyota and Honda. Its luxury car segment took a beating
from BMW, Audi, and Mercedes. Between 1979 and 1991, Detroit shed 150,000 jobs, but only in the late 1980s did it restructure its operation in earnest in the hope of reducing a bloated
cost structure. At the same time, it tried to fight back by adopting lean manufacturing techniques from Japan and, to a lesser
degree, styles from Europe. In the 1990s, the Big Three seemed
to have recovered. Profits were up significantly. The mid-1990s
were a bonanza period for GM and Ford, and even Chrysler enjoyed brisk sales of its minivans. It seemed that Detroit was
saved.

Well, not exactly. Detroit's roaring back was not due to any
serious headway against the competition. It now seems that
what helped the U.S. companies was a booming economy and
a change in consumer preferences toward minivans, SUVs, and
pickups. Since 1995, Detroit has lost an additional ten market
points to foreign-based rivals. Ponder that: Each market point is
worth $4 billion in sales. The result of these lost points is that
Chrysler is no longer an American company, and the fat profits
from trucks are disappearing. Foreign-based competitors
grabbed five market points from domestic trucks in the past five
years alone. With the economic boom over, Detroit is facing
much fiercer competition compared with the 1970s and 1980s.
This time around, all major competitors have bases in the United
States with design centers, manufacturing plants, and nonunionized workforces. Seventeen foreign-owned automobile factories in the United States represent more than $18 billion in
investment. The Koreans have joined the Japanese and the Euro-
peans, and Hyundai intends to open a plant in Montgomery, Al-

abama, with an investment of $1 billion that will be capable of producing 600,000 cars in 2005. The cost advantage of the Japanese versus the U.S. companies is estimated at $1,600 per vehicle, *after* all the restructuring and cost-cutting by the American companies. The flexible manufacturing afforded by nonunionized workers where jobs are not as rigidly defined as in the United Auto Workers–controlled factories of Detroit, the ability to build two or more models on a single assembly line for low-volume niches, which the older and larger U.S. factories lack, and the supplier relationship afforded by doing a lot of preassembly work to which the unions object but which the Japanese use more and more frequently, all conspired against the U.S. companies. General Motors improved its quality the most over the years—in 1987, GM had 180 problems per 100 cars, and Toyota had 127. By 2002, GM had gone down to 127. Alas, Toyota was at 107. In the study of the dependability of four- to five-year-old cars, the Japanese overwhelmingly dominate all segments except full-size cars.[3] U.S. companies have their backs to the wall, *again*.

And what do U.S. makers' executives consider to be their problem? It is not that foreign cars look better, perform better, and are more reliable. It is not that they are still cheaper if one takes into account value for money, and absolutely cheaper if one looks at small cars and Korean models. No, it is the loss of patriotic purchasing. In a speech in May 2002 in New York City, GM's CEO, Richard Wagoner, said: "Once these manufacturers establish a foothold in the U.S., they begin to mimic our broad product lines, eventually become accepted by the public as a 'domestic' brand, and suddenly we lose our home-field advantage."[4] In other words, Americans should prefer mediocre cars with mediocre looks and mediocre performance because they are American brands.

In terms of management action styles, GM and Ford (and Chrysler while it was one of the Big Three U.S. companies) exhibited all three styles over the years. Their late reaction to the Japanese onslaught of the 1970s and 1980s was a classic SPMS. *The* classic SPMS actually. The fact that they focused on competing on cost and price—a strategy that they had no chance of winning given their union restrictions and older plants—was a reflection of MLMS. The coma they have lapsed into since the 1990s, basking in the profits from the SUVs and pickups and completely losing sight of the bigger picture to the point that no other than Ford Motors' chairman, William Ford, Jr., said, "We have absolute collective amnesia in this business"—is none other than black hole mentality, or BHMS. Wagoner's statement shows GM has not learned much. It will continue competing on the same bases as the better-positioned foreign companies rather than introducing innovative cars that will win Americans back. I will not be putting my neck out too much by predicting that in a decade or so, foreign-based automobile companies will dominate the U.S. domestic market.

Even fast-acting companies can lapse into SPMS or MLMS when it comes to issues fundamental to their core concept. Over the past decade, Mattel, the maker of the Barbie doll, has seen the age of their core customers dropping from the 7 to 10 range to the 3 to 6 range.[5] That means that by the time girls reach the age of six, they tend to stop playing with Barbies. Instead, since June 2001, they have played with Bratz, a line of funky-looking dolls from MGA Entertainment, which they seem to consider much "cooler" and more fashionable. Mattel had a whole decade to watch this industry change driver and to act on it. Indeed, Mattel is well known for reacting fast and incorporating features of rival dolls that had threatened Barbie's dominance before. However, the changes were never too radical. A revolutionary change would be lighter face paint and straighter hair—a makeover given to the doll in 2000. The Bratz dolls look nothing like Barbie. They have BIG heads, and much sexier looks. For the first six months in 2002, they were the number-one best-seller in the United States, replacing Barbie and expected to bring $1 billion in sales since their introduction, together with one hundred licensed products created around them. That's a huge chunk of money to be left on the table when the signs had been quite clear for quite a long time that "Barbies were for babies." Yet Mattel did not react until late in 2002, with a doll called My Scene that attempted to appeal to the growing market for fashion dolls for preteens. The new Barbie is still slim, and true to form.

Mattel will survive the Bratz. Barbie is a huge brand that is not going to die any time soon. But the intriguing question is why Mattel didn't act earlier to appeal to the preteen market. Perhaps because questioning the fundamental assumptions on which a whole strategic concept is built is never an easy task, especially in successful and dominant brands. But it must be done if companies want to prosper, and the searchers for the holy grail must persist in their quest. Management with a sense of survival would encourage the continuous critical watch for signals of adverse change or new opportunities and would act to *institutionalize* this search. By the way, Mattel ousted its chairman and CEO, Jill Barad, in 2000 after the ill-fated acquisition of The Learning Company put the company in the red. One can hope that the new chairman and CEO, Robert A. Eckert, will be less preoccupied with big takeovers, and more attuned to early signs of risks and opportunities

Handling SPMS and MLMS

How can a CEW overcome slow response or insufficient or wrong response from management? While the following sections are not meant as a panacea, these are valuable lessons I learned over the years in dealing with management action and intelligence input.

First, it is of the utmost importance that management and the CEW team agree in advance on the following fundamental value added of the CEW:

> **The goal of early warning is not to yield an immediate management action but to force management's awareness. Management's awareness instigates a whole set of actions— debates, discussions, deliberations, further studying, and finally, *at management's discretion*, planning and visible initiatives.**

The rationale behind the above principle is that CEW stimulates management discussions *several months to several years* before those discussions would have taken place in a natural course of management attention and before the banks, the courts, or the institutional investors force management to take action.

If I had a penny for every time I have heard a beleaguered CEO say, "If we had only started looking at it seriously two years ago, we'd be in a very different place," I would never need to work again in my life. Instigating management discussions early on can be a company's lifesaver. Throughout the next section, keep in mind that CEW's value is in *fostering management deliberations*. It makes the effective use of CEW and its structure much more focused. It avoids misleading expectations for quick action, expectations that should not be laid at the door of an analytical process and a monitoring activity, when the ultimate discretion regarding any action is management's. Managing expectations is one of the most delicate and important steps in creating a true early warning mentality in an organization.

Maximizing the Effect of CEW's Deliverables

The following are five basic tenets of delivering early warning to management. They are based on the lessons learned from hundreds of organizations where intelligence professionals attempted (and usually failed) to communicate with management.

1. The deliverables of the CEW should be in the form of irregular management alerts and regular executive briefings.
2. CEW reports should never be only data.
3. The writing of a management alert is an art form; it cannot and should not be done by just anyone with a word processor.
4. In a politically charged environment, a buffer between the analyst and management may be desirable.
5. For worst-case events, use tripwires.

Management Alerts

Management alerts are short (never more than four pages), concise statements of significant risk or opportunity. They can be color-coded (yellow, orange, red) according to the urgency of the required action.

Management alerts should not be reports that land on the

desks of busy executives and never get read. They are not the tidbits of "competitive alerts" issued by market researchers or information professionals and placed on the company's internal Web site at a section typically called "Competitive Newsletter." These are creative syntheses based on observed indicators which provide insights into the future and are written specifically for the consideration of top executives and with the purpose of eliciting a debate.

Management alerts may deal with any subject that was part of the strategic "risk list" agreed upon between the CEW team and management. At the same time, the alert is not confined to an agreed-upon list; if an urgent issue emerges that requires management attention, the team may elect to issue an alert. Often, alerts follow the discovery that a worst-case scenario, or portions of it, is emerging.

Generally speaking, a typical alert follows a significant deviation of reality from a "most likely" scenario shared by top executives, planners, and the CI professionals partaking in the CEW process. It can be the result of one major indicator "lighting up," or more likely a synthesis of many risk signposts becoming active. Significant deviations typically occur when a worst-case scenario, or more generally a risky development, emerges. In an institutionalized CEW process, employees with access to the pertinent information closely monitor indicators derived from worst-case scenarios. Once the monitor sees movement on his or her indicator—a market statistic, a competitor announcement, a political maneuver in Washington, a patent application, construction work on a new plant wing—the report goes back to the CEW team and is processed for implications. When enough indicators accumulate to suggest an emergence of a worst-case scenario, an alert should be issued to management.

Alerts should not be issued lightly. Too many alerts and the CEW team loses credibility. Too few and it will be called upon to explain surprises. This delicate balance is hard to reach and depends to a large extent upon the skills of the CEW team and the politics at the top. Executives who are worth their salaries, such as the CEO of a large energy company, actually take part in the preparation and deliberations leading to an alert. Having an executive or two involved in this process achieves two goals. First, the executive adds pieces of intelligence that combine with the team's data to form a more complete puzzle. Second, the executive may bring a flavor of the executive team's ongoing deliberations and concerns to the CEW team. However, the team should be careful not to let the executives' concerns dominate its agenda.

This last point is far from trivial in a corporate hierarchical environment. CEW does not *need* to know what is on management's mind; an early warning process does not give executives what they *want* to know, but alerts them to what they *need* to know. This point is so fundamental that I expand on it below.

Needs to Know, Wants to Know, What's the Difference?

When Jan Herring retired from the CIA and was recruited by Bob Galvin, then Motorola's chairman and CEO, to head Motorola's Business Intelligence unit in 1985, he revolutionized the unsystematic intelligence activities of Motorola and with it, the whole of corporate America. Herring was the first to introduce the concept of Key Intelligence Topics (KITS) into a business environment. KITS is a familiar government intelligence term for a list of intelligence topics required by decision makers for their decisions. Today, largely due to Herring's teaching, most competitive intelligence professionals use KITS to one degree or another in planning their projects. The mechanisms of drawing KITS vary, but the most popular is a set of questionnaires and/or interviews with top management to determine a list of topics to be addressed by the intelligence professionals during the year. That list is then translated into questions around which a competitive intelligence department can plan its annual collection efforts. If a competitive (or business) intelligence function operates properly, KITS would occupy a central role in its modus operandi.

KITS is but one way to provide management with the information it wants. But even in organizations where the CI function is not that well developed, management has its way of getting its information. It will not come as a surprise to anyone if I state that when a division head wants information, she makes a phone call, and a whole cadre of people is then incited to sometimes frenzied activity until the information is provided.

Combining a systematic KITS list and the power of senior executives to get information, it is safe to say that in most cases management has a way of getting the information it wishes to obtain. The problem is: What about information it does not know it wants—but information it needs?

Considering the rising number of business experts who claim many top executives don't know their business, considering the repeated evidence revealed by the press that top executives are insulated, surrounded by "yes-people," rubber-stamp boards, and advisers with severe conflicts of interest, it is not too outrageous to assume that management *does not always know all that it needs to know,* and the difference between "wants to know" and "needs to know" becomes quite critical.

Since CEW is about driving management discussions before management is fully aware it needs a discussion, using KITS to drive CEW may defeat its purpose. Instead, the method proposed here suggests using analytical frameworks to derive scenarios, using scenarios to drive intelligence monitoring efforts, and using monitoring results to alert management. In this causal chain it is not mandatory that management concerns be included. It may be advisable to obtain management approval for the broad targets derived from the scenarios to prevent political problems later on. However, since the main objective of the CEW is zero surprises, it should be left to the discretion of the CEW leader to decide what will be monitored, when it will be monitored, and how the intelligence resources are deployed. If management keeps in mind that the goal of the CEW is to save its career and performance bonus, and incidentally also save the company, we can only hope it will quickly give the CEW team a free hand to monitor whatever the team considers crucial and will remove any organizational obstacle from its way. Management can still use KITS to drive other information projects in which it has an interest.

While making a conscious effort to prevent executive *domination* of the CEW's agenda is paramount to the effectiveness of the process, knowing management's ongoing discussions and concerns can help in a different direction. Without that privileged knowledge, alerts run the risk of being ignored as "old hat" —"We have been discussing it already for some time" and "These guys are not up to date." The latter label is a death sentence to lower ranks managers. The champion of the CEW, therefore, should gain its analysts access to management deliberations, or the alerts will lose credibility quickly. Once the CEW team loses credibility, the *crucial* alert will be ignored, and the CEO and his team may become the next on the unemployment line (OK, next on the line to the yacht club might be more likely, even in these circumstances).

Executive Briefings

Unlike management alerts, executive briefings are regular, routine reports by the CEW leader to the executive team. These briefings should precede executive meetings dealing with strategic issues. That's a tall order. Many if not most executive meetings deal with putting out fires. They are focused entirely on operational issues, personnel issues, and internal problems; anything *but* strategic discussions. The outside world may have a conception of gentlemen and gentlewomen clad in dark business suits seriously deliberating global trends and deciding the big issues, but this cannot be further from the truth. Then again, sometimes even mundane deliberations are in short supply. I know of executive meetings where no one but the top boss speaks up. Powerful executives can be quiet as rabbits in the presence of an even more powerful executive.

Asking management to devote fifteen minutes every third Monday to hear what scenario is taking root in the real world may be a tough call, but leaders make tough calls. For those who don't, my recommendation is to do an EW briefing, at the least ahead of executive retreats and planning sessions. These EW briefings' objectives are twofold:

1. Bring management up to date on which scenario seems to be unfolding in the market.
2. Get management feedback.

So, together with the creation of a CEW process, management would do well to allocate time for EW briefings—quarterly, bimonthly, or monthly, depending on the pace of change and the competitive pressures facing the company and its industry. I recommend to my clients that they never go without an EW briefing for more than a quarter. My recommendation is completely self-serving—I want their checks to be honored at the bank. . . .

Whether or not a company succeeds in the incredibly delicate task of creating a regular forum where the CEW leader gets his fifteen minutes in the spotlight, it should be clear to any professional business manager that executive retreats—or annual planning sessions, as they might be called to ward off the gossip about the value of these events to the shareholders who pay for them—will be far more valuable if they are preceded by an EW session. I find it to be one of the most absurd corporate rituals when executives meet for days of intensive work sessions on business units' strategy and resource allocation without the slightest bit of help from a systematic intelligence process behind their deliberations. Sometimes they invite an outside expert to present, in essence bringing the outside world to infringe a bit on inside thinking. Adding the systematic CEW is a much more powerful and effective tool to bring an external focus to executive retreats.

Substituting for objective CEW briefings with the self-serving pitches by business units about the "competitive environment" is analogous to consulting horoscopes for business planning. Every business unit's (BU's) presentation must be accompanied by a CEW briefing on the emerging reality of this industry, the most likely projected future, correction to the earlier most likely projected future, and some briefing on the status of the signals for the worst-case scenario. If the BU does not have an EW team, or the BU president does not want the EW team to present, corporate must ask why. Jack Welch was well known for his tough competitive questioning at GE's investment review sessions. Lou Gerstner introduced competitive questioning at IBM's highest level. Both leaders changed their companies' cultures with their insistence on external focus. Bringing CEW into the executive retreat is a good start on the way to such a lofty goal. Since most retreats are held in the winter, it is also charitable to a CEW leader who would otherwise be freezing in Rochester with the rest of the employees while the executives keep warm in a retreat in Arizona. But that's a different story.

Should the BOD Be Briefed Too?

I don't know about you, but if I own stock in a company, I like to think that the board of directors (BOD) is there to guard my investment. The fact that directors' insurance premiums have skyrocketed in recent years may suggest otherwise. One reason boards may not do their fiduciary job is because all the information they are fed comes from the CEO and his lieutenants. Officers' presentations by nature are not meant to be objective intelligence reviews of the state of the nation.

So what are poor board members to do? Assuming that they would like an effective legal defense when being sued for negligence, I suggest they demand a CEW briefing of their own.

The fact that boards can use a CEW briefing is indisputable. The matter of whether or not it can come from a completely objective source is questionable. One solution is for the corporate CEW leader to have dual reporting—to the CEO and the board— but that solution is rife with political landmines. The real issue, however, is not whether or not the CEW team can do an "objective" presentation for the board of directors. The real issue is whether the board is equally informed without one. Consider this:

According to a recent study by *USA Today* and the Corporate Library—a corporate governance tracker—one-fifth (20 percent) of the 1,000 largest companies in the United States share at least one board member with another of the top 1,000. Eleven out of the nation's fifteen largest companies have at least two board members sitting together on another outside board; four of the fifteen share at least two board members with another of the largest fifteen companies. Now, according to Mason Carpenter, professor at the University of Wisconsin-Madison and a researcher of corporate BODs,

> **Boards that are highly linked tend to get "blindsided" by changes in their industry because they do not see them coming. And Eric Bonabeau, a researcher at Ecosystem, a company studying the effect of interlocking boards says: "Directors who sit on different boards together tend to gravitate towards a common way of thinking.**[6]

I rest my case.

Alerts I Would Have Written If I Were . . .

If I were a Rothschild . . . I wouldn't write any alerts, of course. But if I had been working for a telecommunications company in Europe in early 2001, I would have written an alert (or several alerts) bringing up the following issues for management to think about:

Multiple Issues Alert—European Telecom Company O

February 2001

> The market is nearing maturation. Subscribers' growth rate is expected to slow to a crawl (click here for graph). Most growth in phone sales will come from replacements (click here for 2002–2003 forecast).

> Therefore, most growth in revenue must come from profitable new services, specifically data communication.

> The expected rollout (March 15) of our new 2.5-generation package (General Packet Radio Service) in regions 1–5 without wide coverage through domestic and pan-European roaming agreements will significantly reduce the expected sales increase. Customers will have little reason to sign up. (Click here for P&L sensitivity analysis to 2001–2002 sales forecast based on CEW's assumption of customers' sign in rates and percent activating GPRS in 2001–2002.) Implication: There are thousands of roaming agreements that must be signed quickly. *Code: Red. Time horizon for risk: 6–18 months.*

> Recent activity on indicators for Scenario Beta shows wireless Internet connections for PCs and laptops will be fully operational by 2002, offering cheap, reliable, and convenient substitutes to connecting through our cellular phones. (Scenario Beta is our worst-case scenario. Click here for details. Summary report of our TIOTS— Technical Intelligence Operation, Trade Shows—for Comdex' 2001. Click here.) TIOTS report suggests pricing will be as low as $150–200 for an ADSL wireless

packet for a typical notebook. Indicator Hot Spots predicts Starbucks will be first to deploy wireless antennas in coffee shops. Indicator Wireless Network revealed Microsoft in final development stage on wireless networking card. See strategic options' analysis at the end of this alert. *Code: Red. Time horizon for risk: 12 months.*

▶ Our competitors' prices seem to confuse customers. Company X charges vastly different prices for the same package. (Click here for sample of ads and the results of a recent consumer focus group on the failure of the per-byte pricing model.) This presents an opportunity for us. For strategic options' analysis and recommendations, see the end of this alert. *Code: Orange. Time horizon for opportunity: 18–24 months.*

▶ We estimate a high probability that the new technology on the horizon, multimedia messaging services (MMS), will falter, and we predict revenue shortfall in 2003 versus plan. The reason is lack of roaming capability and lack of compatibility between brands of phones, so customers will not be able to send photos and sound files even within the same network. One can expect the same reaction as to the GPRS. *Code: Orange. Time horizon for risk: 24 months.*

▶ Attempts to keep most of the revenue for content will backfire. Scenario Zeta forecasts content providers getting out of the business of providing us with content (click here for Scenario Zeta). The business model of NTT DoCoMo's should be studied. DoCoMo kept only 9 percent of revenues and stimulated the creation of thousands of services, which helped i-mode to become the huge success it is. (For DoCoMo's intelligence file, click here.) First competitor expected to follow DoCoMo: Y (click here for analysis of Y's expected moves in 2002). *Code: Red. Time horizon for threat: 12 months.*

▶ Industry structure analysis suggests room for "rule changing" behavior under a scenario predicting regulatory action. (For Scenario Gamma and its current set of indicators click here. We urge you to add your input and vote on the likelihood of the scenario in the section marked Executive Prediction.) Scenario Gamma predicts regulators will vote to increase portability of cellular numbers when customers switch between carriers. Implication: Rivalry will change from price competition to features competition as switching between carriers becomes hassle-free. See some options analysis at the end of this alert. *Code: Yellow. Time Horizon: 18-30 months.*

Sample of strategic options analysis:
Pricing:
Option 1: Flat rate billing to replace our current per byte deals.
Pro: Simple to understand, attractive marketing point, significant short-term competitive advantage.
Con: Give up short-term revenue (further study recommended).
Estimated competitor response: Reluctance to follow at first. If model succeeds, Company A, C, D will follow within 3–6 months. Company B will not.
Option 2: Improve marketing and advertising support for current pricing by explaining clearly the differences in what customers get if pay *X* Euro and if pay *Y* Euro.
Pro: Attractive to consumers.
Con: Need new advertising campaign; easy to imitate.
Estimated competitor response: Company A will respond quickly, especially if we use price comparison. Company B, C, within weeks.
New data services options: etc.

End of alert

For those readers who say—with full justification—that writing alerts in early 2003 as if I were writing them in early 2001 is less than a thrilling intellectual exercise, I like to remind them that:

1. I am no industry expert. A CEW analyst working for, say, Vodafone or Orange could have written these things in 2001.

I have seen reports by intelligence analysts working for companies in the telecom and other industries, and in retrospect they were amazingly insightful. The power to write a good alert exists inside most companies. The willingness to give it the right place at the mahogany executive table does not—until the repossessors come to remove the table.

2. The purpose of the alert above is not to show off my wisdom but to demonstrate one possible format for an effective alert based on several I've seen and several more I've written. My alert is based on information found in newspaper articles, especially a piece by Andy Reinhardt of *Business Week* magazine, titled so appropriately *Europe's Clueless Wireless Operators* (*BusinessWeek Online*, 23 November 2002). If I had been working for one of those clueless operators, I would have had a hard time resisting using a similar title in my inside CEW report. I am willing to bet the royalties from this book that many, if not all, of the issues and problems identified by Mr. Reinhardt in late 2002 were showing up as *early indicators* in 2001. An effective CEW should have been able to pick them up long before a reporter could.

3. The strategic option analysis and the recommendations deserve an explanation. In the alert above I did not try to spell them out completely. A real alert would have put a bit more thought into them. The important point to remember is that strategic option analysis that includes an assessment of a likely competitor response can improve management deliberations *by magnitudes*. Such assessment can only be produced if the company has a serious professional competitive intelligence capability and has invested in creating and retaining competitors' experts. While beating around the bush is an art form, using it in predicting competitor response can cost the company dearly (and can cost the poor nonexpert chap who had to do it his job).

Alerts That Should Have Been Written . . .

There are some alerts that, in retrospect, should have been written, but that, in reality, knowing the players, the culture, and the lack of management foresight, would have been ignored. Still, they can serve as good blueprints for specific types of alerts. One such alert I would like to have written is for a conference organizer, the media company Key3Media, which bought the Comdex exhibition from Sheldon Adelson in 1996 for a quarter of a billion dollars (yes, $250,000,000). Comdex was founded twenty–three years ago as an exhibition of computer dealers. I would have liked to write this alert at the end of 2000, the best year in the company's history. That year, 210,000 attendees flocked to Las Vegas, filling several hotels and huge convention centers. More than 2,000 exhibitors paid exorbitant prices to present there (a tiny exhibition on the fringe of the conference cost more than $100,000). From my experience, *that's exactly the time to write an early warning.*

Single Issue Alert—Media Company K

November 2000
Code: Orange

▶ The PC industry is maturing (click on graph for sales projections 2000–2008). In maturing industries, consolidation occurs and raises entry barriers (click here for a three-year forecast of global and domestic market share for the five leading companies). Economies of scale become important as differentiation declines and small players are pushed out.

▶ Out of the consolidation, our scenario Obsolete (for worst-case scenario, click here) predicts the following remaining U.S. competitors: Dell (leading), IBM, Gateway, HP, and Compaq. We predict HP will take over Compaq. (What an insight!)

▶ Dell does not use Comdex since it focuses on direct sales, not dealers.

▶ Our own surveys show that the majority of the exhibitors at Comdex are small- to medium-size companies and startups. Consolidation will take many of those out.

▶ The Consumer Electronics Association's international consumer electronics show is forecasted to grow by 20 percent per year for the next five years (click here for CEA file) surpassing Comdex by 2002.

▶ The Cellular Telephone & Internet Association annual spring conference is expected to grow by 35 percent over the next two years (click here for CTIA file).

▶ Against these substitutes (CTIA and CEA), under scenario Obsolete, Comdex's broad-based concept may become unprofitable as quickly as 2002.

Strategic options available to us:

1. Fracture Comdex into three focused exhibitions. See attached detailed proposal. Pro: Lack of focus our main complaint. Saving on smaller facilities (conference halls availability much larger). Con: Lower bargaining power, smaller economies of scale (unless mitigated by group purchasing).

2. Cut cost by 15 percent by January 2001. This is a robust strategy option (surviving scenario Obsolete). See P&L analysis given various cost estimates and attendance rates predicted by scenario Obsolete. Failure to do so may result in bankruptcy by 2003.

End of alert

The alert above would have turned Shining Red in 2002. If someone had written such a CEW alert back in 2000, Key3 Media, Comdex's owner, would have had a chance to better prepare for Comdex 2002, in which the number of paid attendees declined by two-thirds, the number of paid exhibitors went down to 1,000 from 2,500 in 1999, and the company was on the brink of Chapter 11. But no one did write an alert. With all likelihood, Key3Media did not even have a CI analyst on its staff, let alone a systematic CEW process.

Another memo I would love to have written is to the steel industry in the United States. This probably would have been my last alert as an employee since there is very little one can say to mask the huge blindspots of the executives of companies such as LTV and Acme, two of the many that went bankrupt and were bought by the private equity firm WL Ross. Sometimes a CEW is just not enough, and one can see an inevitable end. The benefit of being in a CI position or on a CEW team is that one can see it coming early enough to bolt out. This is what happened to several smart CI professionals I worked with at Lucent, Boeing, and Enron. They were able to spot a blind management team and hopelessly insular culture two to three years (!) before the companies started to sputter and lay off managers or collapsed altogether.

Requiem Alert—U.S. Steel Industry

Any time in the 1990s
No code. Too late.

- The Koreans are here! The Koreans are here!
- The Chinese are here! The Chinese are here!
- The industry is global! Ask the Japanese!
- The contracts terms and work rules you offered to the United Steel Workers Union are simply and squarely unaffordable in a global competitive situation. (No need to click on anything! My eleven-year-old daughter can run the P&L forecast to show you when Chapter 11 is due). The pension and health benefits alone will drag you into bankruptcy.
- On the other hand, the lack of attention to workers' ideas is ill-afforded against more productive competitors.
- Twenty-two executives can run a steel company. What do you do with 500!?
- A capital structure of junk bonds is a recipe for bankruptcy in a cyclical, capital-intensive industry. Interest alone will put you behind the foreign competitors.
- Someone can come in, buy your assets, but not your obligations and union contracts, start over with 31 percent of the workforce, and make money!

> *Strategic option analysis:* I don't know! You've painted yourself into such a corner that no one with your management structure, debt, benefits, and union rules can save itself. My letter of resignation is on your desk. See ya!
>
> **End of alert**

OK, so this is an extreme alert, not often written. But the signs were there for so many years that only severely blinded management could not see them or, alternatively, had no desire or inner strengths to do something about them. Wilbur Ross, a New York financier, eventually swept in, bought the assets of LTV and Acme, but not their obligations or union contracts, and on February 8, 2003, announced the purchase of Bethlehem Steel as well. With this latest deal, Mr. Ross has become the owner of the largest steel company in the United States almost overnight. In an interview he gave to *Business Week*, he wondered what the bankrupted steel industry had done with so many lawyers, so many executives, so many workers, and contracts that were simply unaffordable. He wondered why the management of those companies never actually listened to the workers or their unions when they made good suggestions on improving productivity.[7] After twenty years of running blindspots war games, I have stopped wondering.

Finally, here is an alert that is truly future-oriented. So, no hindsight. Every CEW analyst working for a large company with investments in China should write it. Few will do so because of the allure of the silly belief, held firmly, if not explicitly, by significant numbers of senior executives in the United States, that "if every person in China bought just one of our products. . . ." Never mind that in the meantime the average income of every person is enough to buy a pack of chewing gum.

Single Issue/Silly Issue Alert—Dozens of Industries
NOW
Code: Very Red
  ▶ Chinese banks' total nonperforming loans are estimated at $700 *billion*.

> ▶ **China's biggest banks are technically insolvent.**
> ▶ **High investment rates will not remedy this potential disaster waiting to happen.**
> ▶ **Ignore at your own risk.**
>
> *Strategic option:* **Get out or stay out until a market economy and a non-Communist regime cleans up the mess. Estimated time: Fifty years? Five years? Five months?**
>
> **End of alert**

Options and Recommendations

Should alerts include action options for management? How about specific recommendations? Experts disagree on these issues. My own belief, reflected in the sample alerts above, is that laying out strategic options and making recommendations increases the appeal of the alert to management. Laying out options makes the analysis more "actionable." Recommendations save executive time.

Strategic options are where creativity exhibits itself. One test of management is its ability to come up with creative strategies to fight the structural forces, preempt competitors, etc. (think Michael Dell). One reason I regard executives who delegate strategy formation to the big consulting firms as slackers is that this creativity must be cultivated as a core skill *inside* the company. Giving it up to a team from outside consulting firms is dangerous and shortsighted. This skill dies inside the company as managers realize they have little influence on strategy formation. The consultants walk out with a hefty fee, the executives can blame them ("We used the most prestigious company and paid it $30 million"), and the ones that are short-changed are employees and shareholders. Surprisingly, many shareholders buy into this myth that employing the big consulting firms is a reasonable course of action for top executives.

The ability of the CEW team to propose creative options depends on the people populating it. If the team leader feels her team is composed of some of the best minds in the company, and some of the most outside-the-box thinkers, she must stick her neck out and make strategic options part of her alerts. She should also choose those options that her team believes are the best and recommend them to management. That makes decisions easier and quicker or at least focuses the debate. Management is, of course, free to disagree, consider other options, or send the CEW team to bring in more intelligence. Since the value added of CEW is in driving management debates, options and recommendations help achieve this goal with more efficiency.

The issue of team composition becomes paramount here. I will discuss it in more detail in Chapter 10, but it is clear that executives who believe it is impossible to control strategic risks and opportunities, or prefer to manage by crisis, will find it hard to assign out-of-the-box and/or deep thinkers to a CEW team.

The proposed alternative courses of actions put forward by the CEW team include pros and cons. A pro/con analysis draws on two elements unique to the CEW knowledge pool: understanding the industry structure and where it is going and, crucially for options analysis, understanding competitors' mindset, intentions, drivers, and capabilities. Strategic moves by a company are sure to elicit competitive response. This simple fact escapes the attention of numerous senior executives and project leaders who assume, sometimes implicitly and sometimes explicitly, that competitors will remain passive watchers. When they don't, and when the revenue/profit stream falls short of the rosy forecast, everybody is shocked.

The knowledge pool within the CEW team, if built correctly, will be unmatched on exactly these two aspects. Its value added to the management discussion is therefore superior.

Never, but Never, Give Them Data

Alerts should never be composed of mere data. They must include analysis, interpretation of reality, and prediction of things to come. Data provide the background, the support for arguments, and the graphics for alerts.

There are those decision makers, in government and in businesses alike, who say to their intelligence professionals: "You give me the data, I will make the interpretation." This is a mistake. No matter how wise the decision maker thinks he is—and most think very highly of themselves—his judgment and intuition, experience and sixth sense, broad perspective and immense talent, never can and never should replace a professional analysis and assessment complied by an intelligence network and a CEW team. The reasons are numerous and have been detailed throughout this book. To repeat briefly, executives are insular by the nature of their job and the company they keep, their experience marks them more for blindspots than their underlings, and their systematic memory can never compete with the filing system of a well-run intelligence operation. Moreover, they have little true competitor expertise, even if they call the other side's CEO by his first name on the golf course.

Executives' opinions and analyses can definitely supplement a professional intelligence assessment. In fact, they should. The final decision is theirs, and they are called upon to accept or reject their professionals' work. Executives are not obliged to agree with the analysis in the alert. They can even ignore it completely. This is an executive prerogative. The intelligence professional, however, including the CEW leader, should never succumb to a demand to provide the data only. This will be a betrayal of his or her professional integrity as an intelligence professional. My advice to managers who come to me when they find themselves in this quandary is clear-cut: Find a new assignment. If management wants you to be a data collector, move over to marketing. No one asks you to think there either, but the pay is better.

I know I am wasting my time arguing this point. Executives who think they know best will ignore this warning in the blink of an eye. I also know that no matter how many scandals and silly misdeeds are exposed by the press and the SEC, and no matter how antiexecutive the U.S. culture turns, some of those people who reach the top and make millions are bound to feel pretty confident that they know better than anyone else what's up with their industry.

My concern is not to convince the small portion of CEOs who are arrogant and insular to have a professional risk assessment. My concern is to prevent the CEW team and its leader from wasting its time and effort on alerts that are just data.

It is not that sending a piece of especially significant raw data to management is all that bad. In fact, it is a natural activity within a large corporation. CI managers, marketing managers, and salespeople all chip in with data, some on a weekly basis (sales competitive reports), some more spontaneously. But early warning is not a routine activity, and alerts are not tactical information to be channeled upstairs in the course of a workday. A CEW alert should be a well-thought-out and well-written piece of analysis. Sending in data is a total misuse of the CEW process.

What MBAs Don't Know but a Biblical Tribe Knew

The difference between data and an early warning alert report is the difference between data and intelligence. Intelligence is technically defined as analyzed data. The distinction seems trivial to some executives. It is not taught at the MBA level. "A semantic difference" was how one MBA student put it to me. It is not. The simple failure to distinguish between data and intelligence puts thousands of stakeholders—employees and investors alike—at a higher risk.

The difference between facts and intelligence, or data and analysis, is that the latter is an expert interpretation of the former. This interpretation paints a picture of reality, connecting the facts and allowing the decision maker a better understanding of the "why" and a more insightful guess as to "what next." The best example of this difference can be found in a 3,500-year-old story of the twelve scouts, cited in the Old Testament (Numbers 13). It always amazes me how ancient leaders knew more than some modern-day executives with MBAs from the best Ivy League universities. . . .

In this story, the Israelites had escaped from slavery in Egypt and were wandering in the desert. As they approached Canaan, the Promised Land (modern Israel), God told Moses, the leader of the Israelites, to send twelve scouts to survey the territory. Ten of the scouts came back with the following report:

> We came to the land you sent us to; it does indeed flow with milk and honey and this is its fruit. However, the people who inhabit the country are powerful, and the cities are fortified and very large; moreover we saw the Anakites there . . . and we looked like grasshoppers to ourselves and so we must

have looked to them. . . . We cannot attack the people for it is stronger than we.

The report above lists the following facts: the land was populated by strong tribes who inhabited fortified cities. Some of the tribes were very tall people ("Anakites"), much stronger physically than the Israelites. The scouts recommended that the small tribe of Israelites stay away from the land because they were too weak to win.

However, two of the twelve scouts, Caleb and Joshua (who later became the leader of the Israelites), interpreted the same facts quite differently:

> **And Joshua son of Nun and Caleb son of Jephunneh of those who had scouted the land, rent their clothes and exhorted the whole Israelite community: "The land that we traversed and scouted is an exceedingly good land. If the Lord is pleased with us, he will bring us into that land . . . only you must not rebel against the Lord. Have no fear then of the people of the country, for they are our prey: their protection has departed from them but the Lord is with us. (Numbers 14:6–9)**

According to their report, the tribes in Canaan were fragmented, lacking a unified religion to unite them. The Israelites, being the first tribe to believe in one God, had a strategic strength in their religious underpinning, which would help them against the fragmented locals. Thus, recommended the two, the Israelites should conquer their fears and then the land, which had been promised to their ancestors.

The rest of the story is well known to anyone who has had to sit through Bible class. The Israelites went on to defeat the pagans and conquer the land. Joshua replaced Moses after the latter's death. The important lesson to be learned is that the essence of intelligence is seeing the same facts as everyone else but interpreting them in a way that allows a better understanding of reality. If this interpretation exposes an underlying reality that is hidden from everyone else, intelligence becomes an insight. Not all alerts will be extremely insightful. Not all interpretations will be correct. But to suggest that executive intuition or knowledge is always better than an expert interpretation of the facts is quite arrogant and awfully stupid. As Jim Williams points out, "Good intelligence with bad strategy produces mediocre results. Bad intelligence with good strategy can be catastrophic."[8] He also cites the case of the Singer Company, which in the 1970s hired a new sales force to "push the iron" instead of interpreting the fact that increasing numbers of women were working outside the home to mean the end of the home-based sewing machines.

It is interesting that Larry Bossidy and Ram Charan, the authors of *Execution: The Discipline of Getting Things Done*, define execution in terms related to intelligence: "In the most fundamental sense, execution is a systematic way of exposing reality and acting on it."[9] Exposing reality is the raison d'être of intelligence, and intelligence—not data—is the core of early warning. An alternative to doing diligent intelligence work to expose reality will be to use execution as a way to *test* the assumptions underlying the strategy. I would venture to say that this is an extremely expensive way to find out if you were right or wrong. The problem is aggravated by what Bossidy says is a reality check issue with many top executives: ". . . leaders don't reach out to the rest of the world. They are centered internally instead of externally."[10] Executives who order their professional CEW team to deliver data because no one can interpret reality as well as they can completely miss out on Bossidy's fifth (out of six) success factor for executives of companies who execute well: "Ego containment is crucial."[11]

Evaluation Committees

One organizational tool that works well in some large corporations is the formation of an evaluation committee as a buffer between the CEW analysts and top management. Depending on the company's culture, the nature of the hierarchical relationship dominating discourse between management and rank and file, and the personalities populating the top team, an evaluation committee can provide a more comfortable medium to bring about management action because management may be unaccustomed to working directly with more junior professionals.

An evaluation committee is a body of seasoned and influential managers who assess the output of the CEW team and resolve which alerts go to the top. The composition of this body is critical: It has to carry credibility with the top team. An evaluation committee in a research-intensive company will most likely include a senior scientist or two in addition to several vice presidents. In a marketing company, a director of an influential brand may be called upon to serve on the committee. The litmus test is who has management's ear. Naturally, each company will have its own cadre of people whose word carries more weight at the top than others, and it is not always determined by seniority alone. At times, an experienced, seasoned, respected professional (e.g., a district sales director) may have the ear of the CEO or an executive vice president.

The evaluation committee should meet periodically to review alerts in progress and on an ad hoc basis to review urgent alerts that were not in the queue at the last meeting. The objective of the evaluation committee is to save on executive time and yet keep the company alert and prepared. It is a genuine balancing act, and evaluation committee members may decide to adopt a series of criteria for giving the green or red light to alerts in process. If the company follows the balanced scorecard mentality, the committee may decide to weight the significance of alerts according to the impact on the scorecard's various areas, and the most pressing concern of the top. If the company has a particular crusade dictated by the top (to gain leadership in a particular technological area, for instance), the committee might decide that all alerts touching upon this topic will go upstairs.

Evaluation committees are not ideal—they are a buffer between the CEW analysts and the top decision makers—and buffers are both bad and good. As an intelligence analyst, I always prefer no buffers at all, but in that case the assumption is that top executives will be willing to listen to relatively junior CEW analysts. Alternatively, if management is willing to nominate a very senior person as the head of the CEW team, an evaluation committee may not be needed at all. But in most situations in a typical Fortune 500 company, top management has no idea who Bob the analyst is, and regardless of how bright the analysis is, it may simply fail to register on the executives' retina. Considering that large Fortune 500 divisions may employ many thousands of people, it is hard to expect management to be familiar with and give credence to a relatively unknown CEW analyst even though she may actually save them from an SEC investigation or investors' lawsuit a few years down the road.

While an evaluation committee can produce some very desirable effects, especially in large bureaucratic organizations where "going by the book" is superior to significant insights (and

I know a few of those), executives who understand the need to keep their organizations nimble and responsive may still want to provide an *alternative* route for the CEW analyst to reach the top. That alternative route should not be used lightly. It should be reserved for a minority opinion of an analyst who sees a disaster looming and whose boss (or the evaluation committee) fails to act or outright rejects his interpretation. An example is the practice at one military intelligence agency to allow the individual analyst to write directly to the head of the agency, or in some instances all the way to the prime minister himself in cases where ignoring a signal may cause a catastrophe. In this particular case, this alternative route was created following a very nasty surprise that cost thousands of lives. If such a mechanism had existed inside the extremely bureaucratic FBI, it is at least possible that the September 11 attacks might have been avoided or altered.

Tripwires

Tripwires are mechanisms used to evoke action based on a predetermined plan. They are popular in national security early warning systems but can be easily adapted to business settings. An example of a tripwire is the launch of a missile attack from outside the United States against American targets on the continent. Once such an attack is confirmed, the government has a predetermined action plan, typically known by a code name.

In business, a tripwire may be a statistic—once market share hits a low of x percent, the company will put into effect a new pricing policy. Or it can be a specific competitor's move—a detection of a violation of property rights, for example, might evoke an immediate legal action.

Tripwires represent a way for management to deal with a culture of "paralysis by analysis." Since a tripwire is an indicator normally derived from a worst-case scenario or an indicator for a "hot button" for the company, it should be acted upon quickly. Michael Porter defines hot buttons as "areas of the business where a threat will lead to a disproportionate response."[12] Hot buttons reflect historical roots, strong beliefs, "creed," and pride. Or they may reflect economical underpinnings such as cash cows or the most promising new area for a company. Or they may represent nothing more than a CEO's pet idea. (If you think this is preposterous, read about the acquisition of Sterling Drugs by Kodak and the staunch defense of this silly move.)[13] Regardless of their origin, hot buttons are typically associated with specific tripwires so the company can react quickly.

Tripwires must be agreed on in advance between management and the CEW team. Action-reaction plans must be prepared in advance for the occasion when the tripwires are, well, tripped. It is the responsibility of the CEW leader to make sure that once a wire is tripped, the information gets quickly to the proper decision makers, who then take out the plan and execute it.

Brief Conclusion Regarding the CEW

The competitive early warning process described so far is simple in design but tricky in implementation. A colleague of mine, a brilliant analyst with a membership-based research organization working with Fortune 500 companies, who wrote a report on strategic early warning systems, remarked that it has always amazed him how few companies managed to put forth the consistent effort necessary to make such a practice succeed. There are probably several reasons for this: First, it is a new concept for most corporations. Like quality issues two decades ago, new concepts aimed at improving competitiveness need time to take hold. Second, it is a process that requires scarce management attention and even more scarce management involvement. It is not enough to declare, "Our company is committed to minimizing strategic risks and maximizing strategic opportunities through an early warning system," as one executive client of mine did—and then immediately proceeded to remove it from his vicinity. The test of management is in actually using the process to fundamentally change their own way of making decisions involving the future of the company and billions of dollars in investments. Third, my colleague hit it on the head when he stated that to have a CEW capability, a company must be *consistent* in how it applies its efforts. Consistency requires discipline in execution, and Larry Bossidy has already commented that this is not the strong suit of many executives.

Chapter 9 tells the stories of the few leading-edge companies that succeeded in creating a world-class early warning capability, with consistency, foresight, and impressive results. I am not sure which is the chicken and which is the egg: These companies show impressive bottom-line results in tough times. It may be the result of an early warning mentality of the leaders, or it may be the cushion allowing them to play around with leading-edge organizational processes. Either way, it is worth looking closely at them.

Manager's Checklist—Chapters 5–8

❐ Change drivers that affect structural forces pose high risk. Change drivers against which competitors are better positioned than one's company pose the *highest* risk.

❐ Old competitors' and new competitors' actions and interactions will determine the future of an industry. War games investigate these actions and interactions. Without playing a war game, strategic planning runs the risk of being an interesting hypothesis without a base in reality.

❐ SWOT analysis is a powerful method. Unfortunately, it becomes an exercise in self-delusion in corporate hands. Blindspots Identification Methodology (BIM) is a much more relevant tool for companies.

❐ Getting into competitors' mindsets is the highest art of intelligence. Alas, part-time marketing assignments will not achieve that. Ad hoc project teams will not achieve that either. Highly paid large consulting firms are the most likely to achieve that but cannot share it with their clients. Information centers are not much more useful. A company in a competitive situation needs competitor expertise. It needs competitive intelligence experts. It needs lots of luck without these two.

❐ The central objective of an early warning system is simple and straightforward: Prevent surprises. Toyota pioneered the zero defects measurement when Western "experts" claimed it was not a realistic measurement system. I suggest that a zero surprises measurement for a company's intelligence, planning, and risk management capabilities is a realistic goal.

❐ An external intelligence network may be the best weapon executives have against mental stagnation. But to deploy a powerful external monitoring network, one needs the dissenting voices, the critics, and the objective sources that may not be a natural part of a more classic "internal intelligence network" employed by companies, or the "trusted advisers" surrounding the powerful executives.

❐ The goal of early warning is not to create management action but to force management awareness. Management awareness instigates a whole set of actions—debates, discussions, deliberations, further studying, and, finally, at management's discretion, planning and moving.

❐ An early warning process does not give executives what they *want* to know, but alerts them to what they *need* to know. A small difference, huge implications.

❐ Management does not know what it *needs* to know. It knows what it *wants* to know. The two are not the same, as Ken Lay of Enron proved.

❐ Some companies never mange to conduct a serious, ongoing, strategic discussion. The reader may be shocked to find out how many of them are on the Fortune 500 list (at least until next year . . .).

❐ Executives who delegate strategy formation to the big strategy consulting firms are slackers; they prefer to cover themselves rather than cultivate the strategic skills inside the company. They end up with the latest "cookie recipe" or the latest "consultants' fad" based on what others in the industry think, rather than creative propositions based on the company's real capabilities and unique culture. The skill inside the company dies as managers realize they have little influence on strategy formation. The bank accounts of the consultants fill up nicely.

❐ Intelligence means seeing the same data as everyone else but interpreting them in a way that allows a better understanding of reality. It is this interpretation that executives forfeit when they ask for "the data only."

❐ The test of management is in actually *using* the process of early warning to change the way of making decisions involving the future of the company and billions of dollars in investments. Empty words about "commitment" to risk management are good for the cheerleaders from the popular business press who love "success stories" or the Wall Street crowd that has dubious conflicts of interest.

> In my completely biased opinion, using strategy consulting firms (as contrasted with technology consulting firms), especially the large ones, is a symptom of a serious disease—top managers who are slackers. Do you have horror stories of management that relinquished its role (but not its pay!) to the prestigious consultants with the result that everyone paid for it later on? Send your story to me at bsgilad@net vision.net.il. I will post the most telling stories on my Web site, www.bengilad.com. The consultants will not lose their grip on corporate leadership, but at least we can shame those executives who hire them.

Notes

1. Jan Herring, "Producing Actionable and Effective Intelligence," *Competitive Intelligence Review* 6, no. 1 (1995): 57.
2. The following is based on the article, "Autos: A New Industry," by Joann Muller, Kathleen Kerwin, and David Welch, *BusinessWeek Online*, 23 July 2002.
3. 2002 Vehicle Dependability Index study, J.D. Powers & Associates, www.jdpa.com/studies/pressrelease.
4. "Autos: A New Industry," *BusinessWeek Online*, 23 July 2002.
5. The following is based on the story "Barbie Gets Hipper, Trendier, to Fight the Competition" by Ann D'Innocenzio, reported in *USA Today*, 22 Nov. 2002.
6. Matt Krantz, "Web of Board Members Ties Together Corporate America," *USA Today*, 25 Nov. 2002.
7. Michael Arndt, "The Forging of a Steel Magnate," *BusinessWeek Online*, 22 Nov. 2002.
8. Jim Williams, "Thinking About Thinking," The Williams Inference Center, Long Meadow, Mass., Dec. 2002, p. 3
9. Larry Bossidy and Ram Charan, *Execution: The Discipline of Getting Things Done.* (New York, Crown Publishing, 2002).
10. In a *USA Today* interview, 10 June 2002, p. 4B.
11. Ibid.
12. Michael E. Porter, *Competitive Strategy: Techniques for Analyzing Industries and Competitors* (New York: Free Press, 1980), p. 68.
13. See Benjamin Gilad, *Business Blindspots* (Chicago: Infonortics, 1996), p. 6.

PART THREE

EARLY WARNING AT WORK

CHAPTER 9

Case Studies of CEW in Action

"Take calculated risks. That is quite different from being rash."

—George S. Patton

"Confidence is what you feel before you comprehend the situation."

—Proverb

The companies featured in this chapter are from a variety of industries: energy, pharmaceuticals, banking, aircraft manufacturing, home products, etc. The fact that CEW is needed in all industries—service, manufacturing, consumer, industrial, low-tech, and high-tech—is reflected in the choice of stories below.

Confidentiality issues limited the choice of case studies. Many more companies have excellent capabilities of early warning, and by that I mean the whole process—from identification to quick action. However, companies keep their early warning capabilities under a tight wrap. The ability to decipher weak signals *earlier* than competitors is seen as a capability that confers significant competitive advantage.

Several firms I worked with just see it as a "sensitive" area. *Sensitive* in corporate talk means don't talk about it to the press. Not always a bad policy considering that some less than fully informed writers in the popular business press are inclined to sensationalize stories on legitimate and business-smart intelligence activities into "shady corporate spies" stories to increase the chance their pieces will be picked up by the editor. Editors, for their part, like to slap sexy, sensational, and completely misleading headings onto these stories to increase the chance the piece will be read.[1]

It should be obvious to the astute reader that the stories in this chapter do not guarantee a "happy ending." At least one early warning program described below went out of business following a merger. Changes in management are a number-one problem for companies' core skills, and CEW capability is no different. Thus, as described below, the merger of a German company that had a first-rate early warning program with a French-Spanish consortium of companies resulted in the destruction of the Germans' early warning capability because the business culture of the Spanish and French executives completely discarded systematic thinking and planning. In other cases, the progress of the CEW depends on the particular relationship between a CEW leader and the executive team, a relationship that can be precarious and transitory.

Notwithstanding the caveats above, these stories about smart executives and effective early warning should serve to persuade other smart executives that managing strategic risk is not a matter of luck and that avoiding strategic surprises is not an act of divine power. Moreover, the selection below is sufficient to give the smart manager a feel for how the CEW model can be applied in various environments.

Model 1. Very Large Global Company, Complex Operations: Citibank—Clean Windows

Long before John Reed was forced out of Citigroup by what was allegedly a collaborative effort of Sanford Weill, its co-CEO at the time, and another member of Citigroup's board of directors from AT&T, and long before Citigroup's investment analysts were accused in an embarrassing investigation of distorting reports on stocks to serve Citigroup's corporate finance deals,[2] there was a very large bank called Citibank, part of a company called Citicorp. Bad loans in the early 1990s almost bankrupted Citibank. The bad loans resulted from a culture that decentralized credit-giving decisions and encouraged risk taking by local officers. Under the assumption that Citibank was large enough to sustain a few bad loans, and that bad loans would be balanced out by good loans elsewhere, the bank accumulated an enormous number of bad loans on its books. John Reed, then the CEO, went through his bank's near-death experience and came out with a commitment to manage risk systematically and strategically. That commitment was translated into a program called Windows on Risk (WOR).

"In 1991," says Shelby Davis, a mutual fund manager, "Reed went through hell. He couldn't go to the bathroom without calling the Fed. That's why I like him. He became a better banker. He set up something called Windows on Risk and I think it's for real. Not that there isn't risk, but they're focused on it."[3]

Windows on Risk is indeed for real. And while it had its share of failures and critics, it is still Citibank's prime management tool to systematically monitor the bank's exposure to strategic risks, and when Citicorp merged with Traveler to become Citigroup, Windows on Risk migrated to the new entity with few difficulties. In 1994 it was described as a system that "regularly monitors the state of the economy in different countries and the extent to which the bank's exposure to lending, underwriting, or trading might be affected according to 12 key factors."[4] In 1999, with the appointment of a new chairman to the Windows on Risk committee, it was described in much loftier words: "a forum for reviewing risk tolerance and practices."[5] In his 2002 address to a UBS banking conference, Victor Menezes, chairman and CEO of Citibank NA, described it as part of the organization's Balanced Scorecard discipline. And you know, once you are into the Balanced Scorecard jargon, you are *in*.

Windows on Risk is considered such a high-level and proprietary program that Citigroup guards its information with zeal. The little it divulges can be found in secondary sources. The description below is based on a number of such public sources, especially an excellent report prepared by the Corporate Strategy Board.[6]

- ◗ *Program Location*: Corporate.

- ◗ *Charter*: Responsible for identifying risks for the bank's entire portfolio.

- ◗ *Strategy*: Identify early warnings about the emergence of certain adverse scenarios and act on them. Use a senior committee as the cornerstone of the process.

- ◗ *Rationale Behind*: Need to consolidate business units' risk management views at a higher level to prevent the concentration of risk in one industry, product area, customer group, or geographical region. Prevent a disaster like the real estate lending crisis of the early 1990s, which affected the bank's overall results.

- ◗ *Early Driver and Champion*: John Reed, then CEO.

- ◗ *Established*: Around 1994?

Activities on the Three Steps of the CEW Model

Figure 9-1 depicts the model Citigroup chose to apply for its early warning process. The model's specific choices for each of the three early warning steps of the CEW are described in more detail below.

Identification of Risk

Identification of risk at Citigroup is based on two sets of scenarios: most-likely and worst-case scenarios. The two sets of sce-

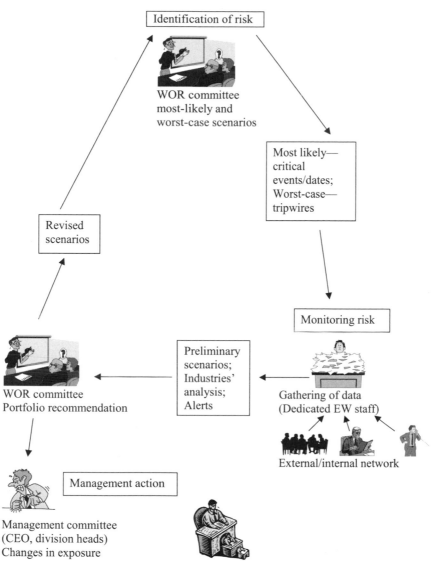

Figure 9-1: Visualization of Citigroup's early warning model.

narios are developed by a senior committee called the Windows on Risk committee. The most-likely scenarios are constructed for countries and for regional markets. They include an outlook for the country and regional economies and, for the most prominent countries in Citigroup's portfolio, a geopolitical outlook as well. The most-likely scenarios extend to eighteen months. The worst-case scenarios define adverse global economic or geopolitical developments for a set of variables known to correlate with Citigroup's performance. They extend to about two years.

The preparation of these two sets of scenarios by the senior committee is backed up by the work of hundreds of people. A team of executives and analysts is dedicated to the task of coordinating the collection of raw data from internal and external sources and analyzing the data to turn them into a usable product for the committee to discuss. Citigroup takes this task very seriously. The collection is based on all key internal reports pertaining to the analysis at hand, culled from 500 senior credit and securities officers and other line managers in the various countries and regions where Citigroup operates. In addition to the secondary research, the early warning team conducts extensive interviews with internal staff analysts, senior lending officers, and outside experts on industries and regional economics and politics.

The data collection is then turned into analysis by the same early warning team. The team prepares alternate scenarios for the global economy for the next two years, with forecasts of major economic indicators. It analyzes country- and region-specific conditions and forecasts their indicators. It analyzes twelve major industries and prepares specific forecasts for them for the next twelve to eighteen months. The material is then fed into the Windows on Risk committee, which meets quarterly to discuss the analysis and agree upon the two scenario sets.

The Windows on Risk committee is not just a formal step used to approve the early warning team's work. It is the most senior committee at Citigroup short of the group's management committee. Its members include the CEO and chief strategist, and it is headed by the organization's most senior risk officer. That officer sits on Citigroup's management committee and reports directly to the CEO. The first head of the committee, William Rhodes, later became Citigroup's vice chairman. His replacement in 1999 was Petros Sabatacakis, a senior banker with a Ph.D. in economics and a wealth of experience at Chemical Bank and Citigroup.

Monitoring for Risk

The Windows on Risk committee delineates a set of critical events that must occur for a most-likely scenario to unfold. Each scenario gets its own set of critical events spanning three to eighteen months ahead. The dates by which these events should occur for the scenario to happen are also determined. If the events do not happen, the scenario may be revised.

The committee also defines a set of indicators for the worst-case scenarios. This set is called tripwires, and each worst-case scenario gets its own tripwires. The tripwires are threshold levels set in advance for the variables identified as critical to Citigroup's performance. If the thresholds are crossed, an "alarm" is sounded. Variables and their tripwire thresholds are determined based on econometrically determined correlations with the company's performance. Though Citigroup does not divulge which variables enter the tripwire list, it is reasonable to hypothesize that leading indicators such as oil prices, interest rates, equity prices, etc., are among them. It is even more reasonable to assume that real estate indexes will be included, since the entire program was created on the heel of old Citibank's disastrous experience with bad real estate loans . . .

The monitoring for risk is done by thousands of line officers who compile reports on the state of the economy and the geopolitical climate in the regions, countries, and markets they serve as part of their daily routine. The early warning team's extensive process of interviewing experts and consolidating internal reports for collation brings this monitoring to a focus for the committee's needs. The team's monitoring is continuous even though the feeding of the committee is done quarterly. This monitoring by a huge cadre of employees and managers, which is carried out as part of their on-the-job routine, is a feature that allows a global company with very complex operations to stay on top of developments in numerous markets and product segments. It is hard to imagine a more centralized monitoring effort with such effective coverage.

Management Action

Perhaps the most impressive aspect of the early warning process
at Citigroup is the way the early warnings are translated into
management action. Here the power of the prestigious Windows
on Risk committee and the credibility of its head, the senior risk
officer of the company, come into focus.

Following the consensus on the most-likely and worst-case
scenarios, the committee reviews the potential effect of the external environment on Citigroup's portfolio exposure. Examples
include review of Citigroup's risk of investment in equity, measured against preset portfolio limits; another risk dimension is
the risk rating of clients. Here the committee examines trends in
these ratings and their effect on the group portfolio's risk. An
especially important perspective is the link of the external environment to the group's exposure in specific industries and products. Here the committee conducts "stress tests" of its exposure
to different market segments. For example, the group's investment in energy-sensitive industries will be tested against a scenario of an oil price hike.

Based on the review of the portfolio exposure and the trends
in the external environment, the committee develops recommendations for changes in the portfolio's composition. Since the
committee is very high-powered, its recommendations carry
significant weight among Citigroup's line managers. Examples
of the committee's successes include tightening of the credit card
standards in the United States based on early identification of a
trend in personal bankruptcy filings. As a result, Citicorp's loss
rate, which was historically high relative to its industry average,
has become more closely aligned with the external environment.
Another example is a tripwire on Asian markets, which was
crossed in early 1997, months before the crisis hit the region.
Citicorp's ability to cut back on its lending exposure to the region
earned it kudos from the press.[7] It also earned Citicorp a higher
credit rating by such rating agencies as Fitch, which quoted the
"impressive approach to management of its global risks."[8]

Windows on Risk is not foolproof though. It did not provide
a warning on Russia's financial trouble in 1998, and as a result,
Citigroup suffered pretax losses of $384 million in the third
quarter of 1998. Interestingly enough, one of Citigroup's board

members, John Deutch, a former director of the CIA, also failed to warn the company in advance.[9] Economic and geopolitical developments are among the most difficult to predict. It is hard to distinguish a trend early. Econometricians and economists have been struggling with forecasting economic shifts for decades with miserable results. The Windows on Risk program does an admirable job considering the difficult uncertainty it has to overcome.

Weaknesses (and a Note on Silly Benchmarking)

One of the knee-jerk responses of companies to the revelation that another company does something *very* well is an attempt to benchmark it. The benchmarking movement means well, and in the 1970s it accounted for some impressively quick adoption of quality improvement practices. However, like most corporate fads, benchmarking has been done to excess and has become silly. Companies guarantee that the benchmarked activity will never be implemented properly by ignoring differences in the competitive landscape of the benchmarked company, its culture, organizational structure, and executive commitment, while focusing on the easy-to-benchmark physical and budgetary elements ("how much do they spend on their sales force?"). This was especially clear with the spread of competitive intelligence activities across U.S. Fortune 500s in the mid 1990s. The "benchmarking" movement adopted CI as a hot thing, and this resulted in many mediocre information centers and none of the excellent features of some of the best functions. In order to fend off the benchmarking frenzy that may result from someone's reading this book with little critical judgment or, worse, asking the big consulting firms to help him do a Windows on Risk inside his firm, I am taking pains to emphasize the obvious: Citigroup's Windows on Risk should be viewed for what it is—a credit-monitoring tool with the specific objective of limiting the portfolio risk for a global financial services company. So, by design and from the outset, it has been a limited application of the CEW model. This is not a weakness per se of Windows on Risk, but since this book is about managing the *whole gamut* of strategic risks, a company looking to create a world-class competitive early warning (CEW) process must carefully modify the concept as follows:

❑ *Change the scope.* While Windows on Risk does look at industries' structural changes, it does not provide early warning on Citigroup's *own* industry. There is no tracking of Citicorp or Travelers or Salomon Smith Barney's competitors. Citicorp's own competitive intelligence capabilities are rather weak, but in that it is no different from its main competitors, such as JP Morgan Chase or Bank One. The banking industry is not known for strong competitive strategies and by implication, strong competitive intelligence. Strategies seem to evolve around acquisitions as *the* principal strategic variable. The ease of imitation of products and services and the difficulty in differentiating one's position contributes to a perception that there is no need for a strong competence in industry-based intelligence analysis. There might be some truth to it though exceptions such as Bank of America, which in recent years demonstrated excellent performance against overall lackluster industry returns, may point to a value in broader intelligence efforts. Citigroup's reading on customers and their preferences, for example, is limited to credit risk. In a CEW, it would include major sociodemographic trends affecting buyers' power for all banking products and the way customers view the offering of competitors. Other than portfolio composition decisions, Windows on Risk does not pretend to affect strategic decisions at the top. That might be a blessing in light of the questionable decisions made by Citigroup's chairman and CEO Sandy Weill—such as what positions his son and daughter get inside Citigroup or what synergies should exist between research on companies' equities and Citi's corporate finance deals—but it is a serious drawback if one is trying to create a strategic early warning capability. It is also a reflection of Weill's management style. Empire builders do not want anyone, not even an early warning committee, interfering in their decisions.

❑ *Tailor to culture and base of business.* Windows on Risk, being an economic-based system, identifies and monitors mostly quantitative variables such as interest rates, currency rates, prices, asset values, industry growth rates, bond yields, etc. While it does include geopolitical events such as election results and tracks them by their expected critical dates, the emphasis is on econometric relationship of quantitative variables to the portfolio's performance. That is fine for a financial institution and a credit-monitoring early warning system. For almost all other companies, and for all CEW programs, qualitative variables will be much more significant, and relationship to performance will be much harder to establish statistically. Instead, history and experience, as well as common sense, will play a much larger role in deciding what signposts to monitor and what critical events to follow. Management should not be hung up on quantitative or numerical thresholds and forecasts.

Strengths

Windows on Risk has several unique strengths. The biggest is:

❐ *Speed.* The use of the committee and the high-level participation in it grants the early warning process the visibility, urgency, and credibility no similar program enjoys. It translates directly into quick management action, an advantage no similar program enjoys either. The direct tie to action means Citi is nimbler and faster than anyone expects from such a behemoth. Executives should pay attention to this terrific result of a simple commitment.

At the same time, Windows on Risk has other strengths deserving close attention.

❐ *Regularity.* The Windows on Risk committee meets quarterly, come sun or snow. It may meet more often, depending on the crossing of a tripwire, but it will not meet *less* often. That makes risk management an institutional feature, something managers must get used to, and they are therefore forced to incorporate it into their mindset.

❐ *Wide Coverage Monitoring.* For a global company with interests on five continents, with loans to all major industries, and therefore with a large number of variables to watch, only a monitoring apparatus embedded deep in the organization can provide the required coverage. While most companies are proud if a few hundred employees belong to an internal network of knowledge and are ecstatic if out of those a few dozen actually have something to contribute, Citigroup seems to have mastered the cooperation of everyone who has something meaningful to say, inside and outside the firm.

❏ *Continuity.* The well-established process, and the constant interaction of the early warning team with the Windows on Risk committee means that the early warning cycle is repeated with feedback from management, revision of most-likely scenarios according to developments in the environment, and tracking of new worst-case scenarios every quarter as needed. In many companies this continuity is far from guaranteed. An initial burst of activity produces some scenarios that are then hardly revisited since management provides little feedback.

Windows on Risk is not perfect. It remains to see how much support it garners once Reed, the mentor, has left, and Weill, the autocratic leader, remains. Nevertheless, it fulfills each and every requirement of the risk identification-monitoring-action model in this book. It is:

1. Systematic,
2. Analytical,
3. Organizationwide, and
4. Involves a serious management commitment.

It allows Citigroup to explore significant threats early on as well as move on new opportunities. As a base model for companies to emulate, it is world-class.

Model 2. Large Company, Several Related Businesses, Long Product Cycle: DASA—Early Warning German Style

The aerospace division of Daimler-Benz (acronym DASA) was a company most would recognize as a member of the

Airbus consortium. It was also involved in manufacturing military aircraft and transport aircraft, as well as related fields. Today it is no longer a division of Daimler, which in July 2000 merged it into the new European Aeronautic Defense and Space Company (EADS) with the French Aerospatiale Matra and the Spanish CASA.

While it was still a division at Daimler, DASA had an elaborate strategic early warning system with some classic German characteristics (highly analytical and systematic process of identifying risk, an attempt to put the world into a clearly defined, fully mapped, orderly system, and *measure* as much as possible).

▶ *Program Location:* Corporate.

▶ *Charter:* Support management and project planning.

▶ *Strategy:* Monitor signposts derived from scenarios. Use business units' evaluation as filters.

▶ *Rationale Behind:* Environment had grown less structured, industry's complexity had increased, and old forecasting tools had failed to deliver. Strategy development was deemed too internally focused. In an industry where product cycles last twenty-five years, planning is extremely complicated.

Activities on the Three Steps of the CEW Model

Figure 9-2 depicts DASA's model. The different choices for the CEW steps are described below. Note the corporate–business units interaction aspect of this model.[10]

Identification of Risk

As expected, this engineering-based German company's strategic early warning system (SEWS) was extremely analytical. At the heart of its methodology for identification of risks was a unique

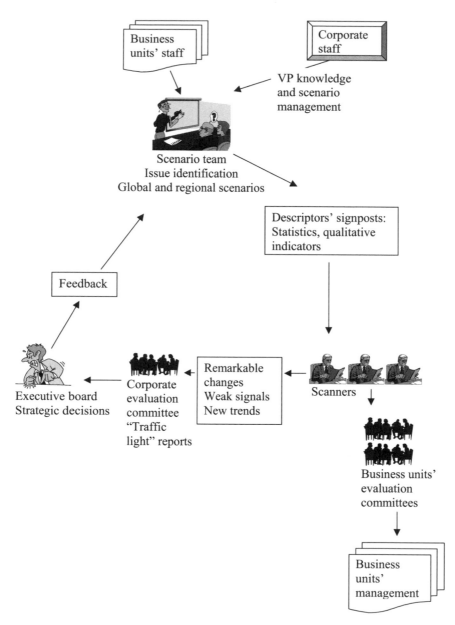

Figure 9-2: Visualization of DASA's early warning model.

"driver-driven analysis," an analysis of the main factors influencing the future (i.e., change drivers) along the lines of system dynamics.

The first step in identifying risks at DASA involved defining the problem the early warning will focus on—as an example, the development of a new, large-capacity aircraft, code name FA-X.

Once the issue was defined, a scenario analysis team analyzed the factors—termed descriptors—that had an influence on its future. Using system dynamics, it focused on the interrelationship between these variables. It thus defined reactive (or passive) and active factors according to their influence on each other. This analysis was transferred into a two-dimensional map and divided into four quadrants, high-low reactivity and high-low activity. Variables in the high-activity and high-reactivity quadrant were deemed the most important in their effect on the system and therefore carried the highest risk. For example, the success of the large aircraft depended on the future of the Asian market, a main customer group for this model. The DASA scenario team developed a scenario for the Asian region. In looking at the system dynamics of the Asian demand for aircraft, the variables of air transport volume and airline profitability were identified as both highly reactive and active, which meant they both affected many variables and were affected by many as well. Variables such as the region's economy, on the other hand, were found to be highly active (influencing other variables) but not under the influence of other variables pertinent to the demand for aircraft, or influenced by any actions of the aerospace industry. The variable replacement policy was highly influenced by other factors but did not influence many other factors. This makes sense: Replacement policy is hardly an independent variable but is influenced by availability of financing, aircraft prices, service concepts of the airlines, etc.

By virtue of their influence on many variables, and the impact of many variables on them, highly reactive–highly active factors have great impact on the system as a whole. Even a slight change in these variables is magnified throughout the system. These variables should therefore be under special scrutiny by the early warning team. That's the essence of working with a system dynamic paradigm.

The descriptors were then projected into the future. Each descriptor received three alternative futures; one of those—termed most frequent—corresponded to Citigroup's most-likely scenario described above. The other values corresponded to an optimistic future and a pessimistic one. Following the influence of descriptors on each other, one can develop a scenario based on a *network* of descriptors. At DASA, two to five such scenarios were selected for further elaboration and presentation to management. For example, volume of air transport received three values: Slower growth than expected (most likely future, 1–5 percent per year), strong growth (optimistic future, >5 percent) and medium term stagnation (pessimistic future in the medium run). Each of those was related to a network of other descriptors to form a scenario. The descriptors included political, economic, and social factors, airline strategies, aircraft industry choices such as product line and pricing, and variables pertaining to the evolution of the whole transport system, including substitution variables such as alternative means of transport and airport capacity growth. If the astute reader sees here a resemblance to the five forces, it is because eventually all those descriptors formed the same industry structure as the five forces. The airlines are the buyers; industry variables relate to rivalry; transport system to substitution and rivalry; and the socio-political-economic descriptors can be easily shown to affect the power of buyers, the intensity of rivalry, and the ease of entry into the industry.

The implications of the three resulting scenarios for the development of the FA-X aircraft were then drawn and the scenarios were also put through a "friction analysis"—a test of the impact on the scenarios of highly unlikely but highly influential factors such as military conflict or an atomic accident.

DASA was a very heterogeneous group of business units. To overcome the issue of relevance of the scenarios, the DASA scenario team was headed by a corporate vice president, who assembled a different team for each scenario depending on expertise, the cooperation of the heads of the business units for which the scenarios were built, etc.

Monitoring for Risk

Once the scenarios were developed, the most important descriptors driving the system were given high priority for monitoring.

Each descriptor was assigned measurable signposts for monitoring. The monitoring was done by low- and mid-level volunteers and sometimes by external scanners. Signposts included statistics characteristic of the descriptors, e.g., financial figures, number of aircraft delivered, etc.; general indicators such as population growth rates and economic conditions; and "weak signals"—signals that could not be classified immediately but were followed until a trend such as a changing pattern in a competitor's activities emerged. Signposts were either quantitative or qualitative.

The scanners were asked to report new developments or "remarkable changes" in their areas. They were given the freedom to decide if short-term developments represented trends that were significant for DASA. Their reporting eventually resulted in modifications to the scenarios as well as more immediate change to operational plans.

The scanners had access to a multitude of internal reports and external information resources. These included secondary sources such as trade and company publications, Internet searches and commercial databases, market studies and reports from industry fairs, branch meetings, primary market research, benchmarking studies (of course), and also information from an internal marketing information system called DAMIS that collected data from DASA's various sales organizations, marketing areas, destinations markets, and competitor analysis teams. Opinion leaders were used occasionally, and students were often recruited to do competitor interviews.*

Management Action

The communication to DASA's management was not as uniform and institutionalized as at Citigroup WOR. The reporting depended on the circumstances: who was doing the monitoring, what the issues were, and what business unit was most likely to face the heightened risk.

The scenario analysis team issued an early warning notice

---

*This practice would have never flown in the United States, where someone on the phone presenting himself or herself as "an MBA student" is a red flag for an attempt to gain competitor information.

once the scanners reported remarkable changes on the most critical descriptors. When the issue was pertinent to a particular
business unit, the notice went to a special evaluation committee
in this business unit. The evaluation committee was composed
of vice president–level executives from the unit's functional
areas—strategy, marketing, business development, and so on.
However, at times the scanners reported new and significant developments directly to their bosses at the business unit or to a
specialist inside the unit who did the actual threat analysis. Since
the scenario team and the scanners were quite often business
units' employees themselves, the demarcation line as to who
raised the flag depended on the threat circumstances. On issues
pertaining to corporate decisions, the reporting and monitoring
were initiated within corporate staff, and the early warning
team did the analysis. If needed, an evaluation committee of corporate executives was involved as well.

One example of this process is the early warning on the economic crisis in Asia. As early as 1997, a scenario team for Asia
was put together, composed mainly of experts from the corporate marketing team at DASA. That team developed a scenario
that looked at the industrial structure in Asia and the level of
government support for the economies. Based on their model,
the scenario predicted a meltdown around 2010. DASA's regional offices in Singapore and Malaysia carried out the monitoring on the most significant signposts. These offices reported
monthly, and their reports were analyzed by the scenario team
and the corporate strategists. Senior executives were given a presentation of the basic regional scenario, and then when the monitors reported activity on the signposts, the combined scenario/
strategists team slapped a color code on it ("traffic light" in their
jargon) and sent it to DASA's senior management for review.

The first color-coded report was yellow—signaling a serious
threat but no call for urgent action required—when the stock
market started deteriorating. Another yellow report was issued
when several large deals between Japan and the United States
fell apart. A red-coded report—meaning immediate action was
called for—was issued when several highly respected companies
in the region became mired in scandals and a few filed for bankruptcy. The red-coded report triggered a big discussion at the
executive board level, which includes DASA's CEO, senior corpo-

rate executives, and business unit managers. The result was a decision to slow down the development of a large aircraft. The crisis in Asia, which exploded full-scale in 1998, did not catch DASA by surprise as it did numerous American and European companies.

A most remarkable early warning was issued on the takeover of McDonnell Douglas by Boeing. The issue again was the development of the large aircraft. As part of the global scenario developed by the scenario team with the help of corporate experts, several descriptors covered competitive activity such as industry concentration and competitiveness indices. "Soft" qualitative factors such as Boeing's motivation to be the largest player were part of the drivers of this scenario, and a possible future direction in which Boeing swallowed up McDonnell Douglas (MD) and changed the competitive landscape was identified. Signposts were developed and monitored by DASA's office in Washington. The evaluation committee in this case was composed of the Airbus unit's manager and the corporate marketing manager.

The first yellow-coded report was based on weak signals. A rise in MD's outsourcing and an increase in the number of meetings held between Boeing, MD, and government officials were the basis for the early warning. At that time, which was more than a year and a half before the takeover actually took place, DASA's management was skeptical. The executive board, which received the report, mandated further monitoring but did not take the threat seriously. The second report, which was coded red, was issued when the U.S. government blocked the negotiations between Lockheed Martin and Northrop Grumman. The executive board was more receptive this time around. Following the recommendation of the evaluation committee, the executive board prepared a postmerger marketing communication plan that aimed at assuring the investment community and DASA's clients of DASA's competitive position. Once the takeover was announced, DASA's quick response was impressive. In the words of Franz Tessun, the head of the scenario process, "the most important effect of the communication plan was that it demonstrated that DASA was not surprised . . . and was equipped to respond quickly."[11]

The early warning process at DASA completed a cycle when

feedback from both the monitoring efforts and management actions were relayed back to the scenario teams. The teams then modified their scenarios and developed new signposts. A completely new scenario was developed only when events showed DASA did not have a scenario in its arsenal to describe them.

Weaknesses

DASA's early warning process was impressive on the analytical side. The signposts' development was creative and inspiring. Monitoring was done on a voluntary basis, which is surprising given the German culture that reveres system and order, but it worked reasonably well as long as the scanners received some feedback on the use of their reports. Naturally, the process could have been strengthened with a more dedicated network, and that could have been done if the mandate for the early warning had come from the top and been applied to all business units uniformly.

When it came to the last leg, influencing management action, the program was weak. Instead of a clearly centralized process whereby management was involved from the outset and evaluation committees carried significant weight, DASA's early warning system was working hard on trying to capture management attention. If the topic was of great interest, management was easily engaged. Otherwise, management stayed on the sideline. There was no standard and regular reporting route like Citigroup's WOR. Scanners could report directly to their business units' bosses, and the head of the scenario process had to fight to get some business units' heads to cooperate with him.

This lack of influence on top management, which may have resulted from lack of a truly strong champion like John Reed at Citicorp, may have contributed to the deterioration of the scenario–cum–early warning once DASA was merged into EADS in 2000. While by that time the head of the scenario process had the impressive title of "vice president knowledge and scenario management" (an upgrade from his 1997 title of "vice president market research"), the lack of senior support was still evident. The process did not survive the cultural clash with the new Spanish and French partners. It will be interesting to see if Airbus continues to win against Boeing without the help of an effective CEW, and what mechanisms the heads of EADS will use to avoid nasty surprises. It does help EADS that its chief rival, Boeing, is even worse when it comes to early warning and management insularity. . . .

Strengths

There is a lot to be learned from DASA's strategic early warning. The value of such a system, which at its core relies on a very sophisticated scenario-building methodology, is especially significant for companies facing a complicated competitive arena with a multitude of drivers that need to be vigilantly watched. In the civilian and military aircraft industries, where government politics and private sector economics interact continuously to modify the rules of the game, a company without a sophisticated SEWS can find itself losing the game. For proof, look no further than Boeing, once the mighty dominant player.

> ## Model 3. Small Size, Domestic Company, Single Product: Pergo North America—The Little Engine That Could*
>
> Pergo's story reads like a fairy tale. Once upon a time . . . there was a big old dinosaur named Perstorp, a Swedish specialty chemical manufacturer. Perstorp was founded back in the nineteenth century. In the 1970s and 1980s it moved to acquire a variety of companies in the areas of laminates, plastics, biotech, and others. Then in 1980, using its technology of specialty chemicals and laminates, Perstorp launched a product for laminate flooring and branded it Pergo. In 1993 it sent a team to the United States to establish a beachhead in this important market. The team was headed by Lars von Kantzow, a Swedish executive with ex-

*I am grateful to Pergo and to David Sheehan, who headed the EW at Pergo NA, for their cooperation in writing this segment. This section is also based on public sources, company Web sites, and the author's knowledge.

tensive international experience, who in a relatively short time was able to make Pergo the number-one brand of laminate flooring in the United States, landing Home Depot as its largest client. From its headquarters in North Carolina, the small U.S. outfit (Pergo NA, with approximately 250 employees) had to fight two battles—one with the market, where U.S. consumers regard carpets as the default choice for flooring, and one with its Swedish parent company, whose idea of product innovation was making the glue a bit better. At the end, in 2001, Pergo AB was spun off from Perstorp and was given a new lease on life.

One reason Pergo NA was so successful was von Kantzow's creation of an early warning system. It was a one-man show, done part-time, and backed by a whole culture of growth and speed. The young man who headed the effort was a product manager with a natural talent for intelligence gathering. The U.S. subsidiary was too small to allocate a full-time position to do early warning, nor did it need a full-time gathering of intelligence, but the product manager's voluntary intelligence efforts resulted in his CEO's assigning him formally to carry out early warning types of activities. Soon everyone who needed competitive data was turning to this manager for help. This bottom-up/top-down simultaneous meeting of needs and minds is not atypical in entrepreneurial cultures. The model that emerged over time can serve as a useful blueprint to many companies with limited resources but a visionary leadership.

- ▶ *Program Location*: Subsidiary.
- ▶ *Charter*: Point to the right strategic option to implement.
- ▶ *Strategy*: Monitor tripwires derived from war gaming.
- ▶ *Rationale Behind*: If you were a 200-person unit fighting competitors twice your size and a gorilla-size customer who could bankrupt you overnight, wouldn't you want a CEW?

Activities on the Three Steps of the CEW Model

Figure 9-3 describes the main components of Pergo NA's EW process. Note the role of war gaming in this process.

Identification of Risk

Pergo NA did not have the funds to keep a full-time scenario team to identify risk on a continuous basis. Moreover, managers were too busy to engage in ad hoc teams working on scenario construction as a side job. The solution was to use war games as a mechanism to draw scenarios on an *as needed* basis. The war games brought various tidbits of intelligence together, allowing participants to analyze emerging trends and developments in a

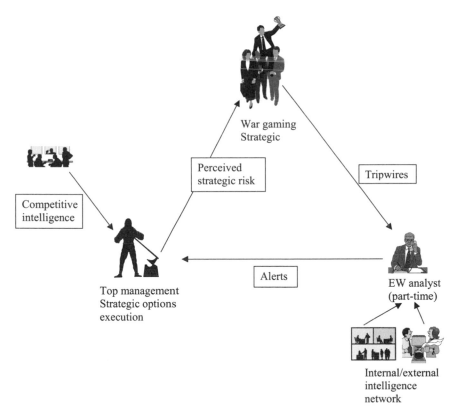

Figure 9-3: Visualization of Pergo NA's early warning model.

concentrated group effort of a day or two and come up with most-likely and worst-case scenarios. At the same time, participants developed strategic options for Pergo NA to fit those same scenarios. What followed was a creation of a slew of tripwires based on those scenarios, which were aimed at informing management which scenario was forthcoming. These wires, when tripped, *forced* Pergo NA to quickly implement a strategic move or, if the strategic move was already in the making, to significantly accelerate its implementation.

Each war game included everyone who had some influence on the direction of Pergo in the United States, so a war game could involve high-ranking Perstorp executives from Sweden as well. Each war game included participants who had some knowledge of the industry and the market and were willing to share it openly with others, leaving politics and power plays aside as much as possible. Von Kantzow, the North American CEO, for example, headed a competitor team rather than his own company in an effort to bring sharp pressure on the group to think competitively. That takes courage, since in essence the CEO was poking holes in his own strategy.

The war games were carried out on as needed basis, triggered by critical events in the market. In that respect, the risk identification process was "stood on its head." Instead of developing a priori long-range scenarios based on sophisticated theoretical modeling of change drivers in the market, Pergo's model initiated a scenario exercise only when enough indicators suggested it needed one. When certain market developments caused enough concern to top management to warrant a war game, it held one, developed scenarios, and came up with specific indicators (tripwires) to be monitored. While this was not as analytical as DASA's or even Citigroup's system, this model is much more suitable to companies with limited resources and a "let's do it" culture. Since war games do not have to be held too often, this model conserves scarce resources. A war game held every five years in an industry where structural changes are not frequent is a reasonable and very cost-effective way to keep strategic risks under control. War games are also typical of companies where "soft" strategic intelligence, which invariably is qualitative in nature, gets as much attention as quantitative indicators and statistics. In engineering or manufacturing-based cultures, where numbers reign supreme, it is hard to get management attention on anything else (unless it is a *rumor* coming from the top executives' closed circle of "trusted advisers"). Pergo's team, composed mostly of young marketing and product people, was much less "numbers-biased" and open to moving beyond financial statement analysis.

It is always intriguing to find out what makes one company, or one CEO, more intelligence-savvy than others. At Pergo NA, it was a lesson from the past. Pergo, the brand, was once the market-leading brand in Europe, where it held a dominant share. The parent company, Perstorp, believed that its proprietary technology would keep out competitors. Yet, in a short few years, larger competitors, mostly wood and board manufacturers with a lower cost structure (remember Pergo was a product of a specialty chemical company, not a large wood manufacturer) were able to enter the market with their own technology and much larger economies of scale. That in itself was not as traumatic as the lag in Perstorp management's perception of the competitive reality. As the early warning manager in the United States described it, "We went to bed one night thinking we had 49% share in the German (market) and woke up next day and figured out it was only 20%."

That trauma was fresh on the minds of the young U.S. team when its CEO decided it would not happen to him. The war gaming and the early warning monitoring followed directly from this experience.

Monitoring Risks

The monitoring of the scenarios' tripwires was done by the part-time CI manager, who was a wizard at human source collection and also close to the market and to Pergo's main customers, by virtue of his other role as a product manager. This manager created a loyal network of internal and external sources with whom he conversed whenever he had the opportunity, looking for information on the tripwires. Being a small company with a relatively cohesive culture, it was not that difficult to engage internal sources. But the monitoring did not stay confined to internal sources. Being a skilled networker, the CI manager was able to establish close relationships with customers, distributors, state officials, and other useful sources of semi-public competitive information.* While the monitoring was not systematic—at crunch times information collection efforts might take a back seat to other duties—nothing of real value escaped this net. In this company, any time someone needed a piece of market intelligence, he knew where to go. So whenever someone *had* a piece of industry news, he also contributed.

Management Action

Management action grew directly from the informal yet pervasive reliance on competitive intelligence created by the CEO and cultivated by his executive team. The war games framed the strategic options that Pergo NA should follow if a particular scenario materialized. The sense of urgency regarding the execution of these strategic options was directly related to the monitoring and reporting of tripped wires. Thus, while a strategic option might take years to evolve and ripen before it was implemented, a report of a particular tripwire got everyone into the action mode. The CI manager, acting as an early warning analyst, had open access to the CEO. His and others' early warnings were discussed during Monday morning executive meetings. The process was simple and straightforward and led to impressive results as the stories below demonstrate.

One event that triggered a war game was an alliance between two of Pergo's biggest competitors. One was a large, vertically integrated manufacturer of medium density fiberboard, whose laminate flooring's strategy relied on a low-cost leadership model, based on efficient manufacturing and economies of scale. The second company was a large flooring company with a controlled distribution channel and a large network of retailers in the United States. It was a one-stop shopper that could offer retailers a low-cost alternative because of cheaper logistics and

*Semi-public information is information that is known in the market but is not in the general public domain like published information. It is information that can be gathered ethically and legally from customers and suppliers, regulators, and industry experts if a company employs skilled professionals and makes an effort to keep its sensors on an alert.

economies of scope. The alliance raised an alarm bell throughout Pergo NA.

The war game that was assembled determined the need for Pergo to form an alliance of its own with a low-cost producer to be able to offer customers competitive products at lower cost. A tripwire involving one of the competitors looking for a manufacturing site accelerated Pergo's strategy and in 2000 Pergo announced the purchase of 25 percent of a German laminate floor manufacturer, Witex. Witex was a low-cost producer based in Germany with plans for manufacturing capabilities in the United States. In late 2002, Pergo AB announced an intended merger with Witex.

Another event that triggered a war game was research findings that Pergo's quality lead in the market was eroding. From 1984 to 1998, Perstorp was essentially making the same products. Improvements were incremental and centered on Perstorp's technology. In the early years, the competition was confined to cheap laminate flooring from board manufacturers. However, over time, those manufacturers improved the quality of their products to a point that the Pergo product did not offer major advantages over the lower-cost ones. The technology they used was different from Pergo's, but Perstorp's management refused to admit the competitor's technology was as good as its own.

Competitors were also able to introduce innovative features that allowed for a different look and texture. For example, competitors' technology created laminate floors that looked and felt like ceramic tiles. New modern designs started to show up in the market, and Pergo's product, which featured old-fashioned planks and no unique designs, was at a risk of losing its differentiation edge.

A war game that pieced together all those bits and pieces of competitive intelligence data from both Europe and the United States revealed the following: First, Pergo needed a concentrated effort in its product development to stay differentiated. Second, the Swedish parent company, where those design decisions were made, was not going to provide new products fast enough to stop a possible scenario of severe erosion in market share. A different strategy was needed.

Following the war game, Pergo NA's team started to form

relationships with innovative companies in the United States. The war game produced several tripwires about the progress of competitors in creating differentiated products. One of the most important tripwires, if not *the* most important one, was the perception of buyers. When a tripwire regarding market perceptions was triggered in 2000 during a trade show, Pergo approached leading-edge producers of differentiated laminate floors to help maintain its leading market share in the United States.

Weaknesses

One shortcoming of Pergo's early warning model was its weak connection to the parent company in Sweden. This was not unique to Pergo—business units' early warning is often not backed up at corporate headquarters, *and vice versa*. To complicate things further, European-owned U.S. companies traditionally have much better CI functions than their European parents. The reason is that European markets, which are defended by protectionist government policies, have for decades lagged behind U.S. markets in competitive pressures. But in Pergo's case the situation was potentially deadly as the energetic U.S. team was straining to break through to a slow and unresponsive European parent with a completely different mentality (manufacturing) and lack of understanding of the U.S. market (not very unusual for a European company). As Pergo's luck went, a new and forward-thinking Swedish top executive rose to power just as Pergo needed a new approach before it lost its lead in the United States. That may not be the fate of many other business units.

Another weakness was the dependency of the early warning effort on the limited availability of one busy manager who was pulled in many different directions. The unique qualities of this manager, coupled with the unique leadership of the CEO, and an industry that was not changing very rapidly allowed the model to function exceedingly well. However, the danger in the lack of a formally institutionalized system is that the process could die as quickly as it was created when either one of the parties involved in keeping it alive leaves the company.

Strengths

Pergo NA's model is an exceedingly good model for companies that cannot afford to throw a whole lot of resources at their early warning system. It is especially suitable for companies that face a relatively uncomplicated industry and technology (yet still face quite severe competitive pressures). It is specifically suitable for companies following a focus product strategy (even if they could afford to throw more resources at early warning).

It is my belief that this particular case study of one small company in North Carolina demonstrates that one person, with the proper training and proper backing by a smart senior executive, can do an excellent job of keeping management secure. In an uncomplicated business, such as one-product companies, there is no need for lengthy negotiations with management on what areas should be monitored, what represents the next big threat, etc. A smart analyst looking out for emerging threats and focusing on a few "hot ones" at a time seems like a very effective approach. A similar model is used in Visa International, another one-product company with a focused strategy, where an analyst following emerging trends provides management with what it terms "comfort intelligence" that keeps it secure.

There is one more anecdote related to Pergo NA that demonstrates the value of smart and frugal management over the popular Fortune 100's strategy of throwing money at an issue. That anecdote has to do with the decision to create a war room.

War rooms are a modern-day fad for rich corporations. They are supposed to be the gathering place for executives who come together to mull over important strategic decisions while all available intelligence is visually laid out in front of them. This information is streamed in from all corners of the world on the latest broadband channel and into the latest electronic displays. The term "war room" brings up an image of flickering TV monitors and computer screens and a group of intense-looking managers huddling together around a display. War rooms would be a great idea if management actually uses them to get informed quickly and efficiently on all internal and external aspects of a given issue, and if that information were true intelligence to begin with. In reality war rooms are nothing more than a fancy waste of a lot of money on glitzy technology and mahogany furniture at a huge investment with little value added. Management does not use the information any more than it uses a paper report, nor does it make decisions in a war room. The information itself is the same old collection of public statistics and graphs. In my experience, a war room is a toy for grown-ups who haven't separated completely from their PlayStations.

Pergo NA did not have any money to invest in a war room. Its CEO wasn't a show-off type. Yet he did want management to be externally focused (one noble goal of a war room). So the CI manager plastered paper posters with the latest competitive data depicting a strategic map of the industry, market share trends, competitors' product positioning, and other valuable intelligence on the walls of one conference room in the company's headquarters. The total cost of the war room? Approximately $10 for materials. The typical cost of a war room for a Fortune 500? $3 million.

Model 4. Very Large Division, Multicultural Company: AstraZeneca—A Cerberus SEWS*

AstraZeneca (AZ) is a global pharmaceutical giant created by the merger of two companies, the Swedish Astra and the British Zeneca, in the late 1990s. The two cultures were not as different as, say, the German and the Spanish at EADS (or the American and French at Vivendi), and the merger was relatively smooth.

In ancient Greek mythology, Cerberus was a three-headed dog that guarded the gates to Hades, the underworld. Cerberus never slept—one of his eyes was always open. It is a very apt description of (and a high compliment to) the relatively young strategic early warning system (SEWS) at AZ. It also describes AstraZeneca's three-headed approach to SEWS, which is aimed at covering the whole range of the

*This section was written by Wayne A. Rosenkrans, Global Intelligence Director, Strategic Planning and Marketing Operations, AstraZeneca Pharmaceuticals. I am grateful to AstraZeneca Pharmaceuticals for allowing Dr. Rosenkrans's contribution to this book.

pharmaceutical value chain. This made AZ's approach a novel one.

One element of AstraZeneca's SEWS was created at the discovery level; another was created for the development process; finally, the commercial level in the United States received its own early warning program. As this book is being written, another program has been developed for the corporate entity, which will make AZ's SEWS even more awake then Cerberus was, assuming corporate leadership actually *uses* it (that is yet to be demonstrated).

- ▸ *Program Location*: U.S. commercial division, global discovery, global development, and corporate.
- ▸ *Charter*: Support discovery, clinical development, and business-level strategic planning and leadership teams.
- ▸ *Strategy*: Monitor signposts derived from scenarios, using shadow teams. Integrate fully with strategy-making at the leadership level.
- ▸ *Rationale Behind*: AZ has ambitions to rise to the top tier of Big Pharma (which includes Pfizer, Merck, and GlaxoSmithKline). To achieve that, it knows it needs a more systematic, better-coordinated, and well-executed strategy in pipeline, clinical testing, and marketing levels of the business. Pharmaceutical firms are not well known for strategy-making skills at the top, and many lag years behind such industries as consumer products. AstraZeneca was about to change that perception, which naturally required a sophisticated SEWS. This is especially clear in the United States, the most important market for AZ and one in which it has a relatively small presence compared with Tier 1. The initiative to establish a SEWS, which started in the technical-research side of the business, quite quickly received support from the U.S. commercial division—the marketing arm that is responsible for fighting tough competition in the U.S. market.

Activities on the Three Steps of the CEW Model

Figure 9-4 depicts AstraZeneca's unique approach to early warning. Note the strong connection to strategy.

The AZ early warning model has a simple yet effective risk identification process. It started on the scientific side of the business, not a typical place for intelligence efforts. Scientists, though, can be surprisingly strategic as compared with their at times insular and more tactically focused commercial counterparts. Since the science and technology risk identification process was created first and was then emulated across the other two heads of the Cerberus, it will be described here in some detail.

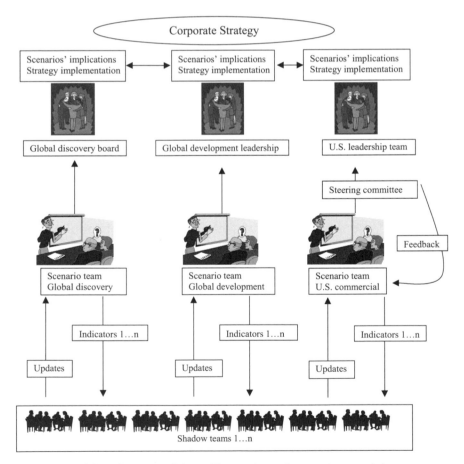

Figure 9-4: Visualization of AstraZeneca's early warning model.

The discovery process for new drugs, a key element for the success of any Pharma firm, is growing increasingly complex and expensive, while its productivity is declining. Yet rapid advances in science and technology are already changing, and will change more significantly, the shape of drug discovery in the next five to ten years. To understand it, let's look at how drugs are discovered.

The process of drug discovery today begins with the selection of biological targets—targets in the pathways leading to disease—that are susceptible to drug intervention and represent a commercially viable area. A crucial factor in this selection is validation of these selected targets both as key elements in the progress of a disease and as elements that are testable in animal and nonanimal-based disease models. Once a target, for example, a specific receptor subtype or cell transport proteins, has been selected, a series of chemical compounds is tested for activity in modulating that target to identify a population of effector molecules or "hits." A make-test cycle is established to define a "combinatorial" library of compounds with increasing potency in affecting the desired outcome. Ultimately, a "lead" series of compounds with the desired effectiveness is identified. These lead compounds must then be optimized in terms of their potency, their relative toxicity, the way the body metabolizes them, and their ability to be produced in large quantities. At the end of the process, a candidate drug and a small series of backup compounds emerge to enter the development process of testing the new drug in humans and gaining regulatory authority approval for marketing. On average, this discovery process takes approximately 3.5 years from target selection to candidate drug. Thousands of hits will have been tested, and something in excess of $250 million expended. (The full process from target selection though launch of a new drug takes an average of twelve years and $850 million, including failed opportunity costs. Only one in ten candidate drugs will successfully traverse the entire process.)

Rapid progress in several areas of science and technology has the potential to substantially change and streamline this current process, *depending on when, and if*, the new technologies can deliver as expected. If it were all to come together, completion of the human physiome, a complete understanding of not only the genetic sequence of humans (genomics) but also the structural and functional relationships of the encoded proteins, will clearly delineate what is now known to be a finite number of "drugable" targets. The structure of these targets will be used to design chemical modulators using fully predictive chemical modeling tools. These will generate compounds with not only the desired activity in genetically characterized responder populations, but also the desired toxicology and metabolic profiles. The resulting set of compounds will be screened for effectiveness using a combination of virtual organ systems and nonanimal biotests fully predictive of their activity in humans. Drug development will consist of an abbreviated clinical trial program, done in collaboration with regulatory agencies and provider groups, designed to confirm the simulations and meet regulatory requirements. On average the "new" discovery process will take approximately a year from target selection to candidate drug. A small number of high-potential hits will have been tested, and something far less than $250 million expended.

This new drug discovery process will have significant implications for the way pharmaceutical firms compete and for the overall structure of the pharmaceutical industry. But—and this is a crucial *but*—it all depends on how fast, how far, and how fully the new technologies deliver. This was the impetus behind the creation of a set of scenarios regarding the speed of technological change. Each scenario carried different implications for AstraZeneca's strategy.

The risk identification process in the technology area had a number of steps:

❐ Following a process of agreeing on the scope and direction of the project with the management sponsors, an extensive interview program was begun to elicit thinking from over a hundred experts in the various drug discovery disciplines. These interviews, both internal and external to the company, were used to identify a list of focal issues and potential change drivers in the environment (issues with high uncertainty and high impact).

❐ To challenge the group's thinking more fully, an exercise was run at an offsite location where highly regarded individuals (ex–heads of R&D, industry commentators, significant academics, etc.) were brought together and engaged in a heavily moderated debate on the nature of future discovery while the SEWS team took copious notes.

❏ Out of both exercises, a number of change drivers affecting the future were identified and characterized, and the extreme positive and negative impacts were suggested.

❏ Once the set of drivers was created, they were used to create a series of "boundary scenarios"—views of the world that were plausible and logical, if not all equally probable, and that delineated the "edge" of the future. To generate a reasonable number of scenarios for evaluation, however, primary drivers were identified through a prioritization process that ranked the drivers on a 2 × 2 matrix of uncertainty and impact.

❏ The SEWS team "tried on" each world generated by the process. Some were really not plausible, some were largely recapitulations of each other, and others yielded a sense of one following the other in how they might play out. A set of scenarios was selected for full workup with complete narrative descriptions (some quite worthy of Hollywood) and sets of characteristics.

❏ Once the scenarios were at hand and had been tested, the team entered into a major interaction with the management team to determine implications for AstraZeneca. We asked the senior managers to "live" in each world for part of a day and tell us what they had to do to be successful in such a world. The team also provided the managers with categories of things such as organization, culture, etc. to think about in generating their strategic implications. The wine at dinner was relabeled "Chateau 2015," place cards reflected the times, and graphic images suggested the alternate worlds. Ultimately, the managers themselves generated very rich sets of strategic implications, consequences of running a discovery organization in various worlds, some of which were not very palatable.

❏ The SEWS team analyzed these sets of implications to generate sets that were common to all worlds, common to a few, or truly independent. Examination of these yielded definable megastrategic imperatives that were fed back to the managers. The management team in turn created task groups, or imperatives teams, to evaluate strategic actions emanating from the imperatives. Ultimately, money and people were moved around—the acid test of strategic implementation.

❑   At this point, the task of the SEWS team evolved to monitor forward risk: Which worlds were emerging? (No one world will ever emerge, but characteristics do emerge over time.) The team's role was to continuously update the drivers and scenarios and act as an ongoing filter for the future robustness of the created strategy.

Entirely analogous processes were followed for allied projects in the Global Development Division and the U.S. Commercial Business (the other two heads of the Cerberus). Several projects also spun out of the Cerberus, some spun up (a project for the corporate senior executive team), others down (a project for the U.S. Operations unit). Great care was taken to ensure commonality of input information, assumptions, process, shared team personnel, and transparent communication between teams to keep the projects in sync and mutually supportive.

Monitoring for Risk

The set of change drivers used to generate the original scenarios provided a rich list of areas to be monitored. Each driver was assigned to a team, called a driver shadow team (DST), whose responsibility was to monitor its progress globally and report to the SEWS team. Individual change drivers themselves are too broad in scope to monitor effectively, so the first task for each DST was to break their driver into its constitutive elements, those monitorable pieces that, when evaluated, together give a picture of the evolution of the driver. Each driver also has an associated set of tripwires, detectable environmental events that would signal a significant change in the driver.

The task of coordinating, motivating, and operating the driver shadow teams, both global and domestic, for three linked but different early warning programs is a real challenge for AstraZeneca's young SEWS team. DSTs monitor all the drivers associated with the Cerberus projects; hence, communication between the teams is critical as none of the drivers is completely orthogonal to any other. Also built into the process are mechanisms for recognizing new and emergent drivers for evaluation and possible constitution of a new team or, conversely, deciding that a driver has become less critical for monitoring.

Management Action

Moving from monitoring to management action has utilized three linked steps involving varying levels of engagement between the SEWS and management teams, and taking different forms depending on how the particular management team likes to receive the input. As an example, for one project the DST evaluations (DST monitoring goes on continuously in all teams) of the relevant drivers are compiled for thorough evaluation by the core SEWS team and generation of an emergent scenario with potential "epilogues" (alternative endings) twice a year. These reports and analysis constitute a semiannual SEWS report that is published for the management team, but also for further use within the company, e.g., brand team strategy. To ensure the linkage of early warning to the developing strategies, the ongoing imperative teams are often monitored by a SEWS member as well. The imperative teams report their status at the same time as the SEWS team, thus demonstrating to the senior managers both the evolving external landscape and those strategic steps the company is taking to address that evolution.

The management team is then engaged in a three-part meeting. The first step, which is largely the province of the SEWS and DST teams, is the presentation and discussion of a brief of the major environmental changes, their implications for the evolving world, and new considerations. The second portion of the meeting, which involves equal participation by the SEWS and management teams, is a review of the strategic imperatives progress seen through the filter of the environmental report. In step three, which is entirely the province of the management team, decisions are taken regarding acceleration, deceleration, or modification of the imperatives, or the creation of new ones. The other two heads of the Cerberus follow slightly different processes for this key management interaction.

In essence, the CEW process at AstraZeneca enabled the semiannual testing of the company's strategy for robustness. Each test is carried out in light of current and future environmental conditions. That testing process is organized and facilitated by the SEWS team, enabling the management team to focus on making the decisions and taking action to implement new strategic direction.

Model 5. Global Company in High-Risk Environments: Strategic Early Warning—The Shell Example*

In today's competitive environment with increased volatility and high uncertainty and risks, a key to success lies in either not being surprised at all or at least being well positioned to react to surprises when they occur. In this context competitive intelligence at Shell makes a significant contribution to corporate strategic planning. One area where this is especially true is strategic early warning.

As a company Shell firmly believes that some of the most important choices we make in the present depend on the assumptions we hold about the future. To succeed we need to make sense of the uncertainties we face and challenge our assumptions about what the future holds. The importance Shell places on the development of scenarios, a technique that has been applied within the company for more than thirty years, reflects the firm belief that success in the future depends on the future success of decisions taken today. In addition to scenario technology, Shell also utilizes competitive intelligence as a tool to identify and analyze risks and emerging patterns in the competitive environment. Being able to spot a pattern with the fewest possible facts—before

*This section was written by Karl F. Rose, Manager, Strategic Intelligence, Shell International Ltd. I am grateful to Shell International Ltd. for allowing Mr. Rose's contribution to this book.

it is too late to respond and before the pattern is so obvious that your competitors catch on first, is a key factor for business success. Shell believes that good use of competitive intelligence for early warning is the best tool for doing this on a sustained basis.

What Are We Looking For?

As Figure 9-5 shows, at Shell we think about early warning in terms of a hierarchy of three layers that need to be monitored: current events, trends and patterns, and underlying fundamental structures.

Any improper focus on a particular layer will cause early warning signals to be either wrong or ineffective. If one monitors only current events, then there is a high risk of "fashion" creeping into the analysis work. On the other hand, looking at structural changes and change drivers in the global environment should be combined with more immediate signals in order to

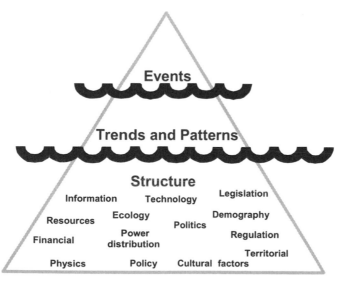

Figure 9-5: Risk identification layers.

produce actionable intelligence. Early warning is of value only when management can take action based on the signals received. The three layers are, of course, interdependent. Trends and patterns are a collection of events and very often constitute the first indication that underlying structures are changing.

Who Does What?

At Shell, CI teams monitor current events and analyze them for trends and patterns. Shell's scenario planning group, on the other hand, monitors developments of fundamental geopolitical, social, and macroeconomic structures, and will compare the signals coming in with the internal assumptions and current scenarios. Those scenarios point out the most important areas for monitoring by the CI community. For both groups the early recognition of trends and patterns is very important. They often force the scenario group to reevaluate assumptions about fundamental structures, and in that respect they act as early warning signals for identifying industry change. For CI teams, early recognition of patterns in the competitive environment almost always triggers an alert or early warning signal. Most recently both groups have started to work together closely on the issue of strategic early warning.

The three layers are also characterized by very different time cycles. Scenarios are potential pictures of alternate futures and allow a better understanding of the relationships between underlying factors, but they tell you nothing about the realistic and short-term trends for those factors. By using both its intelligence and scenario capability together, Shell can monitor changes occurring at very long, as well as very short, time cycles. It is this combination of skills that makes the current early warning effort at Shell complete because it combines strategic early warning, which is more qualitative in nature, with tactical early warning, which is much more quantitative.

How Are We Organized?

Scenario planning is a central effort, and the scenario team operates out of the corporate center in London. The competitive intelligence effort at Shell is more complicated in its organizational setup since capabilities need to exist close to the customers within the individual businesses. Over the years Shell has built a whole network of competitive intelligence teams (Figure 9-6). The current CI landscape within Shell consists of one CI team at the corporate center, six teams within the businesses, some 35 CI focal points in other parts of the Shell organization, a 350-strong strategy, planning, and intelligence community, and some 2,000 registered intelligence network members. Teams are made up of full-time CI professionals, while focal points are staff with part-time CI responsibilities.

Outside of that, there is a large staff base that is encouraged to put information into the system but can also retrieve certain nonconfidential information in return.

The task of strategic early warning for senior executives of Shell rests mainly within the CI group at the corporate center in London, while monitoring of events and patterns takes place in

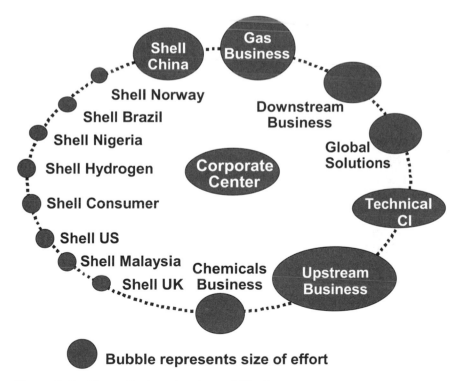

Figure 9-6: CI monitoring structure at Shell.

all businesses, as well as at the center, on a continuous basis. Early warning signals are communicated to executives in the form of CI alerts or special reports if a significant pattern or trend change is discovered.

In addition to ad hoc alerts and early warning reports, Shell also has a system of regular feedback of early warning information to decision makers. Tied into the strategic planning cycle of the company are reviews of the industry structure at both corporate and business levels. These industry structure reviews (ISR) are stress tests of strategic assumptions within an external context and contain information on all three layers of early warning signals.

The Intelligence Team

Probably the most important success factor for intelligence work in general and early warning in particular is the composition and quality of the competitive intelligence team. In our experience intelligence work stands or falls with the skills and experience of the people attempting to do the job. This is one of the reasons why at Shell we believe that intelligence work cannot be outsourced to consultants. There is too much inside knowledge required to come up with cutting-edge analysis of the industry environment in question. And anything less than cutting-edge analysis will not be of much value to the organization and, more important, will not lead to management action. Most CI teams within Shell are set up in a very generic fashion as shown in Figure 9-7.

A team of analysts will report to executives within the businesses or at corporate level. Very often CI teams are also part of the strategy development effort, or are at least located very close to it. At the corporate center the CI effort at Shell is called "strategic intelligence," an indication that the results and products are deemed to be of strategic value to the company and are also used as input for the strategy development process. The manager of strategic intelligence is part of the corporate strategy leadership team and reports to the vice president of corporate strategy for the Shell Group.

Intelligence collection relies on both human resource net-

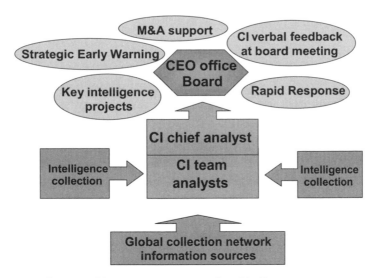

Figure 9-7: Generic CI team structure within Shell.

works and collection from public and electronic data sources. Members of CI teams are almost exclusively coming from within the businesses and are then trained in CI tools and techniques. After spending several years within CI, they will typically return to their parent functions. Within Shell we have, with very few exceptions, no full-time CI career professionals. Over the last couple of years, Shell has spent some effort to try and define what it takes to establish a winning CI team. A number of successful CI practitioners were tested for their skills and behaviors with the help of external experts (Hay/McBer). Results of the Shell sample were compared to a large database of high-performing individuals in similar strategy and competitive intelligence roles in the oil industry and beyond. The purpose of the study was to identify what competencies differentiate outstanding performers in these roles.

What we saw was twofold. First of all, there are certain skills that seem to be common to most good intelligence professionals. They are highly analytical, have a strong focus on improving performance, possess deep and wide information-gathering skills, are future-oriented, are good at communicating and influencing, and are also good at reading others, both individuals and organizations.

Second, four areas differentiate the best from the rest:

1. *Stronger Conceptual Thinking:* They do it at a more sophisticated level, and they do it much more frequently—a source of real competitive advantage to the organization.

2. *Focus on External Dynamics and Forces:* They are not only concerned with relationships and politics within their own organization but are also very concerned about the external world and the impact it has on the organization.

3. *Integrity:* They act with an unusual degree and amount of integrity—being the "conscience" of the organization. This can occasionally require a high amount of courage and is not independent of cultural dimensions.

4. *Leadership:* They demonstrate additional people skills in the areas of leading others, holding them accountable for delivery, and developing their capability.

At least two elements are significantly different compared with requirements of general management roles. For example, the normal emphasis on passion for your own company contrasts with the high requirement for objectivity and dispassionate analysis (integrity). Those differences therefore need to be made explicit and also recognized within the company in order not to derail individuals holding intelligence jobs.

Specific skills for early warning work have also been mapped out at Shell. Within Shell we recognize four CI roles, each with a distinctive suite of capabilities required for excellence in the role (see Figure 9-8).

Note that in this figure, the term "CI department head" refers to line managers with no personal role in CI analysis but with line accountability for CI teams.

Competency development in *CI methods* is acquired through dedicated CI training at the Academy of Competitive Intelligence, EMP Europe, etc. Competency development in the understanding of *CI excellence* can be achieved through CI networking and active membership in SCIP and other regional/local CI organizations. In order to promote CI excellence, the corporate CI team maintains a compilation of CI best practices, which are shared with the CI community. *Customer interface skills* can be partially en-

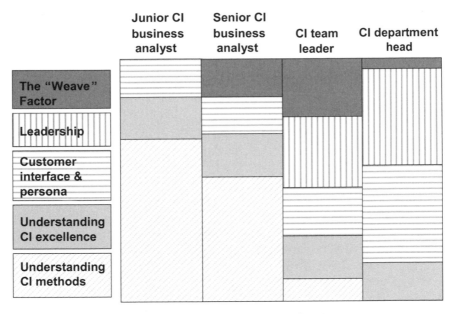

Figure 9-8: CI competencies and CI roles within Shell.

hanced by widely available courses. A technical background in the relevant business aids credibility with the customer base. *Leadership* in the broader sense is also a general management skill that we test and train staff for. What we call the *"weave factor,"* however, cannot be learned through any academic methods we are aware of. This essential cognitive quality of the CI professional is the critical element for pattern recognition and early warning. In our opinion, the weave factor—what Ben Gilad calls "synthesis ability" in Chapter 10 of this book—is the ultimate measure of excellence in a CI professional. We have looked for ways to identify it, and we know that, if present, it is enhanced with time and width of business exposure. Though weave factor is impossible to teach, some of the training by Gilad at the Academy of Competitive Intelligence was also instrumental in flushing out those analysts who possessed this skill. Another way to trace it is to test general management qualities and look for the score on "visualization," a skill that is defined as ". . . the ability to perceive seemingly unrelated relationships within a vast amount of information and correlate these to combine them to a new business insight."[12] We found this to be a rare skill within an otherwise highly analytical staff pool, differentiating the exceptional analysts from the good ones. And only exceptional analysts will be able to produce the high quality of work required for something as important as early warning.

The downside of relying on a skill that is not available in abundance is the problem of succession or replacement. It is very difficult, in our experience, to truly replace experienced analysts in a way that is not detrimental to the intelligence effort. Because a large part of the skill set is also linked to experience and a large amount of actual knowledge accumulated over the years, the problem is compounded.

Special care therefore needs to be taken to ensure that there is a certain continuity of skills within an intelligence team. Too sudden replacement of too many key players can reduce a very experienced, professional CI team to the status of beginners within a very short time frame. At Shell we consequently try to plan the flow of talent into and out of intelligence teams. This is particularly critical for team leader positions requiring a high ability to synthesize. The following tries to demonstrate the importance of a staggered approach when phasing new analysts into an existing CI team. Because Shell does not maintain people in their CI roles for more than three to four years, staff replacement and succession need to be carefully managed, as shown in Figure 9-9.

The value of a CI professional has to be measured on the balance of experience with CI tools and methods, business knowledge, and the weave factor. This will change over time, and experience at Shell has shown that after two years on the job CI analysts reach a plateau of skills, represented in the s-shaped curve for an individual on the left of Figure 9-9. We have also seen that very few people are prepared to stay longer than four years in a CI role. The critical issue is planning the succession of staff within a CI team in a way that, at any given point in time, the sum of the individual experience curves within the team is sufficient to do the job, as illustrated by the curves on the right of Figure 9-9. CI is a very unforgiving profession as far as lack of skills is concerned.

How Do We Communicate?

Crucial for the success of any intelligence effort is the way knowledge and intelligence are shared and communicated.

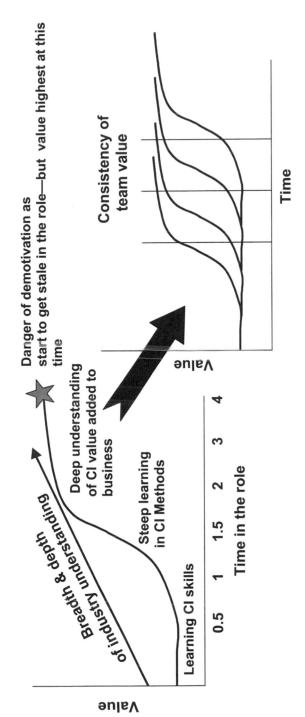

Figure 9-9: Managing CI talent replacement within Shell.

Knowledge is one of the few resources that can increase in value as it is shared. At Shell we use a global intelligence network (IN) that facilitates the exchange of best practices between CI practitioners and also allows the sharing of intelligence within a vast and widespread organization. The latter is of particular relevance for early warning within a large organization like Shell. CI teams and analysts need to rely on the network in order to quickly verify or collect information. However, only in rare cases have we seen the wider network outside of CI teams actually generate an alert or early warning signal. In most cases CI analysts spotted a pattern by analysis of events or information from data sources and then used the network to either verify the correctness or seek supplemental pieces of information completing the pattern.

Because of the size and complexity of the network, it became paramount to switch information efficiently and without too much administrative effort. Shell's knowledge management activities indicate that experts, like CI professionals, need virtual discussions (communities of practice) while day-to-day workers need common solutions to common problems (knowledge bases). The intelligence network offers a platform where members of the Shell CI community can meet and invite others to act as a sounding board for ideas. It is Web based and can be accessed all over the world.

At Shell several such networks exist, and they can have up to several thousand members each. The competitive intelligence network within Shell started with 30 people in 1998 and has grown to its current size of 2,000 members in a careful, incremental way. The network expanded on the back of the expansion of the CI effort within the company, and IT solutions and infrastructure were only introduced whenever the CI effort required them. At this time, the intelligence network seems to have reached a stage where further expansion will require a significant increase in effort and funds, whereas additional benefits are difficult to identify. Shell also believes that tacit knowledge cannot be conscripted—it can only be volunteered—and that we need to create a culture and a simple mechanism to openly encourage this. In the case of the IN, peer recognition and forum discussions seem to be the best driving factors so far.

How Do We Identify and Manage Risk?

The topic of risk identification has always been a critical one in the eyes of Shell. Scenario planning was introduced over thirty years ago to help to identify macroeconomic and geopolitical risks that could form discontinuities for the oil and gas business. Scenarios are alternative futures, meant to challenge business assumptions, focus on key uncertainties, and help to understand drivers and dynamics, and to test the company's strategies and plans. Scenarios alone constitute no early warning system, but at Shell they have proven to be very effective as a tool to generate signals to the organization about changes or developments in the global business environment. They are designed to "think the unthinkable" and to challenge conventional wisdom. If one looks at the early scenarios made at Shell, one can clearly see that they not only told stories about the future, but that they also identified risks, established milestones or indicators to monitor, and in the end sometimes also led to actual management action.

"Scenarios are designed as a tool for understanding the forces that drive the system and the uncertainty that surrounds them. An essential element of this process is the involvement of the decision makers in gaining this understanding such that they are better equipped to make the appropriate business decisions."[13] Because decision makers within Shell are involved in the process of scenario construction, scenario planning is a good first step for early warning, especially as far as industry change drivers are concerned. One of the purposes of building and using scenarios is to help people's awareness of what is changing and also to prepare them to respond faster and more effectively to those changes affecting their business environment. Once they have understood a set of scenarios, people can begin to work with signals. That is, they can scan the environment for indications that the dynamics they have used to create their scenarios, and therefore underpin their decisions or strategy, are actually happening. Watching for early warning signals means that rather than being forced to react to unexpected events after they have happened, decision makers can begin to anticipate the development of situations. By discussing the signals they observe or by trying to understand other people's signals, they can begin to understand the different interpretations that may be placed on the same event, and this can lead them to understand more deeply the assumptions they are making about the future. Through their participation, senior executives are not only aware of the identified risks and uncertainties, but also help to create the early warning indicators in the first place. They are therefore more inclined to act when signals are picked up.

Scenario technology is only one of the tools Shell uses for risk identification. Another important form of risk identification and management is the use of competitive intelligence–based analytical techniques. Within Shell, the existence of a structured and organized CI effort at the corporate center positively influenced the assessment of corporate risks related to business assumptions, senior management failure, and strategic competitive positioning. Especially on the latter, CI and early warning are considered to be a risk response reducing the likelihood of such risks, as shown on an impact/likelihood matrix.

Two main tools for risk identification used by CI teams within Shell are "impact versus risk" matrices and "war maps." An impact versus risk matrix (see Figure 5-5 for a generic form of such a matrix) is a visual representation of sometimes very detailed analysis work on a particular segment of Shell's business environment. This type of analysis is carried out almost exclusively by CI teams within the businesses and is undertaken in close cooperation with the strategy and business development teams of that particular area. A lot of in-depth knowledge is required to come up with meaningful results. That is exactly why we think that consultants cannot deliver cutting-edge analysis and early warning. A matrix displaying the impact and likelihood of potential future events forms the basis for determining the areas of highest risk and exposure or opportunity for the company. Based on the matrix, it is decided which indicators need to be monitored. In a recent impact matrix done for Shell's Asia-Pacific region, all but two events have actually occurred over the last three years.

While scenarios are used to derive early warning indicators for structural change drivers, the impact matrices form the basis for early warning of events that can have a significant impact on our business when coming true. Events being monitored will either be indicative of major impending threats or the opening up of major opportunities. In our experience the discipline required to establish such a matrix forces business leaders to take a very close look at their competitive environment. Experience also shows that the graphical representation of the potential impact of a series of future events can be a powerful tool to stimulate management thinking and action. The target audience for this tool consists of executives responsible for well-defined geographic areas of the business. CI teams will often appoint focal points who shadow such areas and who are responsible for the matrices and the monitoring of the signals coming in.

War maps are a more sophisticated form of pattern analysis and event monitoring. In electronic format, maps of certain geographic areas are being annotated with electronic pages, which can be linked to source data and other pages by hyperlinks, representing events and other information received by the CI team. A variety of relevant information is attached in such form to the map, and then shared with all people knowledgeable in the particular area. Within a short period of time, a very complete picture of the competitive situation is derived, and patterns and trends start to emerge. A war map also constitutes a repository for early warning signals, which can easily be shared, and is often very enlightening to non-CI professionals because all the background information is attached.

Affecting Management Action

Getting top management to base actions on intelligence and early warning alerts is, not surprisingly, the most difficult and also the most crucial step of early warning. The best early warning system is useless if no actions are ever taken based on its results. Since intelligence professionals and practitioners are rarely part of the senior management team of a company, communicating the message becomes a critical success point.

At Shell we determined that combining intelligence work with the strategy development process of the company is one of the cornerstones of success. As Figure 9-10 shows, the different elements of CI work have all become an integral part of the corporate strategy review process and serve as an external stress test of business assumptions and business strategies.

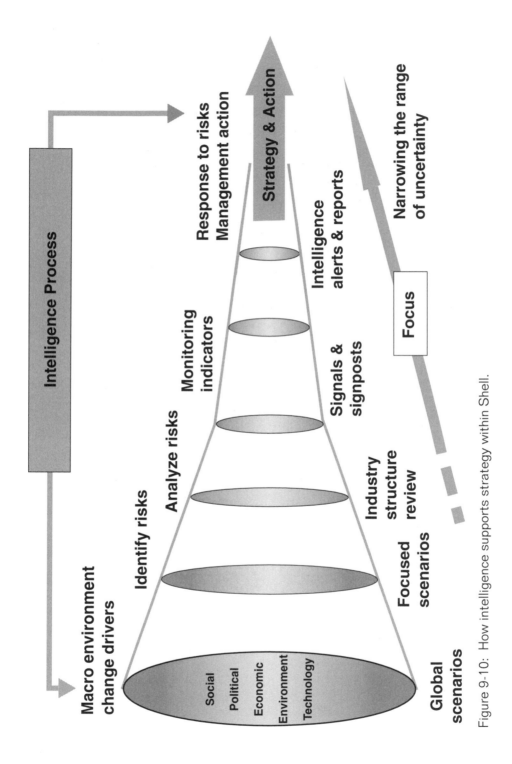

Figure 9-10: How intelligence supports strategy within Shell.

Every element of the company's strategy will at some point be reviewed in the light of its competitive context. During the early stages of strategy setting, the industry structure review at corporate level provides a vehicle to communicate the current set of early warning indicators to top management, including the supervisory board. It raises the awareness of top executives to the main issues, which are currently being monitored by CI teams, and it also allows them to provide feedback and input.

Outside of the fixed strategy development cycle, early warning occurs whenever the situation requires it. In most cases a "CI alert" will be issued whenever a CI team leader concludes that sufficient evidence has been gathered to trigger an early warning report to management. Ad hoc alerts will contain information on the signals picked up, the analysis of the pattern, the conjecture of what it means, and the risks or opportunities this development poses. All those CI alerts end with a paragraph on the significance and importance for Shell. It is also common practice that such alerts are very brief, no longer than one to two pages. Because of that, they are internally often referred to as "One-Pagers." CI alerts are sent to the executives in charge of any potential action to be taken based on the early warning signals. Distribution of such alerts is in most cases rather restricted, and strict confidentiality rules apply.

When communicating alerts to senior executives, it should be the practice to always clearly state what is fact, what is soft information, and what is conjecture. All sources need to be identified and linked to the information forming the basis for the analysis. To issue an early warning alert is the prerogative of any CI team leader at Shell, and there are no rules that would enforce authorization of such an alert by line management, although it is good practice to discuss it beforehand. Since such alerts can reach the very top of the organization quickly, team leaders need to make sure not to engage in alarmism but to issue alerts only in cases where true signals have been picked up and notification of management is warranted. Too many unfounded or unimportant alerts will quickly blunt this otherwise very effective instrument for raising attention to unexpected developments in the external environment.

In case the signals being picked up are "soft" intelligence only and cannot be verified, and especially when the impact on the corporation is large, it is more advisable to follow a different communication strategy. In such a case, practice has shown that verbal briefings between the CI team leader and senior executives are much more effective. It is easier to communicate the confidence or doubts a CI analyst has in his or her conclusions in a dialogue than in written format. In most cases within Shell, verbal communication, or what we call "water-cooler" intelligence, will work as efficiently as a formal report. Often such discussions will be followed by a mandate to keep looking for evidence to either confirm or disprove the hypothesis. But management awareness has been raised nonetheless, and it is not uncommon in our experience that senior executives can actually contribute the missing piece of the puzzle, turning a vague hypothesis into a solid piece of analysis.

Last but not least, let us take a look at the more formal signals and signposts, which are regularly reviewed and are the results of scenario analysis. Scenarios throw off certain signposts, which are then monitored via signals. At Shell, monitoring signals about changes or developments in the global business environment essentially began as early as 1967. Generally, the impetus was on indicators or signposts within scenario stories. Most were described in explicit terms, but occasionally they were implicit within the general themes. The strength of the early signals picked up has tended to vary from extremely empathetic arguments, such as an impending energy gap in the early 1970s, to very casual observations that seem to carry little conviction, as with the possible reunification of Germany in 1989. Overall, the early warning predictions or signposts on the oil industry itself have been remarkably sound, as can be seen in Figure 9-11 on the facing page.

The scenario team monitors the identified signposts on fundamental structures and issues regular reports and updates. Since the introduction of CI at Shell at 1998, monitoring for such industry change drivers takes place also within CI teams: They use scenarios as an indication of where to particularly focus their efforts. The cooperation between the corporate CI team and the scenario group has been greatly intensified as far as early warning is concerned. In most cases CI will take the lead in early warning and monitoring whenever there is a direct business impact or decision, whereas the scenario team will continue to lead

Oil Signals

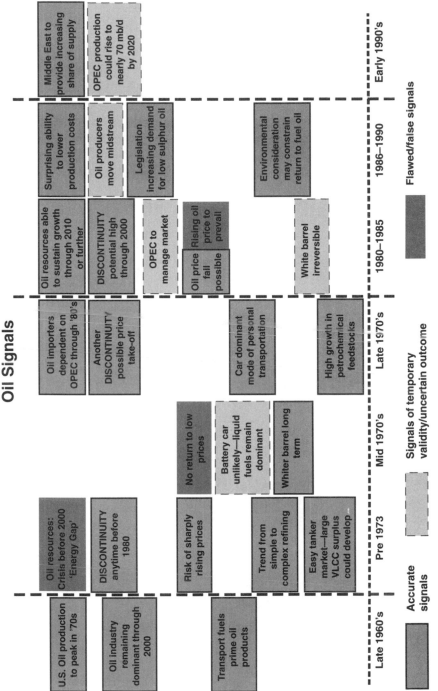

Figure 9-11: Scenario predictions and their accuracy.

the monitoring of underlying structures like global economic indicators, geopolitical developments, etc.

There are several good examples of early warning in action from the period of the early 1970s. Oil companies entered the decade in an optimistic mood, planning and building for unabated volume growth as they had since World War II. In the end, the forecasters proved wrong and the signals were already there in 1972, one year before the first oil shock. Underutilization of refineries was reported for the first time ever and excess capacity was set to increase under the momentum of the building program at hand. Moreover, operating unit costs were increasing significantly. Early warning signposts coming out of the scenarios at that point in time showed the possibility of sharply rising oil prices and a potential for a changed fuel mix in the future as oil consumers switched to other forms of energy. This inspired new thinking at Shell, resulting in a strategy for upgrading refineries and a shift in focus from reducing cost to adding value. First, Shell looked at operational measures to produce a "whiter" barrel, shifting emphasis from low-value fuel oil (very black in color) to high-value distillates. At the same time a building program for thermal crackers was launched to convert fuel oil into distillates.

Two price shocks in the following years led to the tenfold price increase of crude oil. The world economy, already slowing down, moved into recession. Oil demand declined, initially through conservation measures and later through the substitution of other fuels (gas, coal, nuclear). But Shell, with its changed product mix already under way, was better prepared than the competition and less dependent on the sale of fuel oil. Consequently, Shell moved from the bottom to the top of the league of the Seven Sisters. This single shift in mindset, based on early recognition of fundamental changes in the industry environment, ahead of all its competitors, undoubtedly made a significant contribution toward making the company the second-largest energy company in the world today.

A more recent example of early warning followed the attack on the World Trade Center in New York on September 11, 2001. Shell's scenario team worked with other Shell executives and external experts to build a set of three short-term scenarios that described three different ways in which nations and peoples might respond to the attack. Signals were identified under each of the three scenarios. Those scanning used a wide range of publications, looking in particular for maverick viewpoints that readers of more mainstream press and business publications might miss. For three months after September 11, summary reports on signals were produced every week. Thereafter, until May 2002, monthly signals reports were created. Recipients of the reports were already familiar with the three scenarios and so could use the signals to decide for themselves which scenario seemed more or less likely. For an oil company, some major business implications are linked to signals for energy policy, security of supply concerns, energy prices, and disruption of oil markets. Any change in one of those drivers can require a different strategy to respond. An example of an ongoing early warning process in action comes from Shell China. In some of our operating units, early warning has become a fixed part of the way business is done. Figure 9-12 shows how signpost analysis is a regular part of the strategy and planning process within Shell China.

As one can see, key signpost analysis takes place on a quarterly basis, and CI analysis reports looking for trends and patterns are issued on a monthly basis and also shared with the CI team at the corporate center. The CI reports tend to focus on

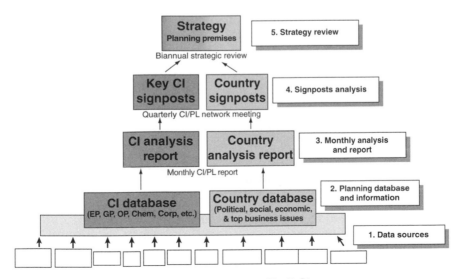

Figure 9-12: The early warning process at Shell China.

local and foreign competitors and new entrants, while the country reports deal with the other forces of the business environment. In China those other forces can be very important and require the special expertise of political analysts, government relations, etc. This setup is not a standard across the Shell Group, but it is promoted as a best-practice process within the CI community as far as regular signposting is concerned.

Cultural Predeterminants of EW

Once an organization has ceased to base its decisions on linear forecasts and extrapolation of trends, it needs another way of bringing the future into the decision making process. At Shell, progress in this direction was accomplished by advancing the hypothesis that the decision making process is a learning process. Circumstantial evidence now indicates that this has been a fruitful way of looking at the issue. Learning and, therefore, decision making consists of:

- A perception, followed by the incorporation of that perception into the way the organization understands the world.

- Drawing new conclusions from this new view of the world.

- Taking action by implementing the new conclusions.

These three points correspond very well to the three main stages of the competitive early warning model (CEW) as described in this book. Therefore, Shell as a company seems to be receptive to the implementation of tools and processes that can be linked to CEW.

Another important cultural component is the acceptance of a certain amount of internal challenge. A guiding principle for good intelligence work is that in order to succeed, executives sometimes need to listen to people who disagree with them. It is a key task for CI to challenge assumptions and blindspots within the organization. Good intelligence work can happen only if that is possible, and at Shell that has been the case.

Manager's Checklist—Case Studies

❏ There are several models of early warning that companies can choose from. Each model fits its specific industry, competitive conditions, company strategy, scope of operations, and the type of product planning required in the industry. The CEW model is as flexible as the mindset underlying it: One can start from any point and move backward or forward. The goal remains management action that manages risk intelligently before it blows up in its face. The examples in this chapter beautifully demonstrate this simple point.

❏ Some less than fully informed writers in the popular business press are inclined to sensationalize stories on business-smart intelligence activities into "shady corporate spies" stories. Neurotic (and not so smart) executives get cold feet.

❏ Changes in management are a number-one problem for companies' core skills, and CEW capability is no different. A merger can kill a first-rate EW capability, as it did when French and Spanish executives got hold of a German analytical process . . . their only hope for a victory is an even worse American competitor.

❏ One person, with the proper training and proper backing by a smart senior executive, can do an excellent job of keeping management secure. The opposite is not true.

❏ War rooms are a modern-day fad for rich corporations who like to throw money away. Management does not use more intelligence just because the company spent $3 million on the latest display toys.

Do you know of a company with a good model of an early warning system? Share it with me. Send details to bsgilad@ netvision.net.il. I'll include it in future writings on this topic.

Notes

1. For a classic example, read "P&G's Covert Operation," *Fortune*, 7 Sept. 2001 by Andy Serwer. Mr. Serwer describes the annual meeting of SCIP

(the professional association of competitive analysts) as a gathering of "corporate spies" and decides that competitive intelligence is just industry jargon for spying. The heading of course is about a "covert" operation, just as in glamorous James Bond stories. . . . With such "knowledgeable" pieces in a respected magazine, no wonder companies prefer to keep mum. I hope the foolishness of such statements is clear: It is just like calling marketing the art of cheating customers of their money or strategy, an industry jargon for luck.

2. Heather Timmon, "Is Citi's Weill Outward Bound?" *BusinessWeek Online,* 15 Nov. 2002.

3. Quoted in "Bank Alarm: Financial Stocks Have Had an Amazing One-Year Run. Now What?" by Roger Lowenstein, *SmartMoney,* June 1998 (Dow Jones News Service, 19 May 1998).

4. James R. Kraus, "Regional Banking Ready for the Next Recession," *American Banker,* 8 Nov. 1994.

5. "Citigroup in the News" from www.citigroup.com, 25 March 1999.

6. Corporate Strategy Board, "Proceeding in Daylight: Frontier Practices for Challenging Strategic Assumptions" (Washington: Corporate Executive Board, 1999), pp. 223–241.

7. Shawn Tully, "Despite Asia's Woes, US Banks Are Standing Tall," *Fortune,* 16 Feb. 1998.

8. "Citicorp's Senior Debt Raised to AA- by Fitch," PR Newswire, 4 Sept. 1997.

9. Carol Loomis, "Citigroup: Scenes from a Merger," *Fortune,* 11 Jan. 1999.

10. The information in this section relies on three sources: "Scenario Analysis and Early Warning Systems at Daimler-Benz Aerospace" by Franz Tessun, *Competitive Intelligence Review* 8, no. 4 (1997); "Strategic Intelligence" by Joel Whitaker, Corporate Strategy Board Executive Inquiry, (Washington: Corporate Executive Board, August 2000) (a superb report, highly recommended for additional reading); and conversations with Franz Tessun, the former EW system head at DASA and its former VP of Market Research.

11. Corporate Executive Board report, p. 19.

12. Source: Description of General Management Competencies, Omega Management Consultants.

13. Reflections on the Evolution of Scenario Planning in Shell. Shell internal report, November 1995.

CHAPTER 10

If You Start from Scratch . . .

> "There is nothing more difficult . . . than to take the lead in the introduction of a new order of things."
>
> —*Niccolo Machiavelli*

Intelligence is a tricky subject. As information, its use is tied closely to a multitude of variables—both personal and organizational. As sometime *speculative* information dealing with an uncertain future, its use is even more temperamental than the use of more "solid" information such as financials or statistics available from commercial databases. To make things worse, its use can be occasion-driven. Would Jack Welch use intelligence? Absolutely. He was an ardent supporter of competitive intelligence at GE. But when it came to his vision of an end-of-career grand finale act of taking over Honeywell, he just could not believe some politically nominated clerk in Europe—the European Union's commissioner for competition affairs, Mario Monti— could foil his plan. Would John Akers of IBM sanction a formal early warning system? Not if his life depended on it, according to people at IBM who regarded his infamous "policy committee" as insular, arrogant, and complacent and held it responsible for leading IBM to the brink of disaster. But under him IBM had first-rate tactical marketing intelligence in the various business units. Each of us uses intelligence according to our own inclinations at any given moment in time. It is both an extremely complicated and an extremely simple prediction to make: Which companies will be good at early warning and which will turn a deaf ear and a blind eye? Which obstacles will be the hardest to remove?

It is extremely complicated because it boils down to a combination of executive personalities and organizational culture, neither of which is a simple, straightforward concept. The use of early warning and the intelligence it is based upon will always be subject to personal vagaries. One executive may be humble and cautious, his replacement overconfident and egocentric, yet on several occasions they will both turn to obsolete prior beliefs and ignore facts and signs in the market, or they may both listen carefully to the intelligence delivered at a meeting. There are experts in the field of organizational behavior and in the field of intelligence who believe in the use of personality profiles and some famous standard tests (such as Myers-Briggs) to predict the inclination to use information (and by inference competitive intelligence and early warning). I am not one of them. I assume NJIT is the New Jersey Institute of Technology, not a useful predictor of the use of early warning. I am keenly aware of the fact that I may be in a minority on that, as every other American manager I met during my twenty-year career as an educator in CI had already scored him- or herself on one of those tests and was willing to release in public, upon the *slightest* bit of encouragement, such statements as "I am an FIPS," "I am a NEJS," and no one burst out laughing. On the other hand, it is one step higher in the evolutionary scale than astrology. . . .*

If the EIFJGP (Extrovert-Intuitive-Feeling-Judgmental-Golden-Parachuted) CEO will or will not listen to an early warning, she may still be only half of the equation. Though top executives may exert significant influence on the behavior of their firm, cultures can be equally as strong. Lou Gerstner, who replaced Akers and was CEO of IBM from 1993 to 2002, was an enthusiastic user of intelligence and early warning and completely revamped

---

* I am sure I am saying that only because I am an Introverted-Intuitive-Judgmental-Thinker, at least for the next two hours.

the competitive culture at the top of IBM. But, according to my friends in the trenches, many middle managers in the vast IBM empire still resist the need to track competitive developments and pay attention to early signs of change. They think IBM should not worry about competition and little issues such as industry structure.

And yet, at the same time, it is extremely *simple* to predict which companies will do a good job on early warning. Use common sense, and score your company on the following test:

The Gilad Test for Early Warning Tendencies

1. Does top management listen to its middle managers? 10 points if it does, 0 if it is the typical Fortune 500 top brass who regard anything outsiders say as valuable and nothing insiders say as credible.

2. How does the CEO perceive his role—a strategist or a statesman? 10 points if the CEO is actively involved in formulating strategies for his company (not just choosing which option to follow) and 0 if he just makes videos communicating vague visions and trite motivational pitches to the employees.

3. How often does the company use one of those big "prestigious" strategy-consulting firms? 10 points if never, 0 if every time the executives run out of creative strategy making skills but prefer not to resign or give back some of their compensation.

4. And finally, how do the company's executives handle those "pests"—stock analysts with a digging mindset (assuming there are some in the crowd!)? 10 points if they admit possible mistakes and alternative scenarios, 0 if they get angry during analysts' calls.

Did your company score forty? You are lucky. Did it score zero? Welcome to the club, this company has no early warning skills and should not be considered capable of detecting surprises. That is an important assessment to make, especially if your company is planning the surprise. Naturally, much of the above information is hard to obtain for an outsider. But if this information *is* available to the observer, predicting those companies that will be surprised (again!) and those that will wake up only when the bomb hits is not difficult at all.

Culture and the CEW

"Culture" is a slippery concept. Though it took over consultants' talk in the 1980s and was mentioned as often as "management by objectives" (remember that?) or "reengineering" (remember this?), for the intelligence analyst it is not always easy to characterize a "culture." Academics define organizational culture to include beliefs, rites, rituals, myths, language, stories, symbols, heroes, and heroines.[1] Some regard culture as a system of beliefs strong enough to be called "ideologies" that determine the way people in the organization relate to, and interact with, each other.[2] Did it help you to translate the concept into a reality in the workplace? Not much? Well, you are not alone.

Since it is not clear what culture actually means, I will use it in a popular way, as just the *typical way* of doing things in a given organization. In that definition, culture has a lot to do with early warning.

Take, for example, General Electric (GE), a company whose culture was praised and appraised by so many popular business stories that no one doubts it *has* a culture. One of the less visible characteristics of this culture is the way intelligence flows throughout GE. Every Fortune 500 manager knows the concept of "information silos." These refer to the very widespread phenomenon of the lack of sharing of information between different units in the same corporation, different departments in the same business unit, and sometime different people sitting across the same room. Under Jack Welch, at GE, intelligence flowed across units, businesses, and divisions. As *Fortune* magazine described it in a story about GE Capital (GE's largest unit), market intelligence poured into Capital "from throughout GE as part of a rich reciprocal relationship."[3] The anecdotes related by the writer included a story about how GE Power Systems, which built power plants for utilities and therefore knew them quite intimately, informed GE Capital about utilities' self-interest in outsourcing customer service functions such as billing and collection. This information led to Capital's Retailer Financial Services forming a whole new business to serve this market. Another anecdote related how the same piece of intelligence was sent to Capital's municipal bond insurance business (Financial Guaranty Insurance Company [FGIC]), which insured utilities' bonds backed by the utilities' expected revenue stream. Deregulation had wreaked havoc on the expected cash flow of many utilities, and GE Power Systems passed on that inside knowledge. Capital FGIC unit pulled out of this market.

With such strong intelligence connections, one can expect GE to have a first-rate institutionalized early warning system. Indeed, the story described a very sophisticated early warning system, using "smoke detectors"—GE Capital's name for tripwires—to identify trouble. The system had been based on a chief risk manger at corporate and twenty-seven risk managers at all twenty-seven business units, all of whom reported directly to the top bosses.[4]

When it came to top management listening to its middle management, the following business development practice at GE Capital can serve as an example. Every Monday morning, the top executive team at GE Capital (at that time all of six people under CEO Gary Wendt) discussed new business ideas brought up from the rank and file. The ideas and the presenters received gentle encouragement until funding discussion time, at which stage the executive team put the idea and its champion at the center of close scrutiny focused on competitive advantage in the given market. Naturally, most ideas died at this stage, but the culture created emphasis on two factors: One, all ideas were welcome and did not have to come from the outside. Second, people needed to have the competitive intelligence before they came up for questioning.

The CEO's perception of his role, in line with my test question, was that of a strategist, not a public figure with ceremonial duties. As *Fortune* reported, "Wendt also happens to be one of the shrewdest people at the company, with an eye for spotting trends." A CEO and an early warning analyst at the same time—one could not ask for more. As a side note, one may bring up the fact that the same Gary Wendt failed miserably at his next job as CEO of the troubled insurer Conseco. This fact reinforces the point that early warning requires both a supportive leader and a supportive culture, and that early warning makes sense early on, before the company is on the brink.

Compare this to the culture at McDonald's, the fast-food king. A poll in 2001 by a fast-food consulting firm of 50,000 frequent eaters from seventy fast-food chains ranked McDonald's dead last overall.[5]

The survey looked at food quality, taste, and temperature, as well as facilities and service. Industry observers concur that McDonald's has failed to innovate for years. However, the early warning signs that something was going wrong had little to do with innovation. How could a company ignore clear signs that 1) the food was not coming off hot enough from its "new and improved" cooking system—sometimes the cheese did not melt on the burgers; 2) service was slower than that of competitors; 3) the facilities were not clean, even though McDonald's claim to fame was that it was the cleanest joint around; and 4) its advertising had gotten stale (a campaign that does not talk about the food at a food place is at best a bit detached, don't you think?).

And these are just the relatively small changes that were missed. The big ones, like the trend toward less sugary, less fattening foods, have been a waste on McDonald's until very recently, as was the change in lifestyles due to the wealth effect that meant, as Peter Oakes, an analyst at Merrill Lynch, observed, "the days of people beating a path to McDonald's door to eat with plastic utensils on immovable furniture are over."[6]

A glimpse at the corporate culture can be found in an anecdote relayed by Gene Galgliardi , a product development specialist who tried to interest McDonald's R&D executives in a steak sandwich. He told *USA Today* that the idea was dismissed outright.

Another cultural telltale at McDonald's is the tenure of its leaders. The recently retired CEO, Jack Greenberg, had been a dominant chairman and CEO since 1999 and was a thirty-one-year veteran of the company. His replacement is a twenty-eight-year veteran of the company. Bringing in fresh blood is not a practice at McDonald's, which has had only four CEOs since 1955. Stability is a wonderful concept, but ossification is not that good.

CEOs and CEW

The acronyms are so close, C-E-O, C-E-W, one would think that every CEO would want a first-rate, *institutionalized* competitive early warning. Not so. The relationship between CEOs and their organizations' early warning capability is a reflection of the CEOs' personalities, backgrounds, belief systems, decision styles, and IQs. This relationship is never simple, but it is rather safe to say that top executives who love listening to themselves more than they love listening to the truth will not be ardent supporters of a reality check tool such as a CEW.

However, there is a new style of CEO shaping up in America, or so the press lets us believe. As Patricia Sellers of *Fortune* puts it so aptly, "The larger-than-life CEO of the past decade is out of fashion (or awaiting prison time)."[7] The new breed, reports *Fortune*, is diligent and cautious with, so far, few self-aggrandizing schemes and little overconfidence bordering on blindness. A risk aversion trait common to so many new CEOs bodes very well for a change in their approach to early warning and strategic intelligence.

Let's look at my commonsense test for early warning appetite and see how the new breed fares.

Question 1: Does top management listen to its middle managers?

According to the *Fortune* article, Ann Mulcahy, Xerox's new CEO "eggs on employees to identify weakness." Mulcahy holds large meetings with her managers and collects from the meeting participants a list of concerns about the company's strategy. Steve Reinemund, PepsiCo's new CEO, holds executive development programs for middle managers at the University of Virginia's Graduate School of Business, and invites PepsiCo's board members to participate and interact with the middle managers during class time.

Question 2: How does the CEO perceive his role—as a strategist or a statesman?

According to the article, the new breed of CEO is completely different from the charismatic, larger-than-life old-boy networker who wrote biographies, gave speeches and interviews, played a lot of golf, and saw himself as a grand visionary leader whose main role was to tell a good tale and do a good spin for his company. Jim Kilts, the new CEO at Gillette, hasn't spoken to the press for two years. Ann Mulcahy is described by *Fortune* as someone who cannot spin "to save her life" and honest to a fault. She gets her entire top executive rank, five hundred in all, involved with her in strategy meetings, talking to eighty people at a time, urging them to find holes in the strategy. Paul Pressler, who replaced Millard (Mickey) Drexler at The Gap, devoted his first hundred days at the company to listening and learning. He told *Fortune*, "the last thing you'll get from me is a grand vision in the first hundred days." Ken Lewis at Bank of America admitted his weaknesses freely to the press and delivered better returns than his predecessor, the famous ego-driven Hugh McColl, who saw himself as an infallible empire builder.

Question 3: How often does the company use one of those big "prestigious" strategy-consulting firms?
    This is tougher to ascertain, as companies do not divulge the facts of their contracts with these firms, but a recent article in the *Economist* suggests the use of such executive-thinking-independently-bypass devices is on the decline.[8] Also, there is evidence that the new breed of CEOs turns to board members for advice and taps certain respected elders—hopefully at the expense of hiring the large "prestigious" strategy-consulting firms and paying them millions for a standard sell of the latest fad. Thus, Jamie Dimon, the CEO of Bank One, brought in John Reed, his former boss at Citibank (and the creator of the WOR early warning system there, described in Chapter 9), to help him with strategic advice. In line with his inclination to use early warning rather than consultants, Reed advised him to focus his board on questions such as "What are the things that could blow up the company?" Finally, A. G. Lafley, the new CEO at P&G, is sending members of his board of directors to visit the business units and alert him to problems—an innovative early warning mechanism.

Question 4: How do the company's executives handle those "pests"—analysts with their digging mindset?
    This is the easiest question to answer, and there is ample evidence that CEOs are changing their old ways. While Joe Nacchio, the former failing CEO of Qwest, was known to blow up at analysts who wanted the detailed facts (such as—can you imagine?—sales figures), his successor, a modest man named Dick Notebaert, is the opposite. Jamie Dimon at Bank One insisted on telling investors the true state of credit losses if a recession hit, a

practice that his colleagues in the industry regarded as insane. Sears chief Alan Lacy fired two top executives from the credit division and explained to analysts that they had provided him with the wrong rosy forecast of the company's future (a practice that should but does not lead to the firing of 90 percent of all division heads) and then gave the analysts an honest view of a tough future. Sears' stock fell sharply following his honesty, but Lacy stood by his act of integrity.

With this new breed, corporate America at least stands a chance of adopting a better posture toward controlling strategic risks and opportunities. Though the new leaders may not be aware of the formal process of early warning, and may never hear of me or this book, they are definitely *thinking* early warning, as evidenced by Jamie Dimon's comment, in the *Fortune* article, about CEOs who are surprised by tough times: "Didn't they know it was going to rain someday?"

Compare these new CEOs' style to the debacle at the famous all-male Augusta Golf Club in Atlanta. When the chairman of the club, one William "Hootie" Johnson, received a letter from the National Council of Women's Organizations (NCWO) asking him to admit a woman into the Masters tournament played at the club, he responded with such a vehement decline that what might have been a no-brainer issue turned into the biggest scandal in the history of the club, bringing tons of bad publicity, threats of protests, and boycotts. Robin Cohn, a PR specialist and a noted writer on the subject, commented to the press that "any time an organization receives a letter like that, they have to get information on what that person wants and who that person is."[9] But that would mean using intelligence—wouldn't it?—and thinking, "Here are some early signs of risk." Not Mr. Johnson's style.

Compare the new CEOs' style to the old and familiar style of John Chambers of Cisco.[10] While his company struggled in the recession of 2000–2002 following the explosion of the Internet bubble, his company's stock was down 83 percent from its peak, 10,000 of his employees had to look for new jobs, and $2.5 billion of his inventory was written off, Chambers dismissed the problems as "A hundred-year flood" and declared that Cisco "got surprised . . . but once we were surprised we executed pretty well against our peers." To that out-of-touch response, Fred Hickey, the editor of the newsletter *High Tech Strategist*, said, correctly, "I don't buy anything he says anymore. He is a cheer-leader. A hypester." Listening to Chambers, who is (was?) a bril-liant entrepreneur and a maverick of strategy, it won't come as a surprise to anyone to learn that Cisco never had a good intelli-gence program and had no early warning capability. Its few CI managers are low-level and without any influence on the execu-tive team.

When it comes to early warning and the attitude toward strategic intelligence, a leader's influence almost always extends to his entire executive team as well. In the same *Fortune* article about Cisco, the writer describes the response he got from Mike Volpi, a senior executive at Cisco, when he mentioned Dell's in-trusion into the networking business. By 2002, Dell had sold more than 100,000 low-end switches, which was a very small amount compared to Cisco, but enough to make Cisco bar it from selling its products. Yet Volpi's response was to scribble on a whiteboard "an illustration why Dell won't succeed." The main argument: In order for Dell to succeed, networks need to become commodity and Cisco believes they are way too complicated for that to happen any time soon (if ever). Dell believes commoditi-zation is happening faster than the industry thinks it is. I don't know who's right, but if Cisco had had an early warning men-tality, it would have never claimed that Dell was bound to fail. That was old IBM/Compaq's claim as well when Dell introduced the direct sell model, which is based on PCs being a commodity that can be sold online. If Cisco's executive team had been *think-ing* early warning, it would not have dismissed challenges to its old operating system, IOS, which was developed in 1985 and is considered a relic, while new upstarts such as Caspian and Pro-cket were working on a better one, by stating, "We have 1,200 people working on IOS. They have to start from scratch." True indeed, but so did Airbus and Genentech.

One does not have to be a true newcomer to the CEO's seat to have a different mentality than the overconfident, chock-full-of-blindspots old guard. Frank Raines, the CEO of the federal mortgage giant, Fannie Mae, has been the company's chief since 1999. He is a former White House budget director and a savvy manager with a knack for early warning. That can probably be traced to his years in the White House. He and his team spend a lot of time looking at long-term industry drivers, such as U.S. home ownership, migration, population, aging distribution, etc. If one runs an analysis of the industry's structure, however, it becomes crystal clear that the force that presents the clearest risk is rivalry, and the most prominent industry driver here is political. Specifically, competitors such as the big banks or other financial institutions have been trying, and would try even harder under a Republican-controlled Congress, to persuade Congress to remove the special privileges enjoyed by Fannie Mae.

Franklin D. Roosevelt founded Fannie Mae in 1938 as a tool to revive the housing market by buying mortgages from private lenders, effectively increasing the availability of funds for lending. It was turned into a government-sponsored private institution in 1968. Today, it is backed by a $2.5 billion conditional line of credit from the federal government, which allows it to benefit from a lower rate on its borrowing; it does not pay state or local taxes. It is a very profitable enterprise, and it draws a lot of fire.

If you are the CEO of this strange half-breed and you have the mindset for early warning and you are the type that believes in questions like John Reed's "What can bring this enterprise down?," what would you do? You would create a world-class strategic early warning aimed at the political arena. That's exactly what Raines has done. When Christopher Shays (R–Conn.) wanted to force Fannie Mae to register with the Securities and Exchange Commission, Fannie Mae got an early warning on his intentions. They tried to set up a meeting with him, but that meeting did not take place. Immediately after Shays introduced the legislation, each House member received a letter containing an impressive list of opponents, from Hispanic-Americans who were opposed to the legislation to the association of realtors who objected to it. That type of letter took time and effort to prepare. The quickness of this action reflected an impressive early warning that moved into action upon the activation of tripwires. An insider at the White House commented to a *Business Week* reporter that Raines "runs the most sophisticated political operation in the universe."[11] Raines actually took this comment as a compliment. As he should. He has a first-rate early warning process that includes a vice president for industry analysis and a vice president for regulatory affairs, both of whom function as

EW analysts. The center of Fannie Mae's early warning, how-ever, is Raines himself, a man whose personal style is that of an intelligence operator. Raines keeps a Rolodex with names of former colleagues from the investment bank Lazard Freres and names of former colleagues from his years as Bill Clinton's bud-get director. In an interview with *Business Week* he said, "I learned when I did the budget that going up and just talking to people long before there are any negotiations—long before there are any demands—goes a long way."[12] Raines also believes in proactive action, a critical factor in the success of early warning processes. In the summer of 2001 he voluntarily registered Fan-nie's common stock with the SEC, even though its statute of ex-emption was not changed in Congress. But he persuaded the SEC not to register Fannie's mortgage-backed securities—the heart of its operations. Representative Richard Baker (R–La.), the House chairman of the government-sponsored enterprises subcom-mittee, and Raines's opponent, gives Fannie Mae the ultimate compliment: "They are without question, the most effective managers of political risk in America."[13] How many companies can say that about their executives and risks their companies face?

Perhaps it takes someone who loves intelligence himself; perhaps it takes a man who has risen to his position from a childhood of hard-working laborer parents who taught him the value of being prepared for the worst; perhaps a stint of training in the White House should be required of all CEOs. There is no doubt in my mind that corporations and the investors who place their money in them would benefit greatly from having more CEOs like Raines.

Other Organizational Considerations

Assume a company decides to develop an early warning capabil-ity. Top management is behind this initiative 100 percent and swears to use the results and listen to the alerts. The CEO herself is an avid believer in intelligence over intuition and beliefs. What other considerations should play a role? Are there specific orga-nizational practices that can hinder early warning? Does size matter? Does it matter which industry one operates in?

The answer to all three questions is yes. There are specific organizational practices that can be particularly detrimental to early warning, size does matter, and different industries will have different optimal models of EW.

Charge-Back

Charge-back early warning is one of those lethal practices. Charge-back is the practice of making an activity pay for itself by making it dependent on funding by customers, instead of overhead's being borne by corporate or business units' top management. At Visa International, for example, regional Visa offices fund the small early warning team composed of a vice president and two analysts.

While, on the face of it, it may seem that early warning could easily withstand a "market" test for the value of its services, a bit of closer scrutiny reveals the inherent irrationality of this model. Assume for a moment that the customers decide they are interested in threats only within their own domain since their annual bonuses are tied to "local" (brand, region, country) market share or profitability. Who then will pay for global early warning that can kill the entire corporation? What incentive exists for an early warning analyst in a business unit to look at the risk to the company as a whole if she is paid by project or product teams?

In a broader perspective, intelligence, and its advance use in early warning processes, should be funded by top management—corporate, unit, and divisional. There are two main reasons for this:

1. Top management—in corporate and business units—is the ultimate client of early warning, which is aimed at keeping its rear end out of trouble. Top business unit management needs a company-wide process to keep a lookout at industry-level changes. Top corporate needs a cross-industry, portfolio EW process. So top management should pay for it.

2. Early warning looks at the big future picture, the dangers looming ahead of the company's existing strategy and its ex-

ecution. The vast majority of managers in corporations who ask for information and are paying for it from their departmental budgets look for *past or current data* to back up their presentations or reports. For example, in the pharmaceutical industry so many managers use IMS data (a commercial vendor collecting market statistics such as market share, number of prescriptions issued, new drug sales, etc.) that one would think the industry might collapse if the data stopped coming. But when it comes to future assessments of the competitive landscape, strategic risks looming ahead or strategic opportunities opening up, very few people are even aware these can be made available, and are so much more critical to their decisions than past–present statistics. Past and present numbers are "facts," and middle managers can clearly understand their use in backing up PowerPoint briefings to management. Management, in turn, wants to know "what's happening" more than anything else. That leaves intelligence analysis and future-looking early warning alerts as a luxury few middle managers would pay for.

One reason from an economist's perspective:

▸ In their personal life, people either buy insurance to protect them from uncertainty, or if they don't, they personally suffer the consequences. But if the individual product manager, or vice president R&D in the company does not buy "insurance" against strategic surprises in the form of funding the early warning program, the *whole company* can go down. Economists call it an externality.

One bottom-line reason:

▸ It just does not work.

One consequence to ponder:

▸ Imagine a U.S. president who decides that national intelligence early warning should be funded at the discretion of state governors. If you can see this model working against terrorists, use the charge-back model, and good luck to you and your company.

Size and Industry

If one starts from scratch, with the right support from the top, with funding from the chairman or CEO or business unit's head office, one still needs to tailor the early warning process to the industry and the company's size. Chapter 9 deliberately presented a variety of models for early warning, suitable for various company sizes and industries. Naturally, the size variable impacts the amount of resources one can devote to early warning. It also affects the culture of information sharing and the formality of a network. Small entrepreneurial companies, where the CEO and twenty-five workers constitute the whole company, do not need to formalize information sharing. Entrepreneurs, unless funded by a lot of venture capital money, tend to be natural intelligence officers, at least in their own narrow domain of activity. Easy funding corrupts, so small companies backed by big money should be extra careful. At least their backers should insist on some kind of an early warning capability (unless they are as careless about losing money as their start-ups). In small companies, therefore, early warning is more a matter of *training* the people to think like intelligence analysts and giving them the tools to see and understand risks when these emerge.

Is there a size threshold for a full-time EW position? I am asked this question more than any other, in line with the obsession of benchmarking by the obvious, not the essential. My answer is yes. The size threshold should be the level at which the CEO feels he and his team are not fully informed or well informed about potential risks, or quickly informed about potential opportunities in the marketplace. A second threshold is event-driven. If a company is strategically surprised more than once every five years, it needs an EW analyst to drive an EW process and be accountable for a zero-surprises performance.

Perhaps the best answer to the size question, though, was the one given by the former CEO and chairman of Best Foods, Charles Shoemate, who placed the goal of "superior anticipation" on his company's balanced scorecard. Under the guidance of Thomas Berkel, a manager in the grocery division, the company built up an impressive intelligence and early warning capability that contributed to a stellar performance. Then Shoemate sold the company at a high premium to Unilever, a much *larger* British-Dutch conglomerate that immediately proceeded to decimate Best Foods' early warning capability. So, size is not everything.

Industry also affects the model chosen for early warning. Long cycles of product life require more attention to the analytical side of the EW model, and fast-changing industries require more attention to intelligence monitoring and quick management action. These are commonsense considerations, which one would assume every manager can come up with on his or her own, but given the lack of common sense among quite a sizable minority of top executives, managers who are into this subject may need to show their bosses they leaned on an outside authority for commonsense advice.

Organizational Location

Is there an optimal location for the EW program? To whom should it report? What level should its leader be? The answers to these questions are more company-specific. I have my favorite and less favorite structures, and I am not one to shy away from generalizations and stereotypes; as an economist, I am a great believer in their value as time-saving cognitive tools. For example, I think intelligence efforts placed under market research are doomed, and I have a file full of cases to prove it, even though I am sure there are individual cases where my generalization is completely wrong. However, since it should be clear from everything I have written so far that I believe the reporting of the early warning staff is less important than the actual *use* of early warning (top management), I will remain mum on this subject. As far as I am concerned, companies can place the EW leader under the cafeteria services—as long as they make sure the CEO gets an EW briefing while he eats breakfast, I will be happy.

Who Makes the Best Strategic Risk Analyst?

This is the million-dollar question. Naturally, I have an answer. First, though, I have to define exactly what I mean by an analyst of strategic risk. In most large companies, the role of the analyst and role of the manager might not be the same. However, in the early warning system, the manager should also be the chief competitive analyst for the company (or chief industry analyst, for those who confuse competitive and competitor analysis). That's because in an analytically based process such as early warning, someone who just "manages" the process as a coordinator is not the heart and soul of the activity and therefore does not matter to its ultimate success. The analysis of strategic risks determines whether the system performs or fails, and therefore, the manager of the competitive early warning process must be the best analyst the company can put forward. This is the person who guides the scenario construction or war gaming risk identification process, and this is the person who makes sense of the numerous monitors' reports, and, most important, this is the person who issues the alerts and persuades management or an evaluation committee that it is not just another case of a bearer of bad news. So now the question is: Who is the *best* risk analyst?

My finest answer is as follows: The best strategic risk/early warning analyst is someone who is a detail-oriented big-picture type of person, fearless and full of self-doubts, a great political networker introvert, analytical to a fault with a sixth sense (he does not have to see the dead, though), and, finally, a broad-minded, focused person. The reason I am making little sense is that I've known and trained an early warning manager/analyst who excelled at his job and was detail-obsessive and a focused fearless fanatic and I've worked with a soft-spoken, big-picture type of risk analyst who was a broad-based intellectual, quoted Shakespeare, and had a significant influence on the success of his division. I've seen a brilliant communicator with very shrewd political senses who had no social skills but built an early warning so advanced his organization needed years to catch up, and I've met and worked with an intuitive woman who could grasp the essence of a very complicated scenario in seconds and thrived on uncertainty but was never too far from doubting her own insights, even though her boss, the CEO of a large division, thought the world of her. And I worked with and befriended another EW manager who was liked by all and could get any information he wanted but had no political talent, which resulted in his lack of promotion, yet he succeeded in creating a world–class often benchmarked early warning process at his business unit. In short, there is no one profile. Still, there are four variables that operate to define the "best" early warning manager:

1. The company's culture
2. The top management team's decision-making style
3. The CEO's personality
4. The analyst's skills and personality

The success of the early warning analyst/manager depends on the interaction of all four variables, which makes it impossible to characterize a person simply as a certain type on this test or another. Since companies differ in cultures, top management's styles, and their CEO's personalities, there can be not one but many "best" profiles of an EW analyst.

In my experience, there are some *cognitive* qualities (not personality or temperament) that are a must in early warning type work. Two stand up in my view as the most critical to the success of the process and the survival of the firm:

1. Synthesis ability
2. Integrity

Synthesis Ability

The strategic risk analyst must be able to paste together a puzzle of emerging reality from a variety of unrelated bits, a strategic picture made up of many tactical details. That is not an analytical skill as we define analytics, since analysis is the breakdown of a complicated whole into its components. Sure, a risk analyst must be able to break down a complex issue and see its components during various stages of the risk identification process, but more important, she must see the whole. The skill of seeing the forest from the trees is called synthesis. Some call it insight, or creativity.

Unlike analytical ability, which is relatively well understood and tested with standardized tests, synthesis ability is a relatively unknown quantity. Don't be misled by simple perceptual tests of putting together puzzles. Conceptual synthesis is very different. We might not know how to diagnose it, but we sure know when we encounter it. Great early warning analysts make themselves known in the community through insight-based predictions. In various intelligence services of the spying kind, great analysts are cherished. In many companies, they are wasted, either because they are labeled troublemakers, or they are not team players, or they do not exhibit the type of mindless loyalty required of peons by many top managers. I once rescued a brilliant strategic risk analyst from being fired by an engineering boss who thought he was asking too many nagging questions for his junior position. But not all is bleak: Bright risk analysts have a way of standing out in a crowd, and in several companies, where the search for merit overcomes the search for mindless loyalty, they rise quickly.

Integrity

The second essential quality is integrity. Some experts may claim this is not a cognitive characteristic but a personality trait. I disagree. Integrity is a choice, based on values and beliefs.

Integrity is important in every aspect of life, but even more so in analyzing strategic risks. The role of an EW analyst is to cry "Wolf!" It calls for the taking of sometimes unpopular, sometimes politically sensitive positions. Naturally it is not a job for an optimist or a cheerleader; but since overkill is as bad, it is not a job for a doomsday prophet either. It is a job for a realist. Facing reality and putting it straight on the table takes guts and integrity. Jamie Dimon, Bank One's CEO and John Reed's student, said to his investors, "Excuse me. This is reality. Deal with it!"[14] Sure enough, the stock took a tumble, but Dimon survived. OK, you say, but he was the almighty CEO and was not about to lose his job for standing up for his views. That's true. But strategic risk analysts should be made of the same stuff that makes up CEOs, or their companies will end up like France Telecom.

The Best Practice for Raising First-Rate Strategic Risk Analysts

Though brilliant risk analysts tend to stand out, companies can help them do that. The best way to ensure that the early warning process receives the attention and skills deserving its mission of saving top management careers, and the company's wealth and competitive position, is to make the position of EW manager an executive development position. There are several reasons why this makes perfect sense, and at least one giant energy company is moving in this direction:

▶ Would you not want those who later lead the company to be able to see the big picture and grasp emerging trends, both risky and opportunity affording? Gary Wendt, the former CEO of GE Capital, was described as a shrewd trend spotter.

▶ Identifying structural changes in the industry early enough is the only insurance a company has against strategic surprises and performance decline. Wouldn't you want the best minds in that position, and would they not be the natural talent to move up later to senior positions?

▶ Some say that formulating strategies is not as difficult as implementing them. The early warning manager is the person who continually monitors the actual success of implementing a company's strategy. His or her position provides unbiased and unparalleled access to information about how well the strategy works. Would you not want an executive to be aware of the real-life difficulties in implementing a strategy?

▶ Finally, the early warning manager needs guts *and* integrity. Would you not consider those essential qualities for senior execs (as well as accountants, yes) in post-Enron corporate America?

I know I would.

Manager's Checklist

☐ To the adoring fans of Myers-Briggs and other popular standardized tests of executive personality and temperament I can only say, for me NJIT is still the New Jersey Institute of Technology, not a useful predictor of the use of early warning. I know, it's blasphemy.

☐ A glimpse at the Gilad test for early warning tendencies: Does top management listen to its middle managers? 10 points if it does, 0 if it is the typical Fortune 500 that regards anything outsiders say as valuable and nothing insiders say as credible.

☐ The acronyms are so close, C-E-O, C-E-W, one would think every CEO would want a first-rate, institutionalized CEW to ensure his company's survival. Not so. The relationship between the CEO and the organizational capability of early warning is a reflection of the CEO's personality, background, belief system, decision style, and IQ. This relationship is never simple, but it is rather safe to say that top executives who love listening to themselves more than they love listening to the truth will not be ardent supporters of a reality-check tool such as CEW.

☐ There is a new breed of CEOs rising in the United States. Compare these new CEOs' styles to the debacle at the famous all-male Augusta Golf Club in Atlanta, where the CEO "Hootie" Johnson did not bother to gather a bit of intelligence about the woman who sent him a letter asking for gender representation in the Masters tournament and instead aggressively attacked her. Ruined a perfectly good game, poor chap.

☐ Compare the new CEOs' style to the old and familiar style of John Chambers of Cisco, a CEO who admits his company was surprised by the burst of the Internet bubble, but dismisses it as a once-in-a-lifetime event. His executives proceeded to dismiss Dell as a nonthreat. See a connection?

☐ The risk aversion trait common to so many new CEOs bodes very well for a change in their approach to early warning and strategic intelligence.

❏ Charge-back early warning can be lethal. The analogy of a market mechanism for insurance (of any type) does not work out. Think: Buying insurance in the market is an individual decision, because the individual pays if he makes the wrong decision. But if the individual product manager, or vice president R&D, or a business unit head in the company does not buy a minimal "insurance" in the form of funding an early warning program, the whole company pays. Therefore, making the future of the whole company dependent on internal clients' desire to pay for CEW through charge-back makes as much sense as walking backward in a minefield.

> **Have I missed some obstacles? Share your experience with me. I'll post it on my Web site, www.bengilad.com. Send an e-mail to bsgilad@netvision.net.il.**

Notes

1. Fred David, *Strategic Management* (New York: Macmillan, 1991), p. 165.
2. James B. Quinn, Henry Mintzberg, and Robert M. James, *The Strategy Process* (Englewood Cliffs, N.J.: Prentice-Hall, 1988), p. 344.
3. John Curran, "GE Capital: Jack Welch's Secret Weapon," *Fortune*, 10 Nov. 1997, p.79.
4. *Fortune*, op. cit., p. 81.
5. Bruce Horovitz, "Ten Things McDonald's Must Do to Get Its House in Order," *USATODAY.com*, 12 Dec. 2002.
6. *USATODAY.com*, 12 Dec. 2002, p. 3
7. Patricia Sellers, "CEOs Under Fire: The New Breed," *Fortune.com*, 3 Nov. 2002.
8. "Consultant, Heal Thyself," *Economist*, 2 Nov. 2002.
9. Michael McCarthy, "All Male Augusta Hires Crisis Expert to Do PR," *USA TODAY.com*, 6 Dec. 2002.
10. The following segment and its quotes are taken from "Can Cisco Dig out of Its Hole?" by Fred Vogelstein, *Fortune.com*, Dec. 9, 2002.
11. Laura Cohen, "Protecting Fannie's Franchise," *BusinessWeek Online*, 9 Dec. 2002.
12. Laura Cohen, "The Prospects of Housing Are Terrific," *BusinessWeek Online*, 9 Dec. 2002.
13. "Protecting Fannie's Franchise," op. cit.
14. "CEOS Under Fire," op. cit.

Epilogue

"What we see depends mainly on what we look for."
—John Lubbock

In a 2002 interview on CBS's *Face the Nation*, Senator Bob Graham, cochairman of a joint congressional committee examining the failure of U.S. intelligence agencies to detect and prevent the September 11 attacks on New York and Washington, stated that "We found, in looking at the specific questions of what happened before Sept. 11, that one of the major causes, in terms of the intelligence community failures, were the fact that people weren't talking with each other."[1] Richard Lugar, another member of the committee, describes the culture at the government agencies as full of "firewalls."

The irony, of course, is that when it comes to intelligence and putting it to optimal use, many corporations can only envy the government. If government—where multiple well-financed agencies fall over each other trying to obtain intelligence—fails to keep tabs on what's happening out there, how can companies that don't have more than a rudimentary capability keep an external focus? Most companies pay lip service to the concept of external focus—it is good in theory and in executive speeches, but it is rather low on their agendas and receives scant funding compared with other activities. Several functions are *supposed* to keep management tuned to the outside world—marketing, sales,

market research, investor relations—but none is in charge of the
early detection and analysis of strategic risks or opportunities.
Without anyone in charge, "firewalls" and "silos" are common.
Keeping tabs on a complicated and dynamic industry's structure
is far from a simple task. Assessing its future is even less simple.
Managers will always prefer the comfort of using present market statistics to estimating an uncertain future. Intelligence professionals, when they are appointed, have little influence on that
task and no access to the top. External focus falls between the
cracks more often than not.

The problem gets worse the higher one climbs. Whether by
design or by natural selection, business units' executives tend to
surround themselves with "yes" people, or people who share
their visions of the external world. No one is told, "Your job is to
poke holes in our strategic thinking about the competitive landscape, making sure we do not fall into the trap of industry dissonance and do not get strategically surprised." This is a tall order,
and without a guiding hand, it takes a second seat to operational
issues. "Let's solve our known problems first," says the extremely busy executive, "before we worry about future problems." Unfortunately, future problems don't wait for current
problems to be solved.

Corporate executives are in the worst position—their insularity is almost total—despite their claims to the contrary and
their highly publicized visits to a few important customers.
Their attention is narrowly focused on here and now, as they are
pulled in a thousand directions by dozens of fires they need to
put down. They have no source of independent intelligence judgment to check on business units' forecasts and industry analyses. They have no early warning of their own. Boards are even
weaker in this regard. Furthermore, their highly paid prestigious
consultants know exactly which side of the bread has the butter,
and their motivation is to provide agreeable input that will extend their contract. Crying, "The emperor has no clothes!" will
not get them a second year.

Sometimes employees just don't know what intelligence is
important, and no one trains them in what to look for. Sometimes people withhold intelligence deliberately for political reasons, to preserve power, which is often based on the exclusivity
of knowledge. Sometimes the bits and pieces get lost in the daily

shuffle and never reach the right place. The result is that 92 percent of companies faced strategic surprises in the past five years.

Below are a few litmus-test statements that reveal a potential problem in early warning. If your company or you yourself make these statements often, seek help or a new job *before* the inevitable earthquake.

- ▶ "In our company, early warning is *everyone*'s responsibility." Translation: No one is in charge. There is no early warning.

- ▶ "Unlike employees in other companies, our people do talk to each other." Translation: I haven't been down in the trenches for a decade.

- ▶ "We have several task forces that meet regularly and keep tabs on what's happening." Translation: They meet every Tuesday of the third week in March in the year of the rabbit if everyone has the time, and no one listens to them anyway.

- ▶ "In our company, early detection of risks and opportunities is a bottom-up approach." Translation: The bad news has not reached us yet at the top.

- ▶ "We have processes up the wazoo. What we need is better execution." Translation: What, another process? Early warning, shmerly warning, if we could only sell more to the idiots who for some strange reason don't want to buy our products.

- ▶ "Our new Knowledge Management initiative addresses just these issues." Translation: I seriously don't understand strategic risk control, but I sure as hell hope the thirty million I am paying the consultants will do something about it!

One related question I am asked on the speaking circuit is whether government can do more to mandate early warning programs to protect investors. This question seems to become more frequent these days as America is busy trying to clean up its corporate culture. Do business leaders owe their investors an oath of *external focus*? After all, CEOs now have to swear their accounting is accurate.

The oath of accounting accuracy is symbolic, of course. The irony is that the act addresses a tiny problem with a tiny fraction of corporate executives who defrauded their investors. *Many* more CEOs have no idea what's brewing in the external competitive arena where their companies play with obsolete strategies, and have few if any serious assessments of future conditions. However, one cannot force a CEO to be intelligence-savvy and pay attention to early signs of change and make sure his strategy is refined quickly and decisively on a continuous basis when industry dissonance seems to develop. In other words, Congress cannot outlaw stupidity, arrogance, wishful thinking, or large egos.

But the market can, and the market *eventually* does. If a company does not demonstrate a clear competence in managing and controlling strategic risks and moving quickly on strategic opportunities, the market always knows at the end. However, the smart investor should know *before* it is obvious to all other, less observant investors. This may be the most important message of this book to investors. Instead of waiting for the crisis, call the company. Ask how specifically they control strategic risks and how they identify changes *early on*. If the answer is "Trust us, we know what we are doing," run for your life!

The congressional committee studying the September 11 intelligence failure recommended that the president appoint an intelligence czar to ensure that communication and coordination failures of such magnitude and consequence will not recur. Should companies appoint a czar for their early warning? Time will tell. Just paying attention to the *process* can be a huge improvement for many.

Note

1. "Congressional Committee Calls for Intelligence Czar," *USATODAY.com*, 9 Dec. 2002.

Index

About the Author

Dr. Benjamin Gilad is the founder and president of the New Jersey–based Academy of Competitive Intelligence (ACI). Established in 1996, ACI is a consulting firm specializing in corporate early warning processes. Its training affiliate, the Fuld-Gilad-Herring ACI, is the leading competitive intelligence training institute in North America.

A former associate professor of strategy at Rutgers University's School of Management, Ben is a pioneer in the field of competitive intelligence and a "guru" among competitive intelligence practitioners worldwide. His prior books and articles on the subject established him as the most outspoken advocate of competitive intelligence practices for better strategic risk management. Based on his experience creating early warning processes for some of the world's leading firms, as well as running dozens of business war games, Ben finds it intuitively silly to trust intuition instead.

Ben can be reached through his Web site, www.bengilad.com.